THE LOVECRAFT
ANTHOLOGY
volume I

THE LOVECRAFT ANTHOLOGY

volume I

A GRAPHIC COLLECTION OF
H.P. LOVECRAFT'S SHORT STORIES

EDITED BY
DAN LOCKWOOD

First published 2011
by SelfMadeHero
5 Upper Wimpole Street
London W1G 6BP
www.selfmadehero.com

This edition published 2012

© 2011 SelfMadeHero

Edited by: Dan Lockwood
Cover Image: Dillon
Cover Design: Dillon
Layout and Lettering by: Andy Huckle
Editorial Assistant: Lizzie Kaye
Marketing Director: Doug Wallace
Publishing Director: Emma Hayley
With thanks to: Jane Laporte

A CIP record for this book is available from the British Library

ISBN: 978-1-906838-53-9

10 9 8 7 6 5 4 3 2 1

Printed and bound in Slovenia

CONTENTS

The Call of Cthulhu

Adapted by Ian Edginton • Illustrated by D'Israeli

The Haunter of the Dark

Adapted by Dan Lockwood • Illustrated by Shane Ivan Oakley

The Dunwich Horror

Adapted by Rob Davis • Illustrated by I.N.J.Culbard

The Colour Out of Space

Adapted by David Hine • Illustrated by Mark Stafford

The Shadow Over Innsmouth

Adapted by Leah Moore & John Reppion • Illustrated by Leigh Gallagher

The Rats in the Walls

Adapted by Dan Lockwood • Illustrated by David Hartman

Dagon

Adapted by Dan Lockwood • Illustrated by Alice Duke

f O R E W O R D

"The oldest and strongest emotion of mankind is fear, and the oldest and strongest kind of fear is fear of the unknown."

H.P. Lovecraft, *Supernatural Horror in Literature*

My first exposure to the works of H.P. Lovecraft stemmed from a brief spell working in a bookshop as a teenager. Browsing along the shelves of their small horror section one quiet afternoon, I came across a three-volume omnibus collection of his tales, featuring covers so lurid in their detail that I could barely tear my eyes away. A few minutes later, I found myself standing at the counter, handing my meagre earnings back to my employer. I can't pretend that I remember much about the days that followed, but they certainly didn't involve much work.

"All my stories," Lovecraft wrote, "unconnected as they may be, are based on the fundamental lore or legend that this world was inhabited at one time by another race who, in practising black magic, lost their foothold and were expelled, yet live on outside, ever ready to take possession of this earth again." Something about this chilling, pessimistic view of a world under constant threat from alien beings and their meddling human minions completely captured my imagination. Whether it was Lovecraft's descriptive, florid language, or the wonderful, haunting stories themselves, I was swiftly hooked. I left that bookshop behind years ago, but have been reading and rereading those same editions ever since.

The more genre fiction I have encountered over the years (whether in prose or in graphic form), the more I have come to realise the extent to which Lovecraft's tentacles have wormed their way into the minds of my favourite writers and artists. This wide-ranging influence is a testament to the power of his imagination, as is his continued popularity with a devoted readership. My hope is that the adaptations in this volume will entertain and unnerve both established fans and those who are new to Lovecraft's weird tales.

The unknown awaits...

Dan Lockwood
Editor

THE CALL OF CTHULHU

Adapted by Ian Edginton • Illustrated by D'Israeli

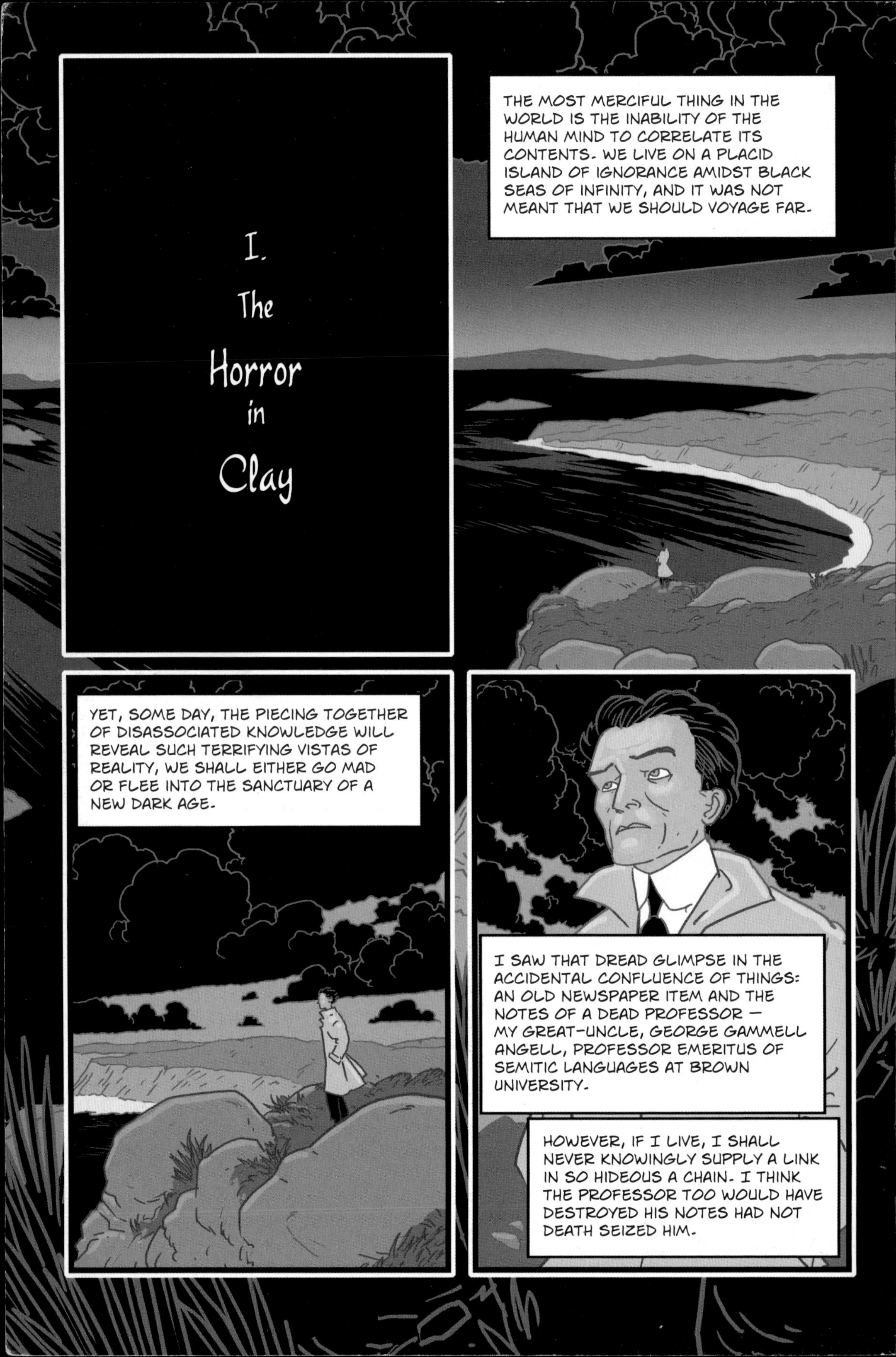
I. The Horror in Clay
THE MOST MERCIFUL THING IN THE WORLD IS THE INABILITY OF THE HUMAN MIND TO CORRELATE ITS CONTENTS. WE LIVE ON A PLACID ISLAND OF IGNORANCE AMIDST BLACK SEAS OF INFINITY, AND IT WAS NOT MEANT THAT WE SHOULD VOYAGE FAR.
YET, SOME DAY, THE PIECING TOGETHER OF DISASSOCIATED KNOWLEDGE WILL REVEAL SUCH TERRIFYING VISTAS OF REALITY, WE SHALL EITHER GO MAD OR FLEE INTO THE SANCTUARY OF A NEW DARK AGE.
I SAW THAT DREAD GLIMPSE IN THE ACCIDENTAL CONFLUENCE OF THINGS: AN OLD NEWSPAPER ITEM AND THE NOTES OF A DEAD PROFESSOR — MY GREAT-UNCLE, GEORGE GAMMELL ANGELL, PROFESSOR EMERITUS OF SEMITIC LANGUAGES AT BROWN UNIVERSITY.
HOWEVER, IF I LIVE, I SHALL NEVER KNOWINGLY SUPPLY A LINK IN SO HIDEOUS A CHAIN. I THINK THE PROFESSOR TOO WOULD HAVE DESTROYED HIS NOTES HAD NOT DEATH SEIZED HIM.

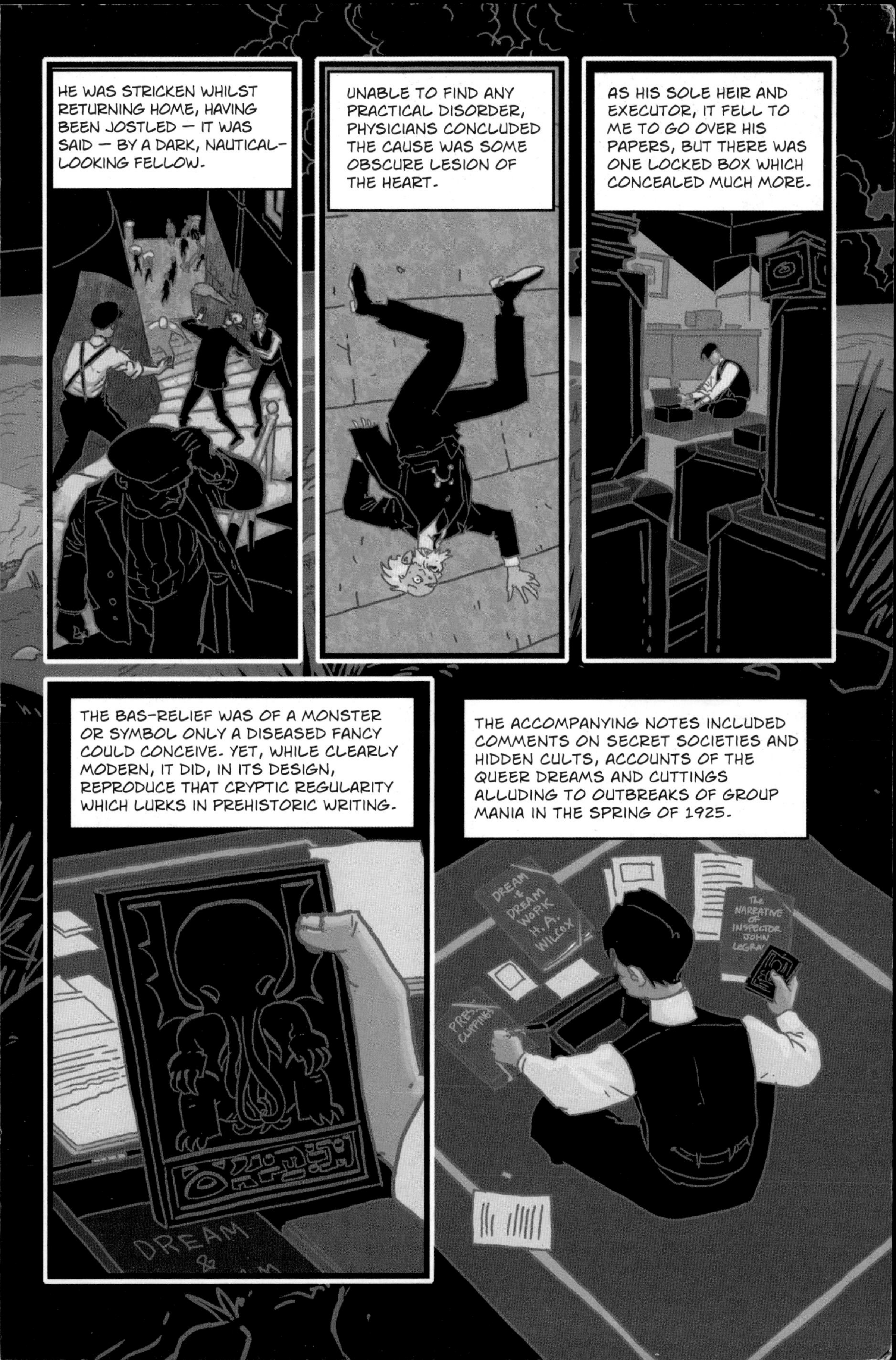
HE WAS STRICKEN WHILST RETURNING HOME, HAVING BEEN JOSTLED — IT WAS SAID — BY A DARK, NAUTICAL-LOOKING FELLOW.
UNABLE TO FIND ANY PRACTICAL DISORDER, PHYSICIANS CONCLUDED THE CAUSE WAS SOME OBSCURE LESION OF THE HEART.
AS HIS SOLE HEIR AND EXECUTOR, IT FELL TO ME TO GO OVER HIS PAPERS, BUT THERE WAS ONE LOCKED BOX WHICH CONCEALED MUCH MORE.
THE BAS-RELIEF WAS OF A MONSTER OR SYMBOL ONLY A DISEASED FANCY COULD CONCEIVE. YET, WHILE CLEARLY MODERN, IT DID, IN ITS DESIGN, REPRODUCE THAT CRYPTIC REGULARITY WHICH LURKS IN PREHISTORIC WRITING.
DREAM
THE ACCOMPANYING NOTES INCLUDED COMMENTS ON SECRET SOCIETIES AND HIDDEN CULTS, ACCOUNTS OF THE QUEER DREAMS AND CUTTINGS ALLUDING TO OUTBREAKS OF GROUP MANIA IN THE SPRING OF 1925.
DREAM & DREAM WORK H. A. WILCOX
The NARRATIVE OF INSPECTOR JOHN
PRESS CLIPPINGS

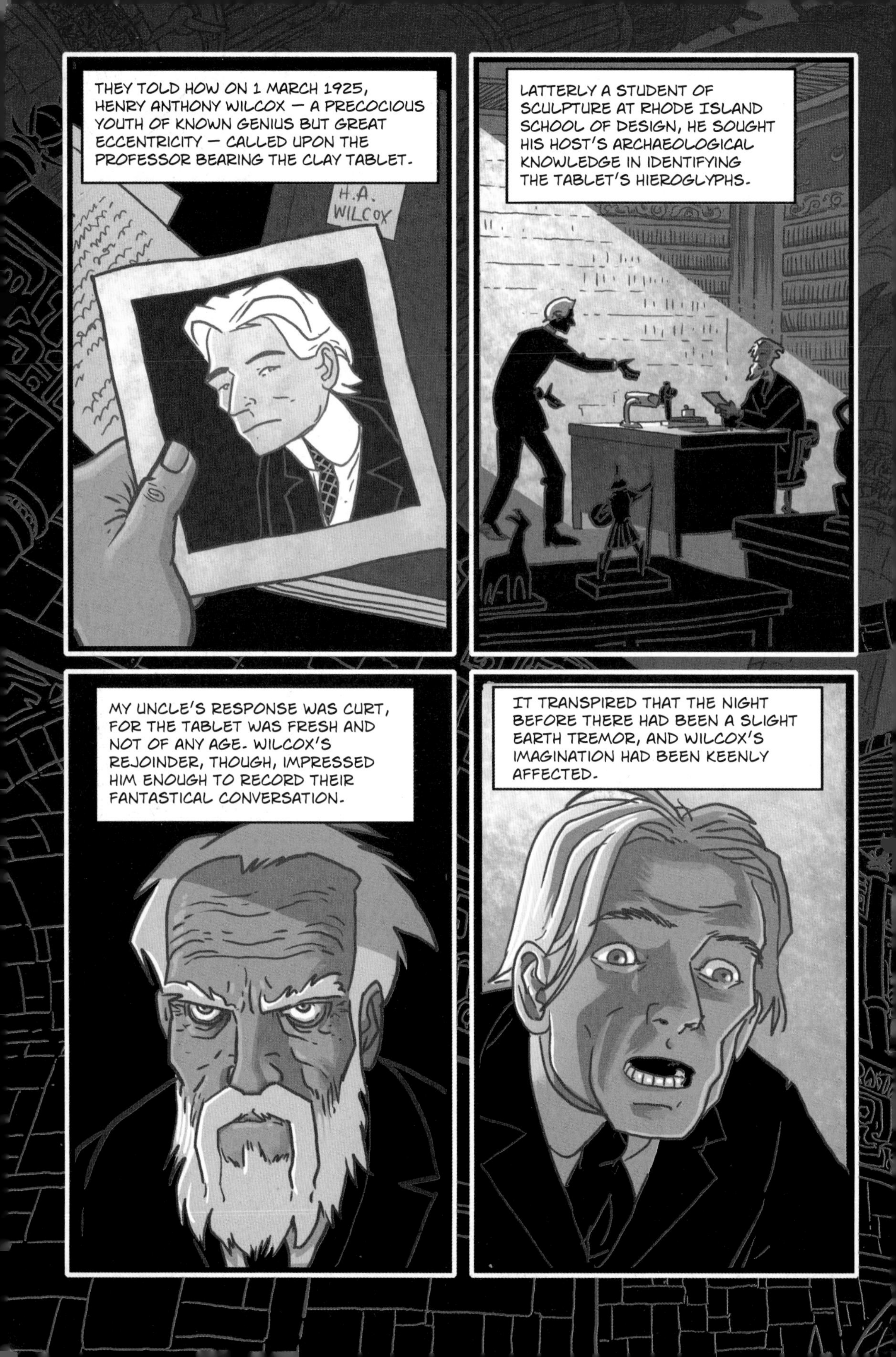
THEY TOLD HOW ON 1 MARCH 1925, HENRY ANTHONY WILCOX — A PRECOCIOUS YOUTH OF KNOWN GENIUS BUT GREAT ECCENTRICITY — CALLED UPON THE PROFESSOR BEARING THE CLAY TABLET.
H.A. WILCOX
LATTERLY A STUDENT OF SCULPTURE AT RHODE ISLAND SCHOOL OF DESIGN, HE SOUGHT HIS HOST'S ARCHAEOLOGICAL KNOWLEDGE IN IDENTIFYING THE TABLET'S HIEROGLYPHS.
MY UNCLE'S RESPONSE WAS CURT, FOR THE TABLET WAS FRESH AND NOT OF ANY AGE. WILCOX'S REJOINDER, THOUGH, IMPRESSED HIM ENOUGH TO RECORD THEIR FANTASTICAL CONVERSATION.
IT TRANSPIRED THAT THE NIGHT BEFORE THERE HAD BEEN A SLIGHT EARTH TREMOR, AND WILCOX'S IMAGINATION HAD BEEN KEENLY AFFECTED.

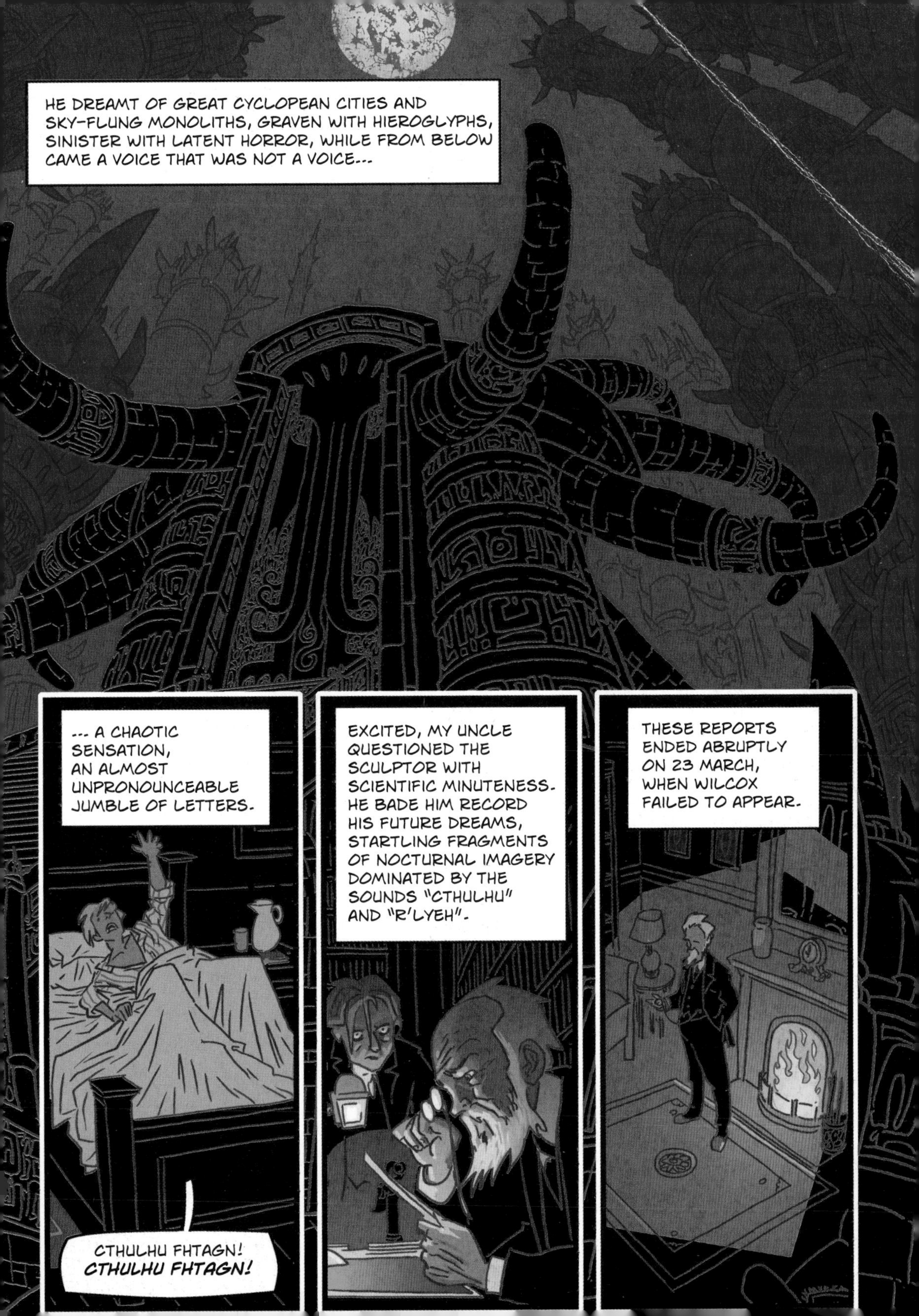
HE DREAMT OF GREAT CYCLOPEAN CITIES AND SKY-FLUNG MONOLITHS, GRAVEN WITH HIEROGLYPHS, SINISTER WITH LATENT HORROR, WHILE FROM BELOW CAME A VOICE THAT WAS NOT A VOICE...
... A CHAOTIC SENSATION, AN ALMOST UNPRONOUNCEABLE JUMBLE OF LETTERS.
CTHULHU FHTAGN! CTHULHU FHTAGN!
EXCITED, MY UNCLE QUESTIONED THE SCULPTOR WITH SCIENTIFIC MINUTENESS. HE BADE HIM RECORD HIS FUTURE DREAMS, STARTLING FRAGMENTS OF NOCTURNAL IMAGERY DOMINATED BY THE SOUNDS "CTHULHU" AND "R'LYEH".
THESE REPORTS ENDED ABRUPTLY ON 23 MARCH, WHEN WILCOX FAILED TO APPEAR.

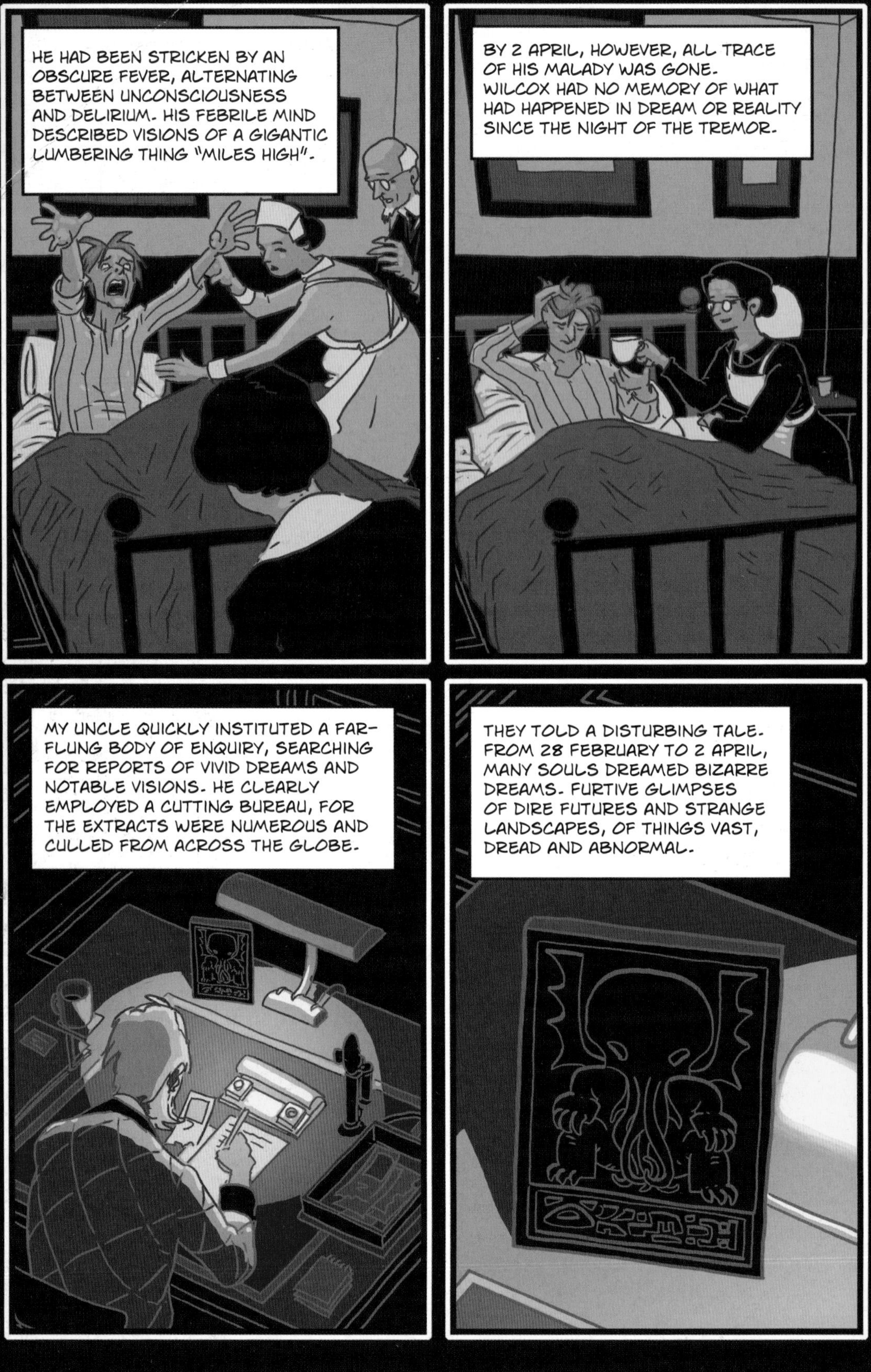
HE HAD BEEN STRICKEN BY AN OBSCURE FEVER, ALTERNATING BETWEEN UNCONSCIOUSNESS AND DELIRIUM. HIS FEBRILE MIND DESCRIBED VISIONS OF A GIGANTIC LUMBERING THING "MILES HIGH".
BY 2 APRIL, HOWEVER, ALL TRACE OF HIS MALADY WAS GONE. WILCOX HAD NO MEMORY OF WHAT HAD HAPPENED IN DREAM OR REALITY SINCE THE NIGHT OF THE TREMOR.
MY UNCLE QUICKLY INSTITUTED A FAR-FLUNG BODY OF ENQUIRY, SEARCHING FOR REPORTS OF VIVID DREAMS AND NOTABLE VISIONS. HE CLEARLY EMPLOYED A CUTTING BUREAU, FOR THE EXTRACTS WERE NUMEROUS AND CULLED FROM ACROSS THE GLOBE.
THEY TOLD A DISTURBING TALE. FROM 28 FEBRUARY TO 2 APRIL, MANY SOULS DREAMED BIZARRE DREAMS. FURTIVE GLIMPSES OF DIRE FUTURES AND STRANGE LANDSCAPES, OF THINGS VAST, DREAD AND ABNORMAL.

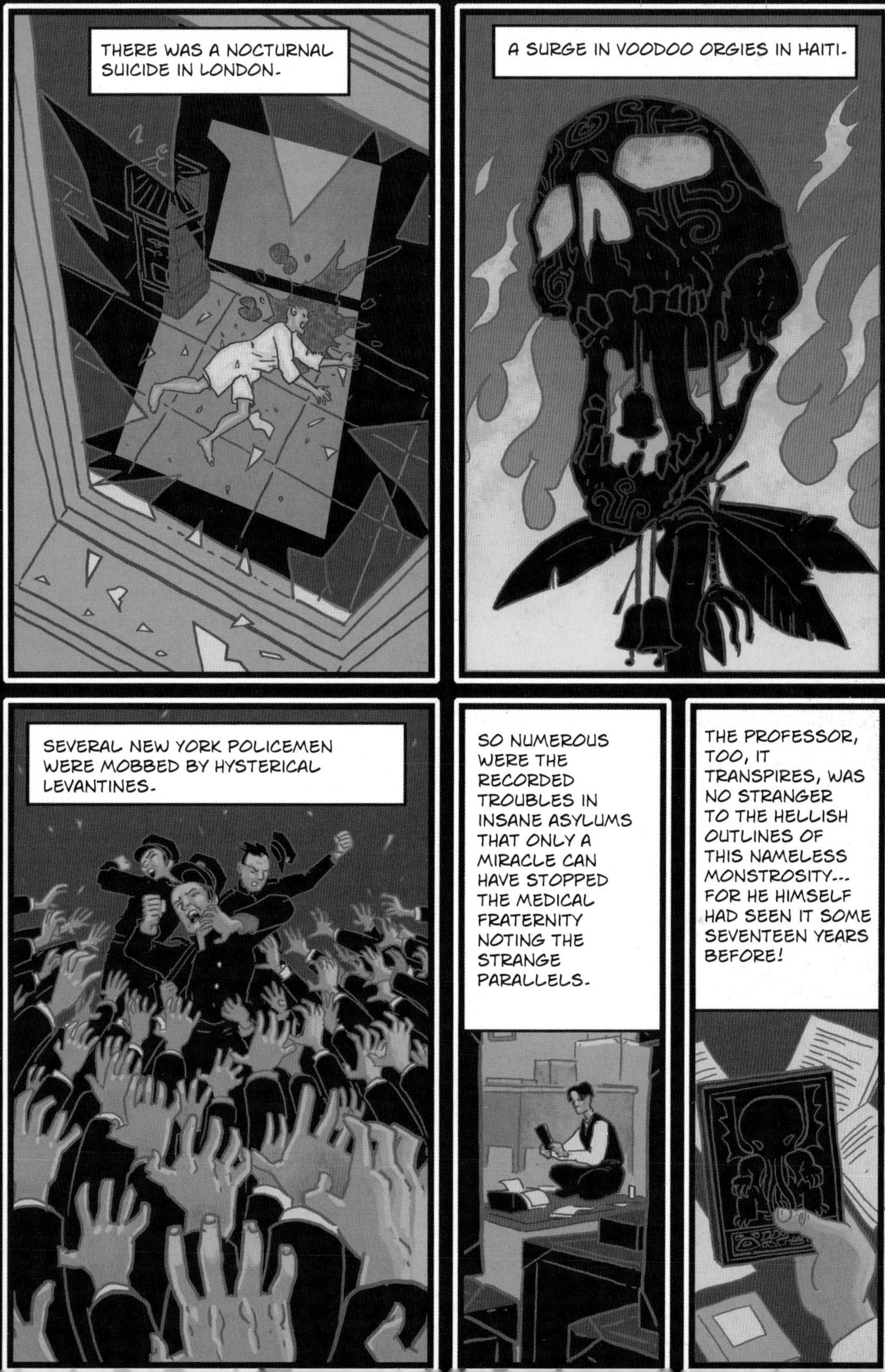
THERE WAS A NOCTURNAL SUICIDE IN LONDON.
A SURGE IN VOODOO ORGIES IN HAITI.
SEVERAL NEW YORK POLICEMEN WERE MOBBED BY HYSTERICAL LEVANTINES.
SO NUMEROUS WERE THE RECORDED TROUBLES IN INSANE ASYLUMS THAT ONLY A MIRACLE CAN HAVE STOPPED THE MEDICAL FRATERNITY NOTING THE STRANGE PARALLELS.
THE PROFESSOR, TOO, IT TRANSPIRES, WAS NO STRANGER TO THE HELLISH OUTLINES OF THIS NAMELESS MONSTROSITY... FOR HE HIMSELF HAD SEEN IT SOME SEVENTEEN YEARS BEFORE!

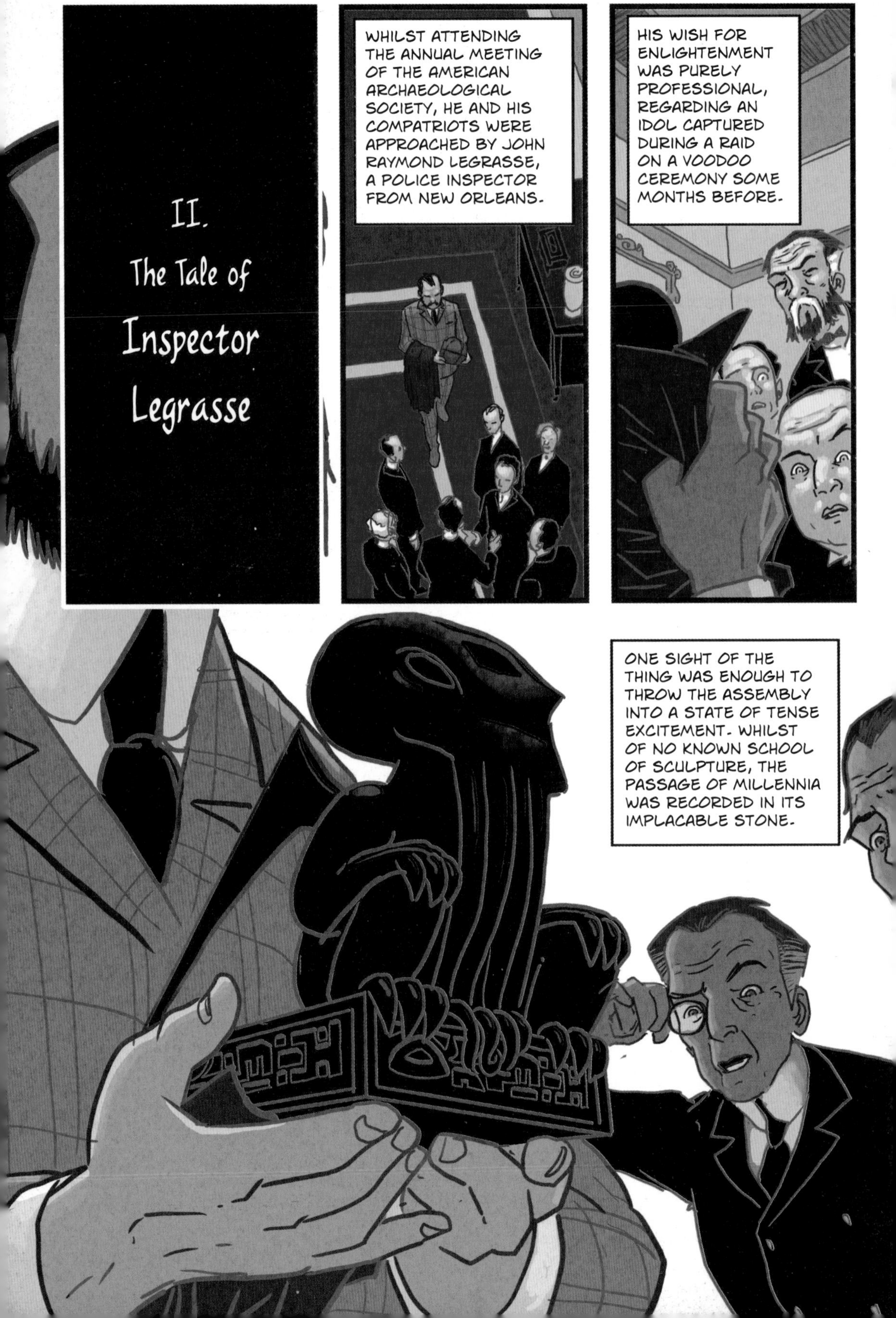
II.
The Tale of
Inspector
Legrasse
WHILST ATTENDING THE ANNUAL MEETING OF THE AMERICAN ARCHAEOLOGICAL SOCIETY, HE AND HIS COMPATRIOTS WERE APPROACHED BY JOHN RAYMOND LEGRASSE, A POLICE INSPECTOR FROM NEW ORLEANS.
HIS WISH FOR ENLIGHTENMENT WAS PURELY PROFESSIONAL, REGARDING AN IDOL CAPTURED DURING A RAID ON A VOODOO CEREMONY SOME MONTHS BEFORE.
ONE SIGHT OF THE THING WAS ENOUGH TO THROW THE ASSEMBLY INTO A STATE OF TENSE EXCITEMENT. WHILST OF NO KNOWN SCHOOL OF SCULPTURE, THE PASSAGE OF MILLENNIA WAS RECORDED IN ITS IMPLACABLE STONE.

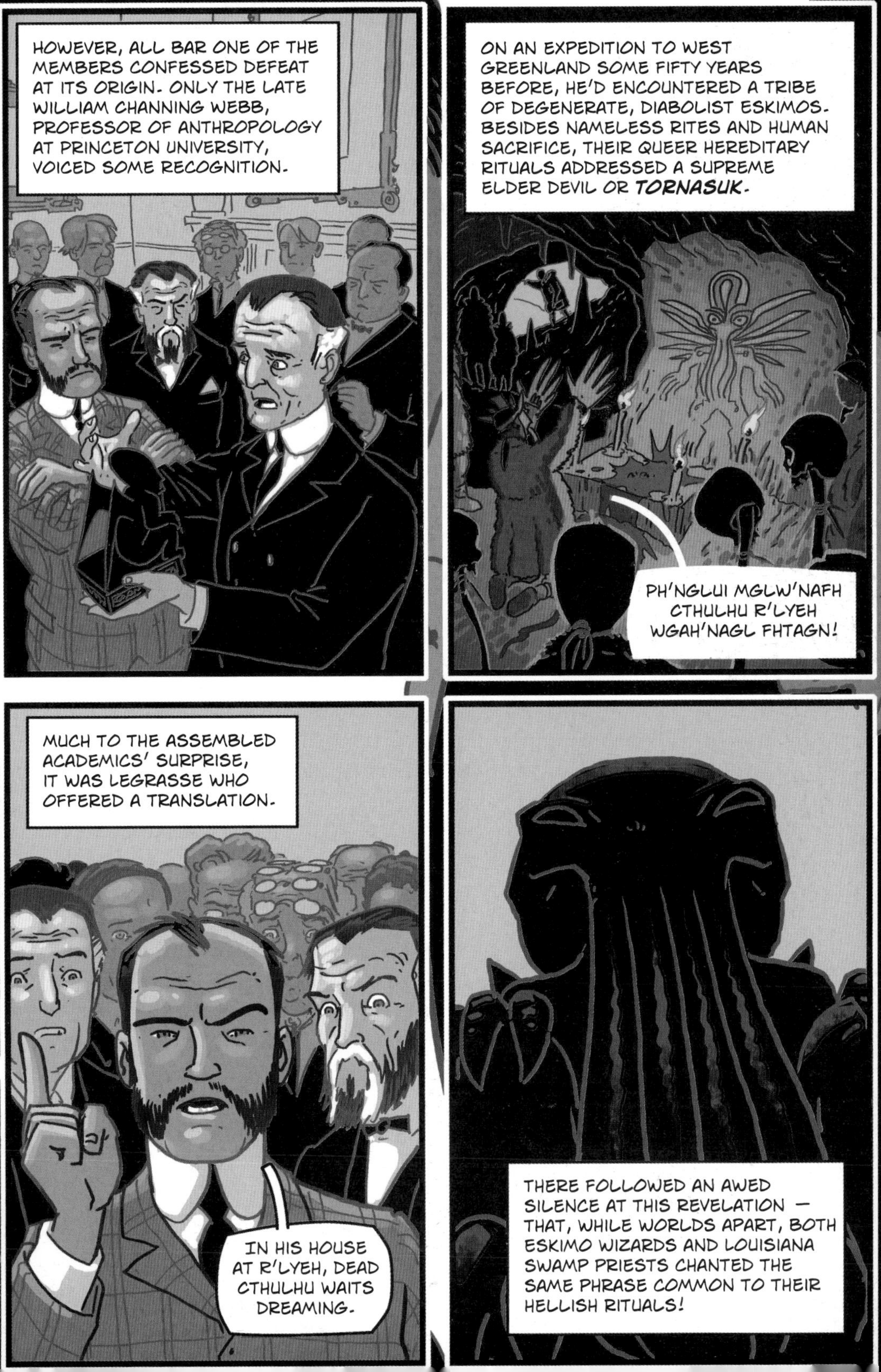
HOWEVER, ALL BAR ONE OF THE MEMBERS CONFESSED DEFEAT AT ITS ORIGIN. ONLY THE LATE WILLIAM CHANNING WEBB, PROFESSOR OF ANTHROPOLOGY AT PRINCETON UNIVERSITY, VOICED SOME RECOGNITION.
ON AN EXPEDITION TO WEST GREENLAND SOME FIFTY YEARS BEFORE, HE'D ENCOUNTERED A TRIBE OF DEGENERATE, DIABOLIST ESKIMOS. BESIDES NAMELESS RITES AND HUMAN SACRIFICE, THEIR QUEER HEREDITARY RITUALS ADDRESSED A SUPREME ELDER DEVIL OR TORNASUK.
PH'NGLUI MGLW'NAFH CTHULHU R'LYEH WGAH'NAGL FHTAGN!
MUCH TO THE ASSEMBLED ACADEMICS' SURPRISE, IT WAS LEGRASSE WHO OFFERED A TRANSLATION.
IN HIS HOUSE AT R'LYEH, DEAD CTHULHU WAITS DREAMING.
THERE FOLLOWED AN AWED SILENCE AT THIS REVELATION — THAT, WHILE WORLDS APART, BOTH ESKIMO WIZARDS AND LOUISIANA SWAMP PRIESTS CHANTED THE SAME PHRASE COMMON TO THEIR HELLISH RITUALS!

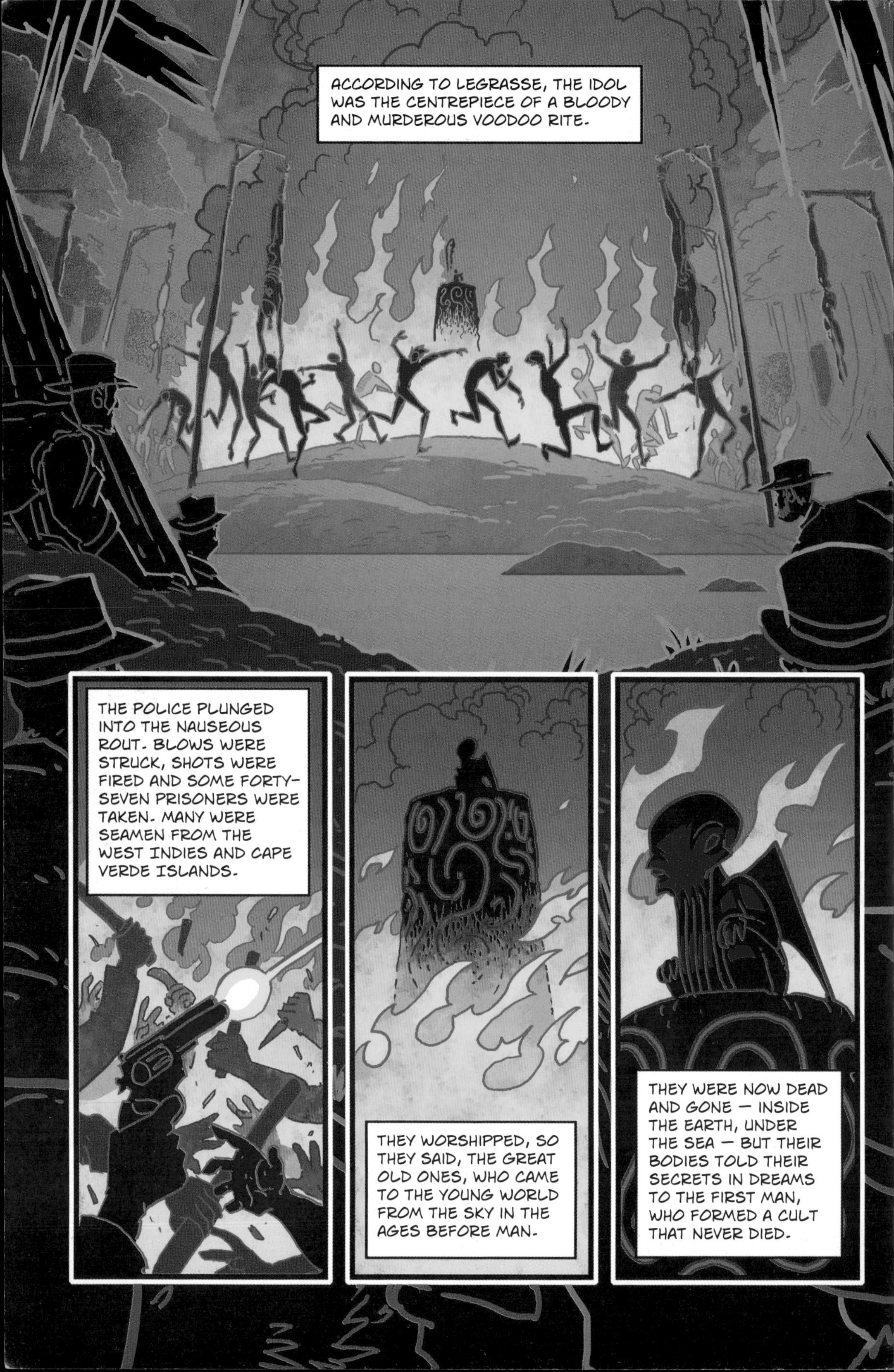
ACCORDING TO LEGRASSE, THE IDOL WAS THE CENTREPIECE OF A BLOODY AND MURDEROUS VOODOO RITE.
THE POLICE PLUNGED INTO THE NAUSEOUS ROUT. BLOWS WERE STRUCK, SHOTS WERE FIRED AND SOME FORTY-SEVEN PRISONERS WERE TAKEN. MANY WERE SEAMEN FROM THE WEST INDIES AND CAPE VERDE ISLANDS.
THEY WORSHIPPED, SO THEY SAID, THE GREAT OLD ONES, WHO CAME TO THE YOUNG WORLD FROM THE SKY IN THE AGES BEFORE MAN.
THEY WERE NOW DEAD AND GONE — INSIDE THE EARTH, UNDER THE SEA — BUT THEIR BODIES TOLD THEIR SECRETS IN DREAMS TO THE FIRST MAN, WHO FORMED A CULT THAT NEVER DIED.

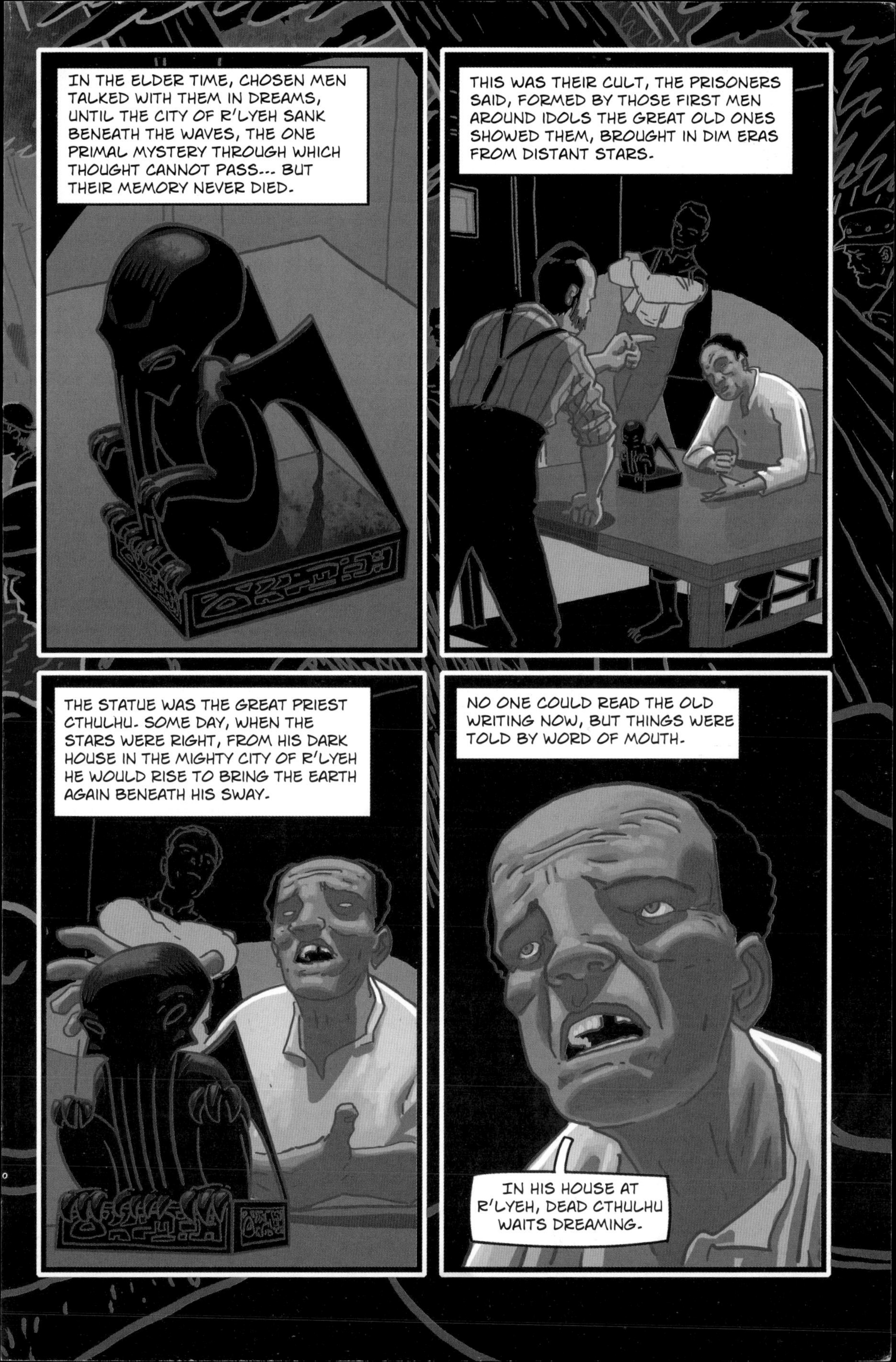
IN THE ELDER TIME, CHOSEN MEN TALKED WITH THEM IN DREAMS, UNTIL THE CITY OF R'LYEH SANK BENEATH THE WAVES, THE ONE PRIMAL MYSTERY THROUGH WHICH THOUGHT CANNOT PASS... BUT THEIR MEMORY NEVER DIED.
THIS WAS THEIR CULT, THE PRISONERS SAID, FORMED BY THOSE FIRST MEN AROUND IDOLS THE GREAT OLD ONES SHOWED THEM, BROUGHT IN DIM ERAS FROM DISTANT STARS.
THE STATUE WAS THE GREAT PRIEST CTHULHU. SOME DAY, WHEN THE STARS WERE RIGHT, FROM HIS DARK HOUSE IN THE MIGHTY CITY OF R'LYEH HE WOULD RISE TO BRING THE EARTH AGAIN BENEATH HIS SWAY.
NO ONE COULD READ THE OLD WRITING NOW, BUT THINGS WERE TOLD BY WORD OF MOUTH.
IN HIS HOUSE AT R'LYEH, DEAD CTHULHU WAITS DREAMING.

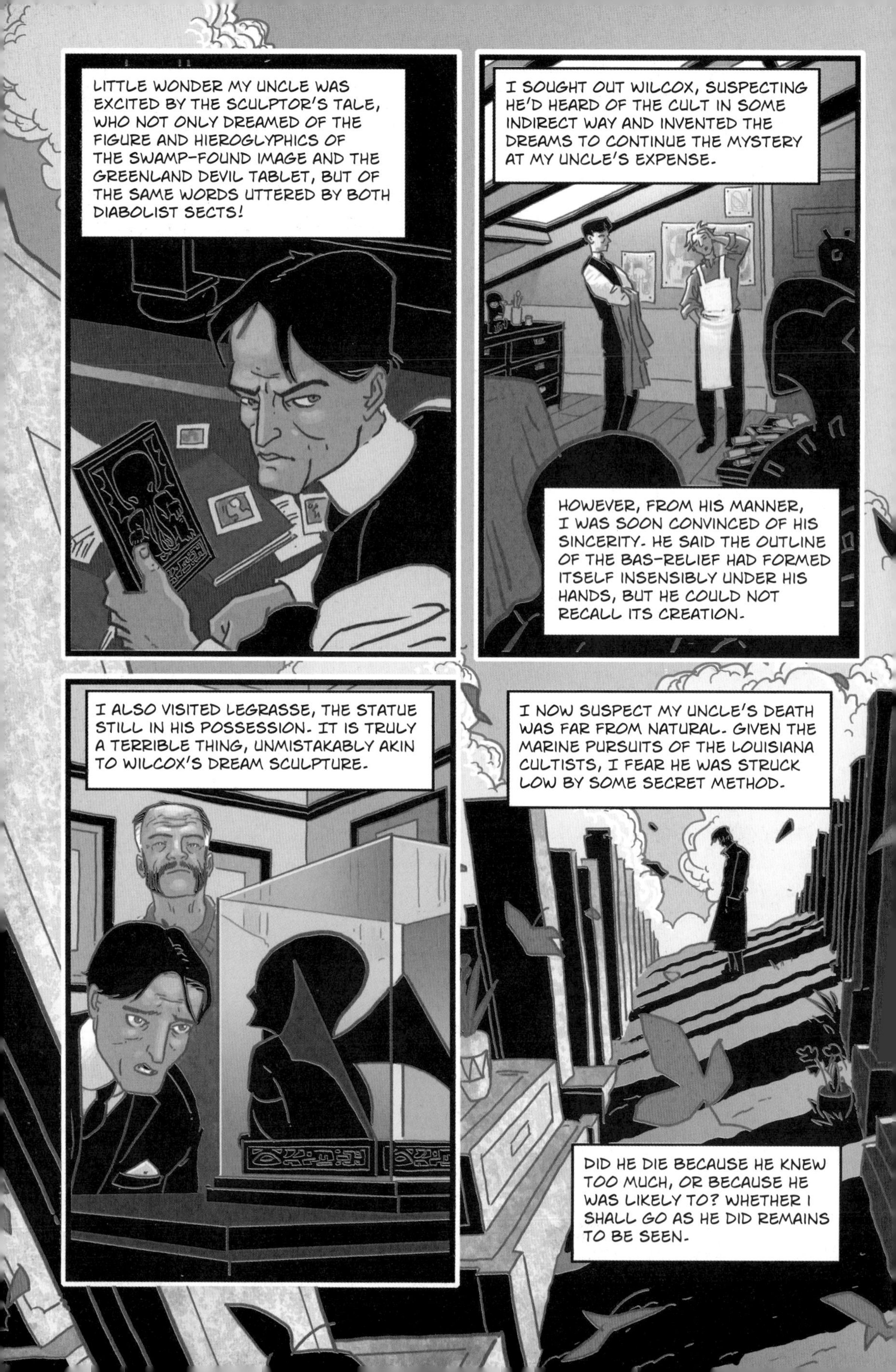
LITTLE WONDER MY UNCLE WAS EXCITED BY THE SCULPTOR'S TALE, WHO NOT ONLY DREAMED OF THE FIGURE AND HIEROGLYPHICS OF THE SWAMP-FOUND IMAGE AND THE GREENLAND DEVIL TABLET, BUT OF THE SAME WORDS UTTERED BY BOTH DIABOLIST SECTS!
I SOUGHT OUT WILCOX, SUSPECTING HE'D HEARD OF THE CULT IN SOME INDIRECT WAY AND INVENTED THE DREAMS TO CONTINUE THE MYSTERY AT MY UNCLE'S EXPENSE.
HOWEVER, FROM HIS MANNER, I WAS SOON CONVINCED OF HIS SINCERITY. HE SAID THE OUTLINE OF THE BAS-RELIEF HAD FORMED ITSELF INSENSIBLY UNDER HIS HANDS, BUT HE COULD NOT RECALL ITS CREATION.
I ALSO VISITED LEGRASSE, THE STATUE STILL IN HIS POSSESSION. IT IS TRULY A TERRIBLE THING, UNMISTAKABLY AKIN TO WILCOX'S DREAM SCULPTURE.
I NOW SUSPECT MY UNCLE'S DEATH WAS FAR FROM NATURAL. GIVEN THE MARINE PURSUITS OF THE LOUISIANA CULTISTS, I FEAR HE WAS STRUCK LOW BY SOME SECRET METHOD.
DID HE DIE BECAUSE HE KNEW TOO MUCH, OR BECAUSE HE WAS LIKELY TO? WHETHER I SHALL GO AS HE DID REMAINS TO BE SEEN.

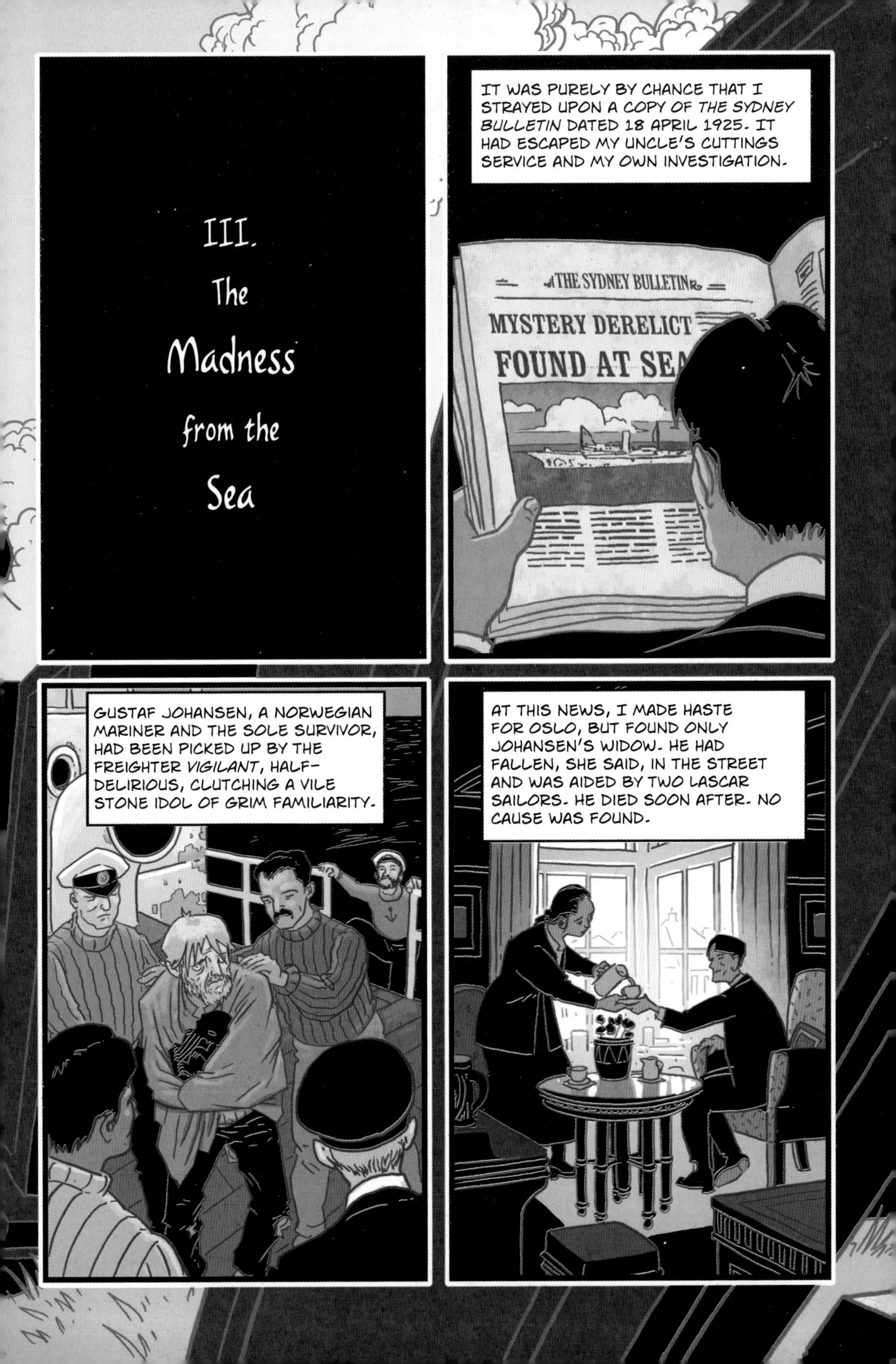
III.
The Madness from the Sea
IT WAS PURELY BY CHANCE THAT I STRAYED UPON A COPY OF *THE SYDNEY BULLETIN* DATED 18 APRIL 1925. IT HAD ESCAPED MY UNCLE'S CUTTINGS SERVICE AND MY OWN INVESTIGATION.
THE SYDNEY BULLETIN
MYSTERY DERELICT
FOUND AT SEA
GUSTAF JOHANSEN, A NORWEGIAN MARINER AND THE SOLE SURVIVOR, HAD BEEN PICKED UP BY THE FREIGHTER *VIGILANT*, HALF-DELIRIOUS, CLUTCHING A VILE STONE IDOL OF GRIM FAMILIARITY.
AT THIS NEWS, I MADE HASTE FOR OSLO, BUT FOUND ONLY JOHANSEN'S WIDOW. HE HAD FALLEN, SHE SAID, IN THE STREET AND WAS AIDED BY TWO LASCAR SAILORS. HE DIED SOON AFTER. NO CAUSE WAS FOUND.

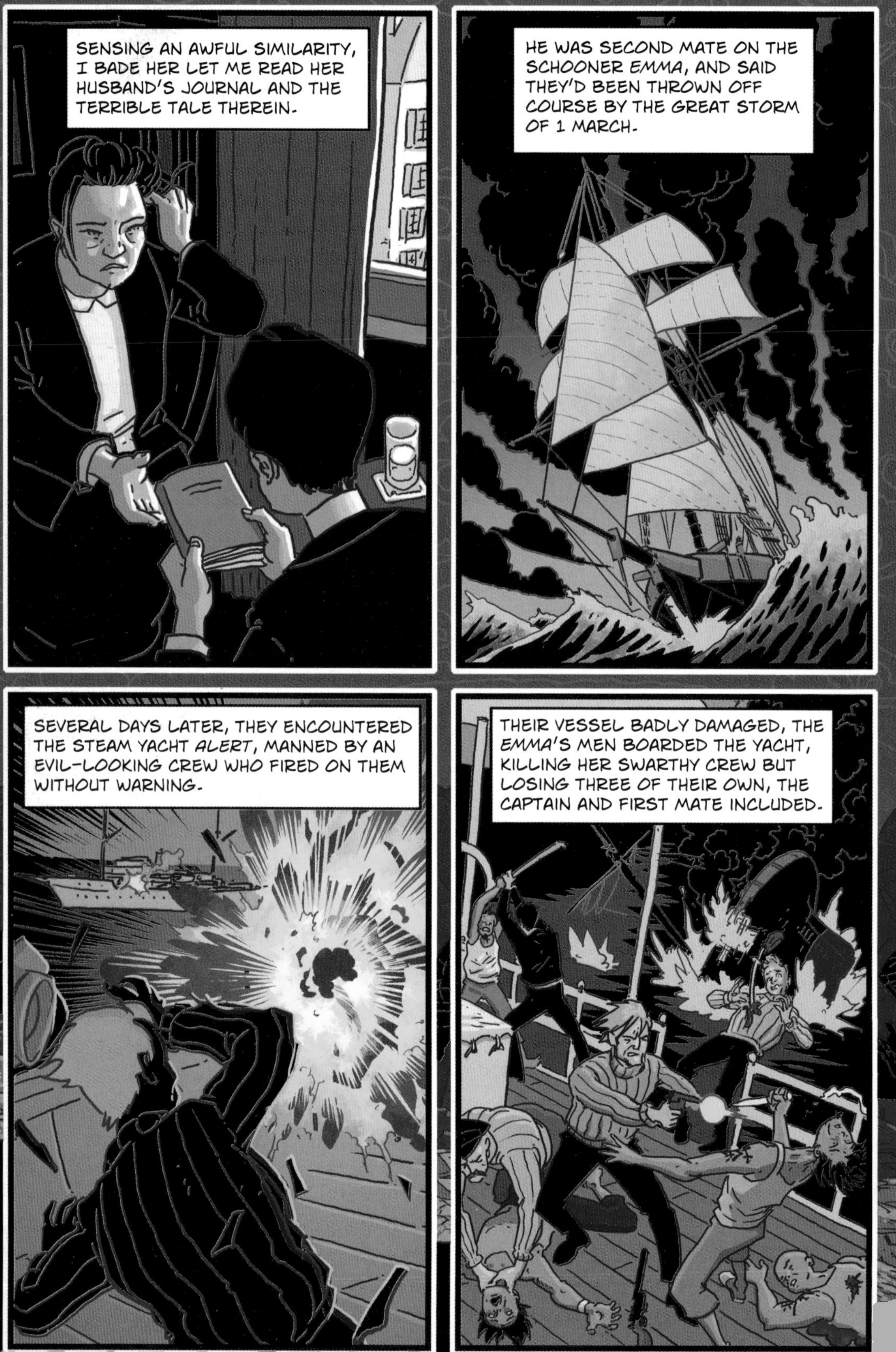
SENSING AN AWFUL SIMILARITY, I BADE HER LET ME READ HER HUSBAND'S JOURNAL AND THE TERRIBLE TALE THEREIN.
HE WAS SECOND MATE ON THE SCHOONER *EMMA*, AND SAID THEY'D BEEN THROWN OFF COURSE BY THE GREAT STORM OF 1 MARCH.
SEVERAL DAYS LATER, THEY ENCOUNTERED THE STEAM YACHT *ALERT*, MANNED BY AN EVIL-LOOKING CREW WHO FIRED ON THEM WITHOUT WARNING.
THEIR VESSEL BADLY DAMAGED, THE *EMMA'S* MEN BOARDED THE YACHT, KILLING HER SWARTHY CREW BUT LOSING THREE OF THEIR OWN, THE CAPTAIN AND FIRST MATE INCLUDED.

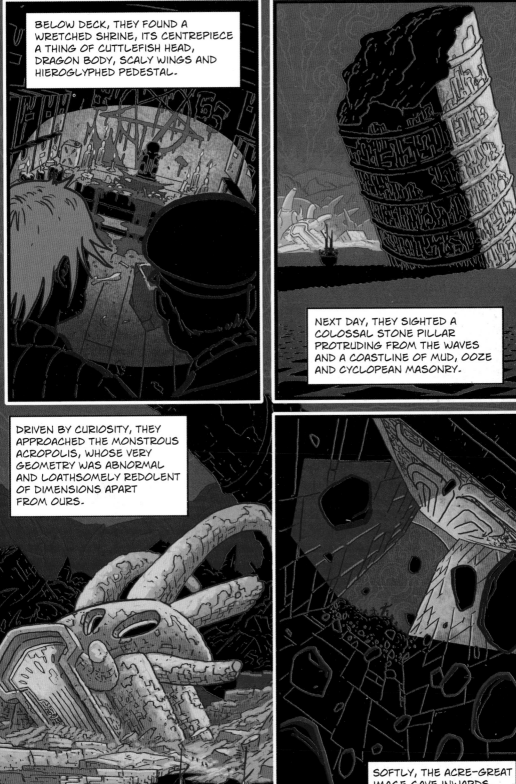

BELOW DECK, THEY FOUND A WRETCHED SHRINE, ITS CENTREPIECE A THING OF CUTTLEFISH HEAD, DRAGON BODY, SCALY WINGS AND HIEROGLYPHED PEDESTAL.

NEXT DAY, THEY SIGHTED A COLOSSAL STONE PILLAR PROTRUDING FROM THE WAVES AND A COASTLINE OF MUD, OOZE AND CYCLOPEAN MASONRY.

DRIVEN BY CURIOSITY, THEY APPROACHED THE MONSTROUS ACROPOLIS, WHOSE VERY GEOMETRY WAS ABNORMAL AND LOATHSOMELY REDOLENT OF DIMENSIONS APART FROM OURS.

SOFTLY, THE ACRE-GREAT IMAGE GAVE INWARDS.

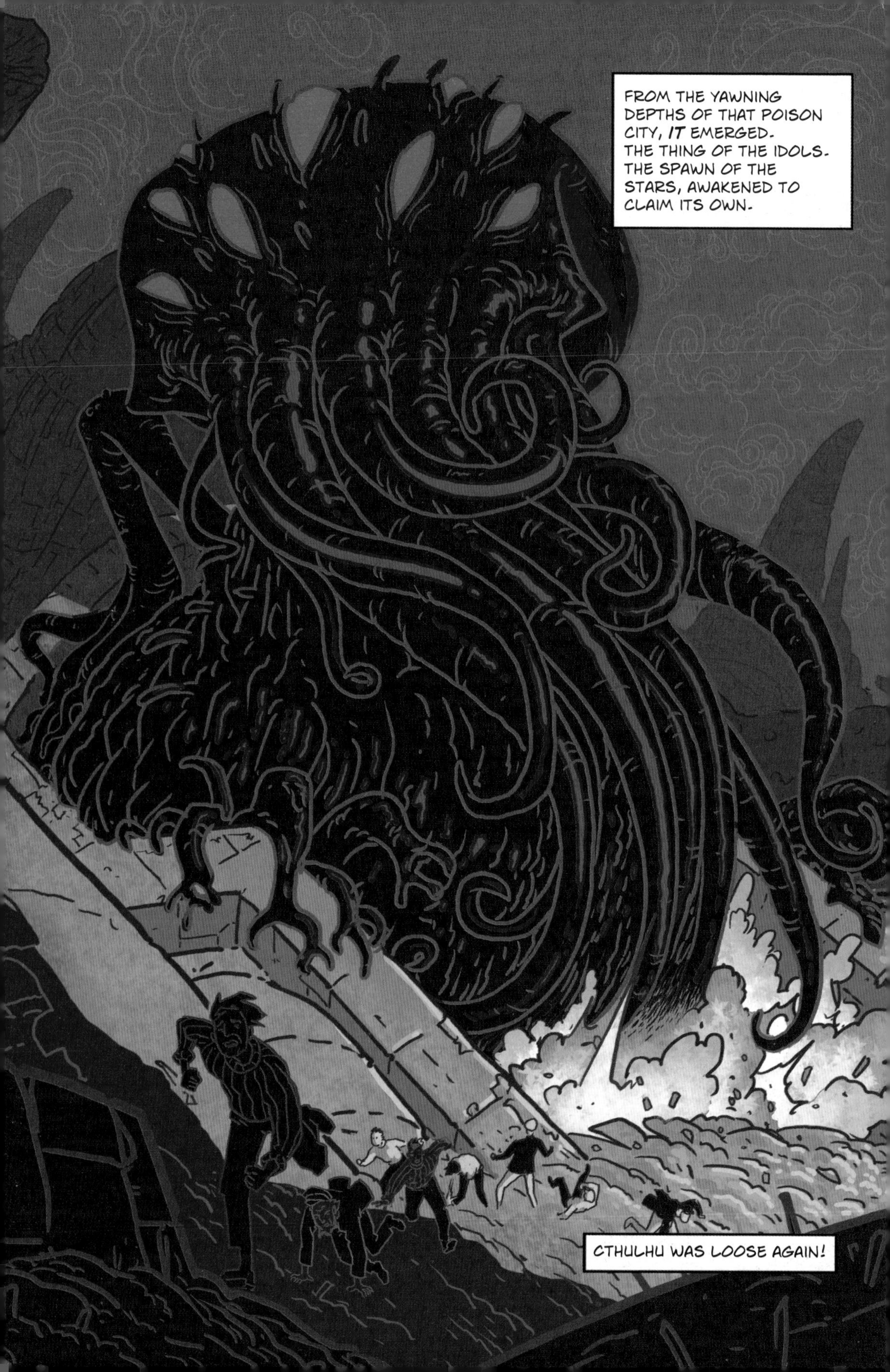
FROM THE YAWNING DEPTHS OF THAT POISON CITY, *IT* EMERGED. THE THING OF THE IDOLS. THE SPAWN OF THE STARS, AWAKENED TO CLAIM ITS OWN.
CTHULHU WAS LOOSE AGAIN!

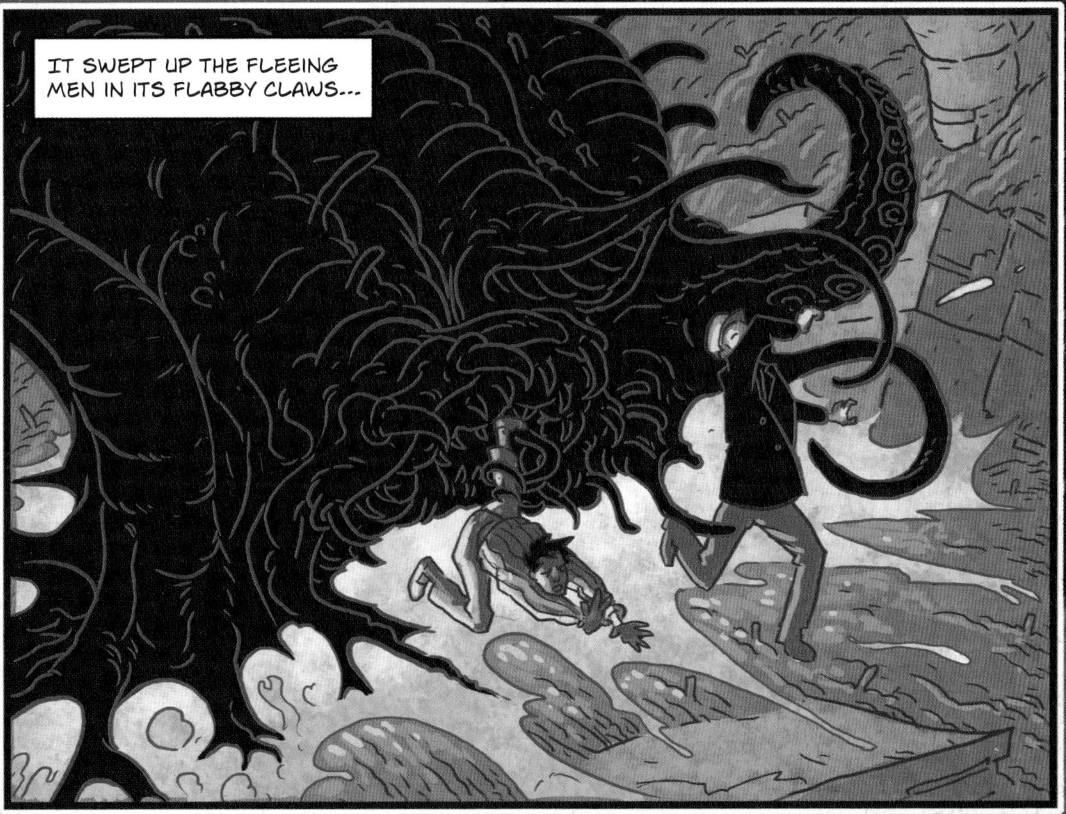
IT SWEPT UP THE FLEEING MEN IN ITS FLABBY CLAWS...

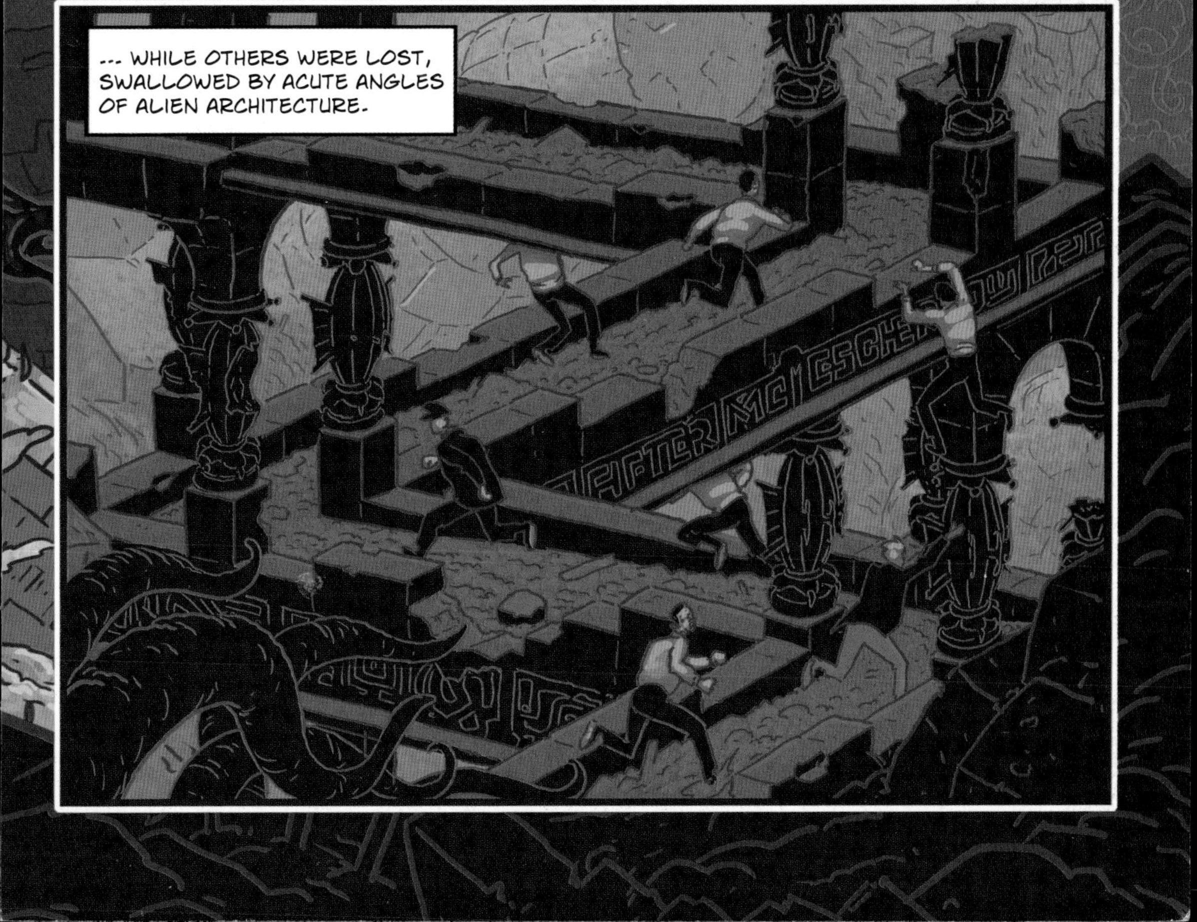
... WHILE OTHERS WERE LOST, SWALLOWED BY ACUTE ANGLES OF ALIEN ARCHITECTURE.

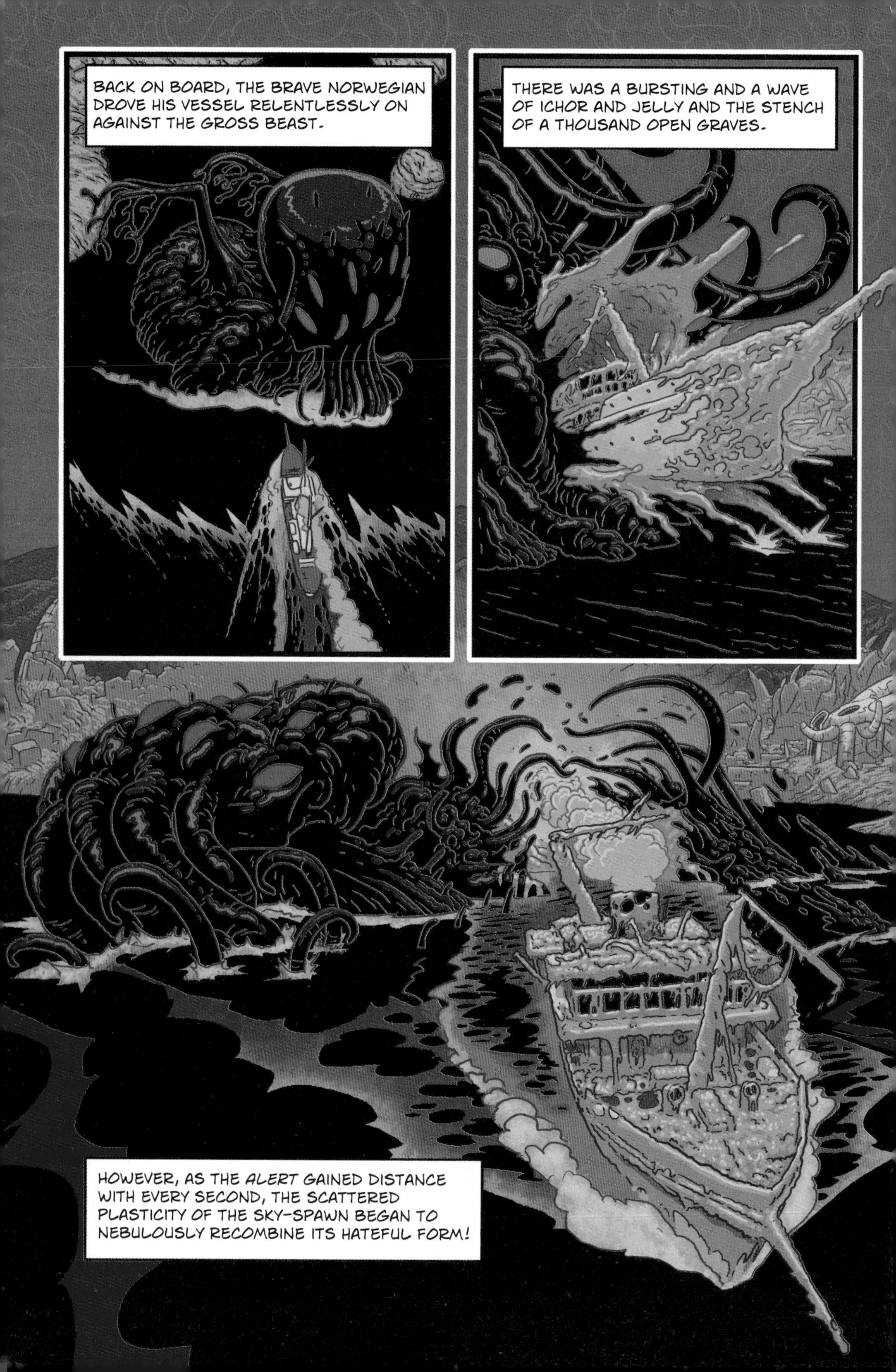
BACK ON BOARD, THE BRAVE NORWEGIAN DROVE HIS VESSEL RELENTLESSLY ON AGAINST THE GROSS BEAST.
THERE WAS A BURSTING AND A WAVE OF ICHOR AND JELLY AND THE STENCH OF A THOUSAND OPEN GRAVES.
HOWEVER, AS THE *ALERT* GAINED DISTANCE WITH EVERY SECOND, THE SCATTERED PLASTICITY OF THE SKY-SPAWN BEGAN TO NEBULOUSLY RECOMBINE ITS HATEFUL FORM!

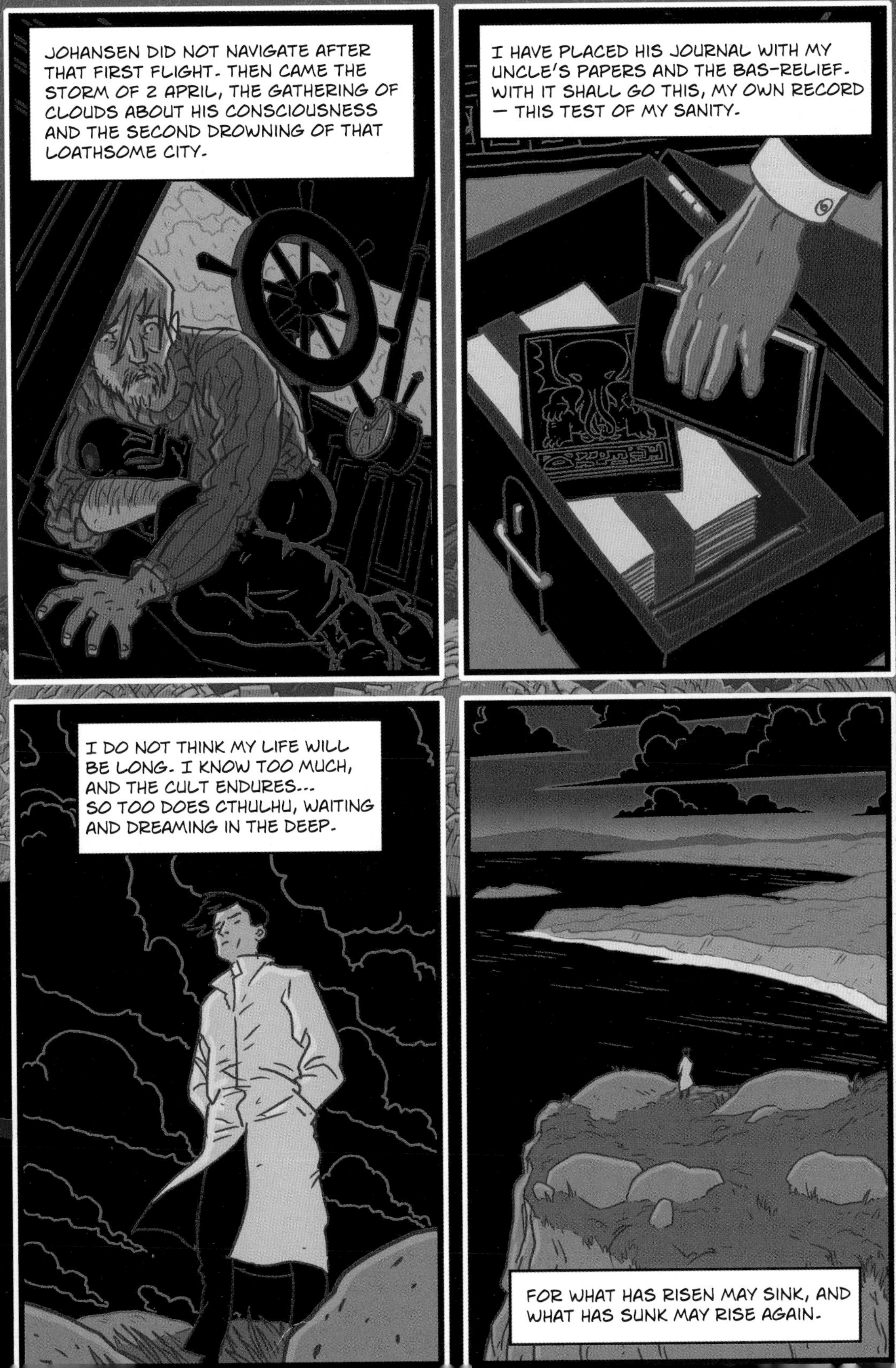

JOHANSEN DID NOT NAVIGATE AFTER THAT FIRST FLIGHT. THEN CAME THE STORM OF 2 APRIL, THE GATHERING OF CLOUDS ABOUT HIS CONSCIOUSNESS AND THE SECOND DROWNING OF THAT LOATHSOME CITY.
I HAVE PLACED HIS JOURNAL WITH MY UNCLE'S PAPERS AND THE BAS-RELIEF. WITH IT SHALL GO THIS, MY OWN RECORD — THIS TEST OF MY SANITY.
I DO NOT THINK MY LIFE WILL BE LONG. I KNOW TOO MUCH, AND THE CULT ENDURES... SO TOO DOES CTHULHU, WAITING AND DREAMING IN THE DEEP.
FOR WHAT HAS RISEN MAY SINK, AND WHAT HAS SUNK MAY RISE AGAIN.

THE HAUNTER
OF THE DARK

Adapted by Dan Lockwood • Illustrated by Shane Ivan Oakley

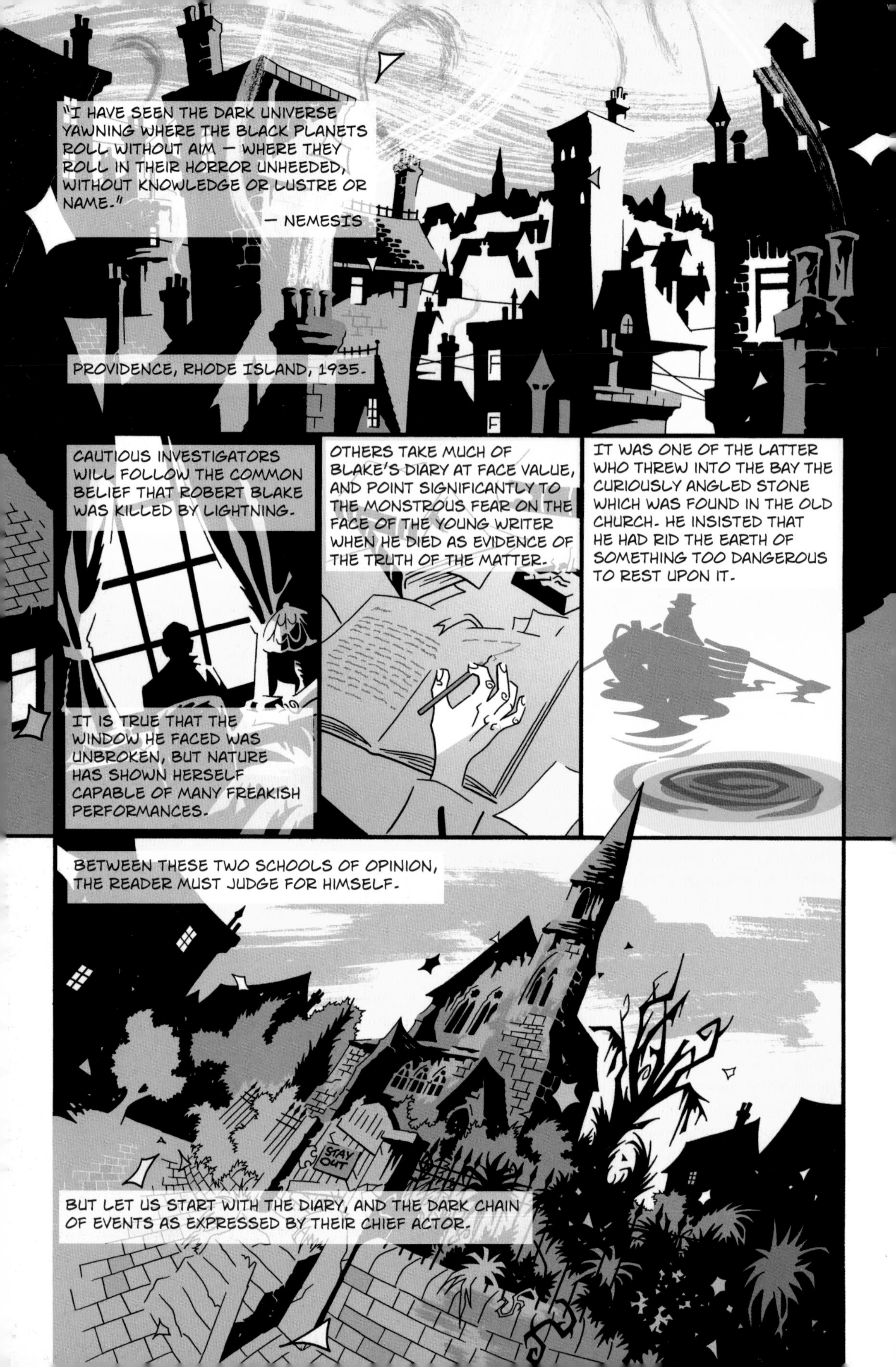
"I HAVE SEEN THE DARK UNIVERSE YAWNING WHERE THE BLACK PLANETS ROLL WITHOUT AIM — WHERE THEY ROLL IN THEIR HORROR UNHEEDED, WITHOUT KNOWLEDGE OR LUSTRE OR NAME."
— NEMESIS
PROVIDENCE, RHODE ISLAND, 1935.
CAUTIOUS INVESTIGATORS WILL FOLLOW THE COMMON BELIEF THAT ROBERT BLAKE WAS KILLED BY LIGHTNING.
IT IS TRUE THAT THE WINDOW HE FACED WAS UNBROKEN, BUT NATURE HAS SHOWN HERSELF CAPABLE OF MANY FREAKISH PERFORMANCES.
OTHERS TAKE MUCH OF BLAKE'S DIARY AT FACE VALUE, AND POINT SIGNIFICANTLY TO THE MONSTROUS FEAR ON THE FACE OF THE YOUNG WRITER WHEN HE DIED AS EVIDENCE OF THE TRUTH OF THE MATTER.
IT WAS ONE OF THE LATTER WHO THREW INTO THE BAY THE CURIOUSLY ANGLED STONE WHICH WAS FOUND IN THE OLD CHURCH. HE INSISTED THAT HE HAD RID THE EARTH OF SOMETHING TOO DANGEROUS TO REST UPON IT.
BETWEEN THESE TWO SCHOOLS OF OPINION, THE READER MUST JUDGE FOR HIMSELF.
STAY OUT
BUT LET US START WITH THE DIARY, AND THE DARK CHAIN OF EVENTS AS EXPRESSED BY THEIR CHIEF ACTOR.

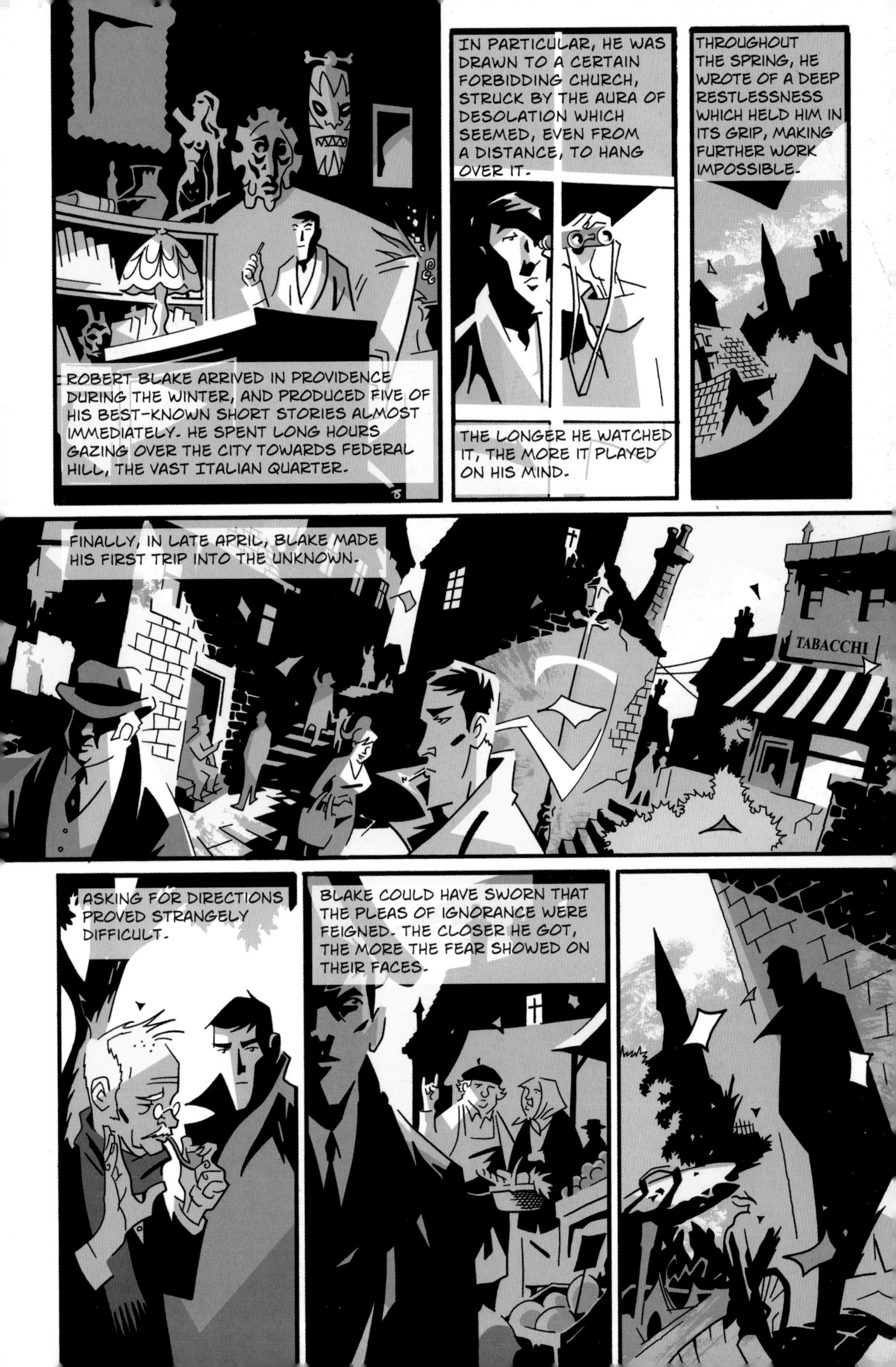
ROBERT BLAKE ARRIVED IN PROVIDENCE DURING THE WINTER, AND PRODUCED FIVE OF HIS BEST-KNOWN SHORT STORIES ALMOST IMMEDIATELY. HE SPENT LONG HOURS GAZING OVER THE CITY TOWARDS FEDERAL HILL, THE VAST ITALIAN QUARTER.
IN PARTICULAR, HE WAS DRAWN TO A CERTAIN FORBIDDING CHURCH, STRUCK BY THE AURA OF DESOLATION WHICH SEEMED, EVEN FROM A DISTANCE, TO HANG OVER IT.
THE LONGER HE WATCHED IT, THE MORE IT PLAYED ON HIS MIND.
THROUGHOUT THE SPRING, HE WROTE OF A DEEP RESTLESSNESS WHICH HELD HIM IN ITS GRIP, MAKING FURTHER WORK IMPOSSIBLE.
FINALLY, IN LATE APRIL, BLAKE MADE HIS FIRST TRIP INTO THE UNKNOWN.
TABACCHI
ASKING FOR DIRECTIONS PROVED STRANGELY DIFFICULT.
BLAKE COULD HAVE SWORN THAT THE PLEAS OF IGNORANCE WERE FEIGNED. THE CLOSER HE GOT, THE MORE THE FEAR SHOWED ON THEIR FACES.

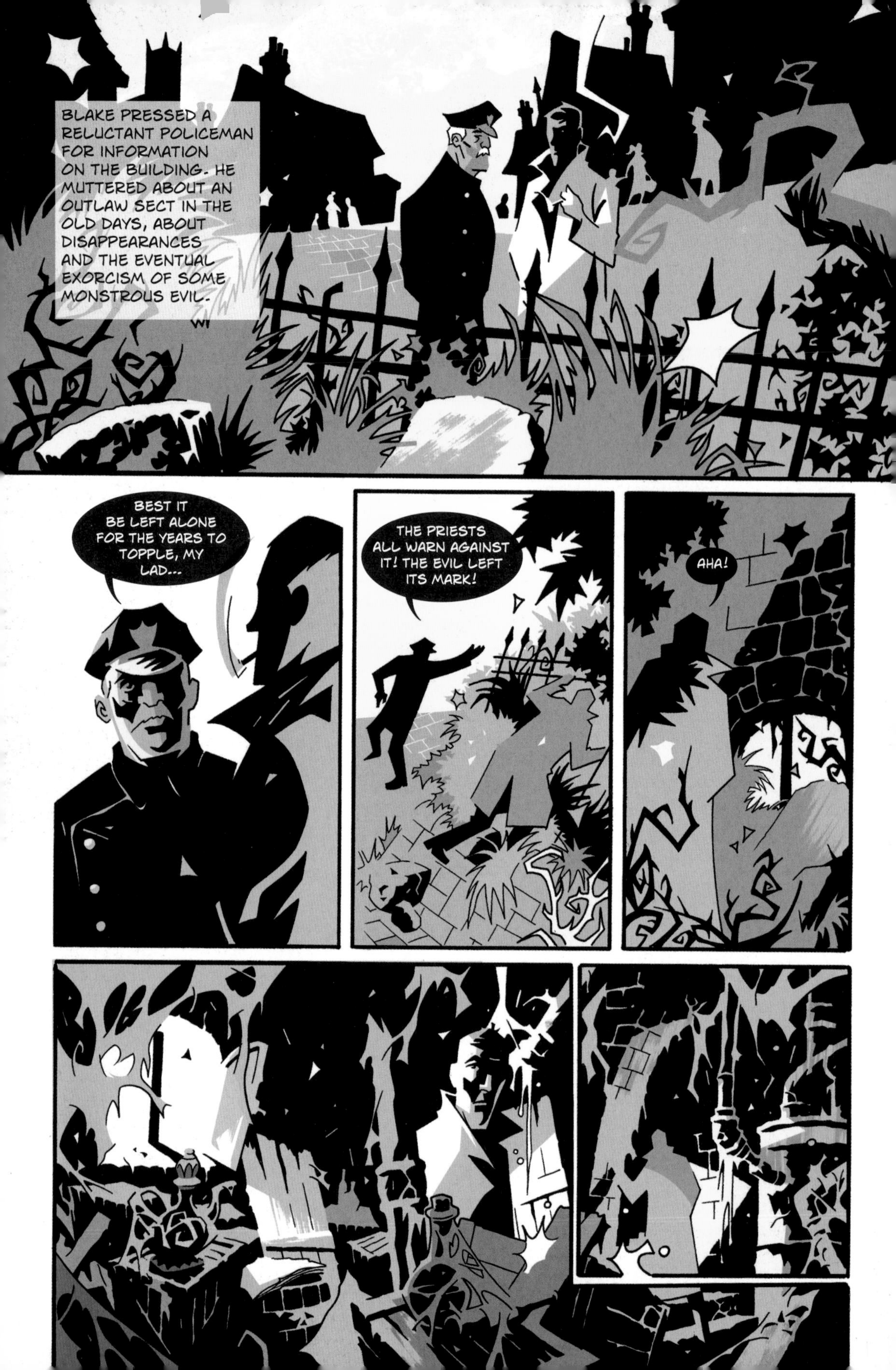
BLAKE PRESSED A RELUCTANT POLICEMAN FOR INFORMATION ON THE BUILDING. HE MUTTERED ABOUT AN OUTLAW SECT IN THE OLD DAYS, ABOUT DISAPPEARANCES AND THE EVENTUAL EXORCISM OF SOME MONSTROUS EVIL.
BEST IT BE LEFT ALONE FOR THE YEARS TO TOPPLE, MY LAD...
THE PRIESTS ALL WARN AGAINST IT! THE EVIL LEFT ITS MARK!
AHA!

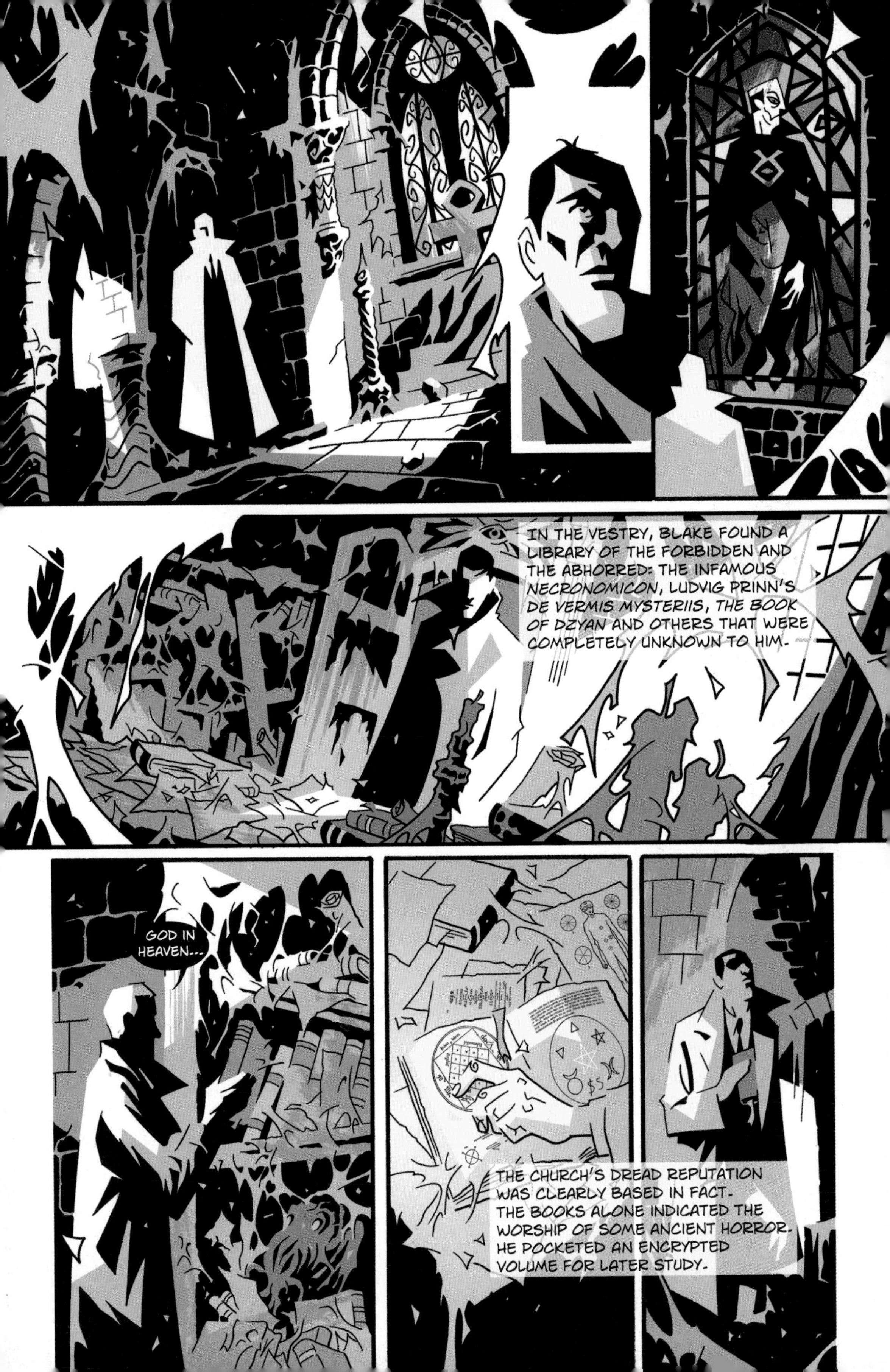
IN THE VESTRY, BLAKE FOUND A LIBRARY OF THE FORBIDDEN AND THE ABHORRED: THE INFAMOUS *NECRONOMICON*, LUDVIG PRINN'S *DE VERMIS MYSTERIIS*, THE *BOOK OF DZYAN* AND OTHERS THAT WERE COMPLETELY UNKNOWN TO HIM.
GOD IN HEAVEN...
THE CHURCH'S DREAD REPUTATION WAS CLEARLY BASED IN FACT. THE BOOKS ALONE INDICATED THE WORSHIP OF SOME ANCIENT HORROR. HE POCKETED AN ENCRYPTED VOLUME FOR LATER STUDY.

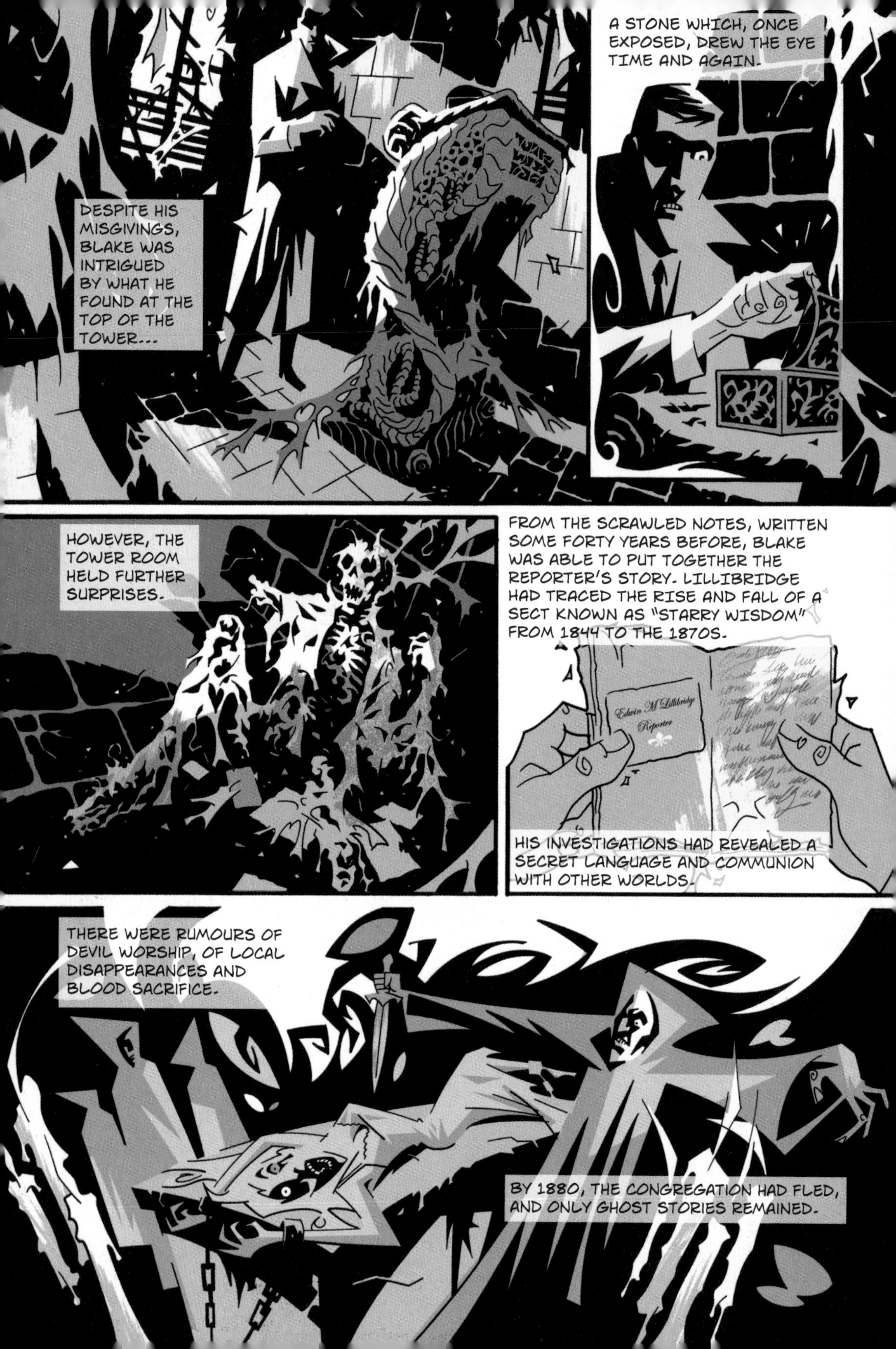
DESPITE HIS MISGIVINGS, BLAKE WAS INTRIGUED BY WHAT HE FOUND AT THE TOP OF THE TOWER...
A STONE WHICH, ONCE EXPOSED, DREW THE EYE TIME AND AGAIN.
HOWEVER, THE TOWER ROOM HELD FURTHER SURPRISES.
FROM THE SCRAWLED NOTES, WRITTEN SOME FORTY YEARS BEFORE, BLAKE WAS ABLE TO PUT TOGETHER THE REPORTER'S STORY. LILLIBRIDGE HAD TRACED THE RISE AND FALL OF A SECT KNOWN AS "STARRY WISDOM" FROM 1844 TO THE 1870S.
Edwin M Lillibridge
Reporter
HIS INVESTIGATIONS HAD REVEALED A SECRET LANGUAGE AND COMMUNION WITH OTHER WORLDS.
THERE WERE RUMOURS OF DEVIL WORSHIP, OF LOCAL DISAPPEARANCES AND BLOOD SACRIFICE.
BY 1880, THE CONGREGATION HAD FLED, AND ONLY GHOST STORIES REMAINED.

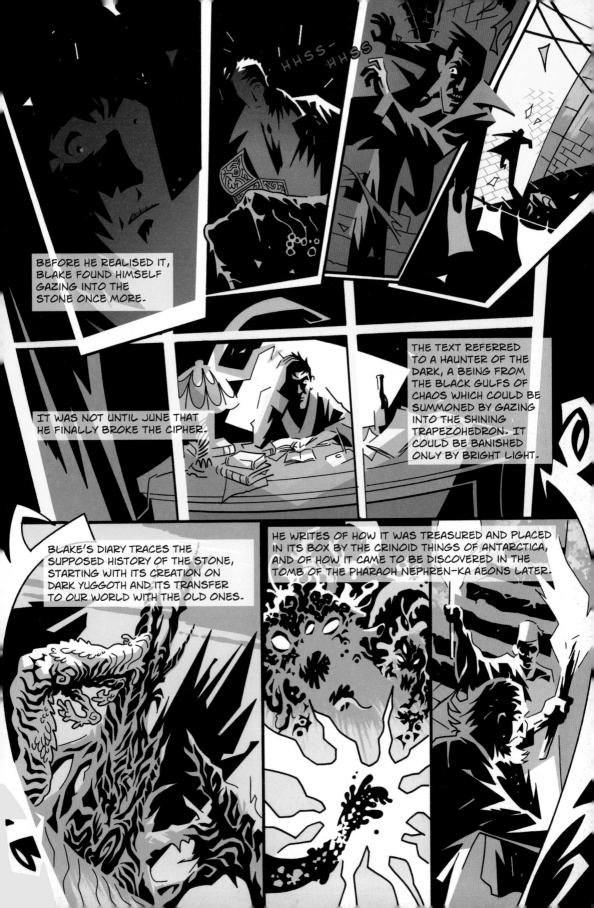

BEFORE HE REALISED IT, BLAKE FOUND HIMSELF GAZING INTO THE STONE ONCE MORE.

IT WAS NOT UNTIL JUNE THAT HE FINALLY BROKE THE CIPHER.

THE TEXT REFERRED TO A HAUNTER OF THE DARK, A BEING FROM THE BLACK GULFS OF CHAOS WHICH COULD BE SUMMONED BY GAZING INTO THE SHINING TRAPEZOHEDRON. IT COULD BE BANISHED ONLY BY BRIGHT LIGHT.

BLAKE'S DIARY TRACES THE SUPPOSED HISTORY OF THE STONE, STARTING WITH ITS CREATION ON DARK YUGGOTH AND ITS TRANSFER TO OUR WORLD WITH THE OLD ONES.

HE WRITES OF HOW IT WAS TREASURED AND PLACED IN ITS BOX BY THE CRINOID THINGS OF ANTARCTICA, AND OF HOW IT CAME TO BE DISCOVERED IN THE TOMB OF THE PHARAOH NEPHREN-KA AEONS LATER.

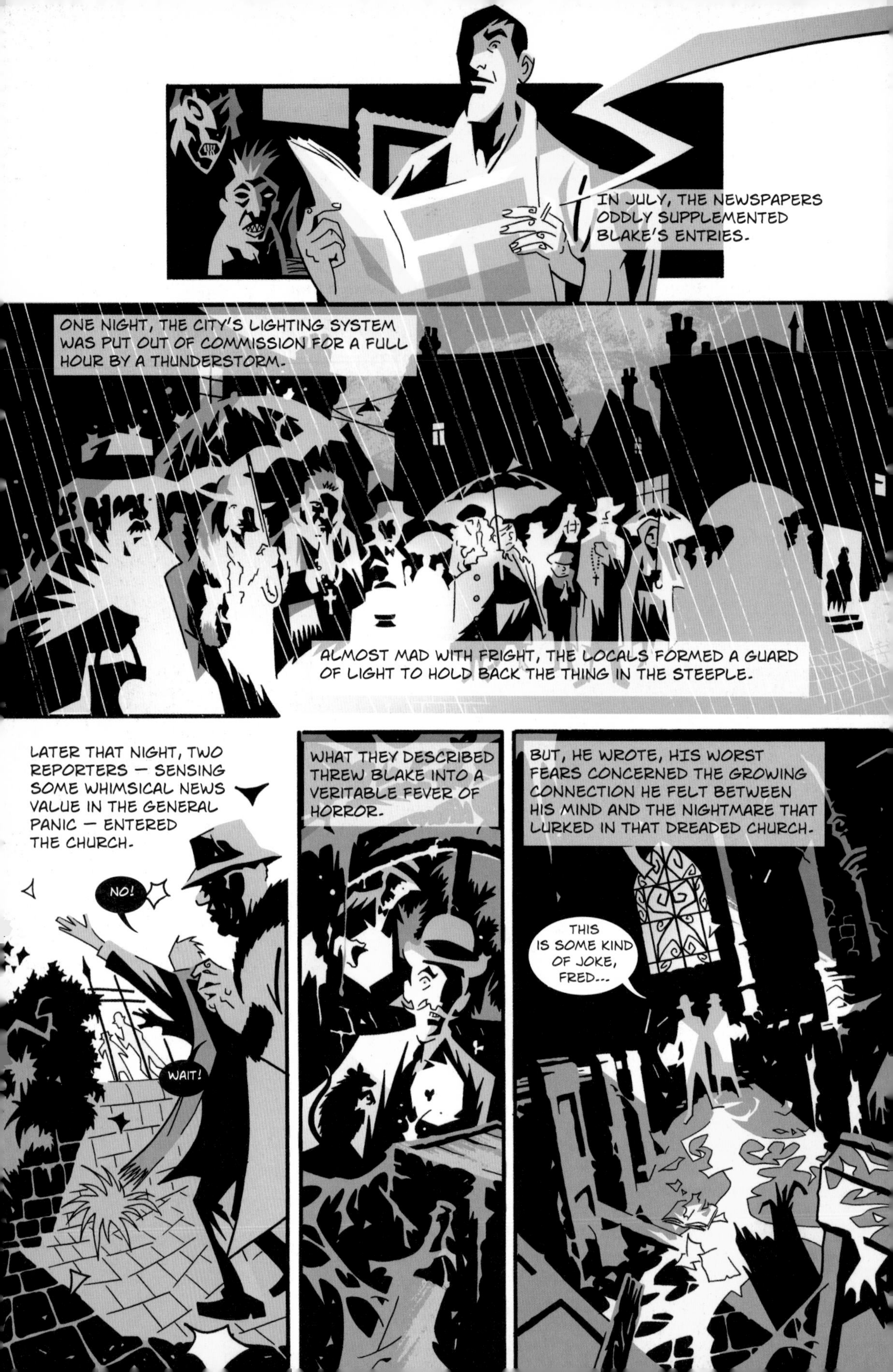
IN JULY, THE NEWSPAPERS ODDLY SUPPLEMENTED BLAKE'S ENTRIES.
ONE NIGHT, THE CITY'S LIGHTING SYSTEM WAS PUT OUT OF COMMISSION FOR A FULL HOUR BY A THUNDERSTORM.
ALMOST MAD WITH FRIGHT, THE LOCALS FORMED A GUARD OF LIGHT TO HOLD BACK THE THING IN THE STEEPLE.
LATER THAT NIGHT, TWO REPORTERS — SENSING SOME WHIMSICAL NEWS VALUE IN THE GENERAL PANIC — ENTERED THE CHURCH.
NO!
WAIT!
WHAT THEY DESCRIBED THREW BLAKE INTO A VERITABLE FEVER OF HORROR.
BUT, HE WROTE, HIS WORST FEARS CONCERNED THE GROWING CONNECTION HE FELT BETWEEN HIS MIND AND THE NIGHTMARE THAT LURKED IN THAT DREADED CHURCH.
THIS IS SOME KIND OF JOKE, FRED...

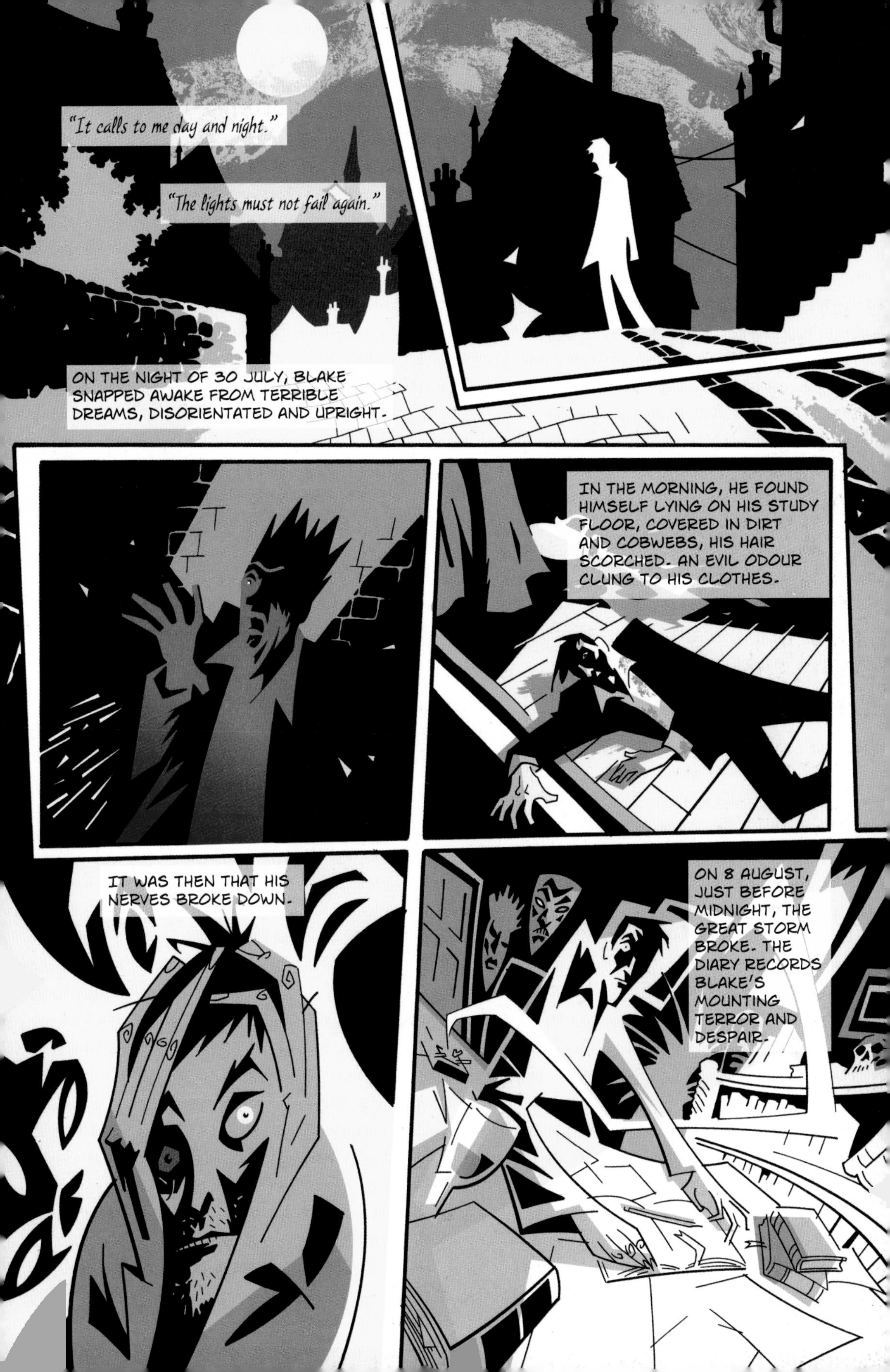
"It calls to me day and night."
"The lights must not fail again."
ON THE NIGHT OF 30 JULY, BLAKE SNAPPED AWAKE FROM TERRIBLE DREAMS, DISORIENTATED AND UPRIGHT.
IN THE MORNING, HE FOUND HIMSELF LYING ON HIS STUDY FLOOR, COVERED IN DIRT AND COBWEBS, HIS HAIR SCORCHED. AN EVIL ODOUR CLUNG TO HIS CLOTHES.
IT WAS THEN THAT HIS NERVES BROKE DOWN.
ON 8 AUGUST, JUST BEFORE MIDNIGHT, THE GREAT STORM BROKE. THE DIARY RECORDS BLAKE'S MOUNTING TERROR AND DESPAIR.

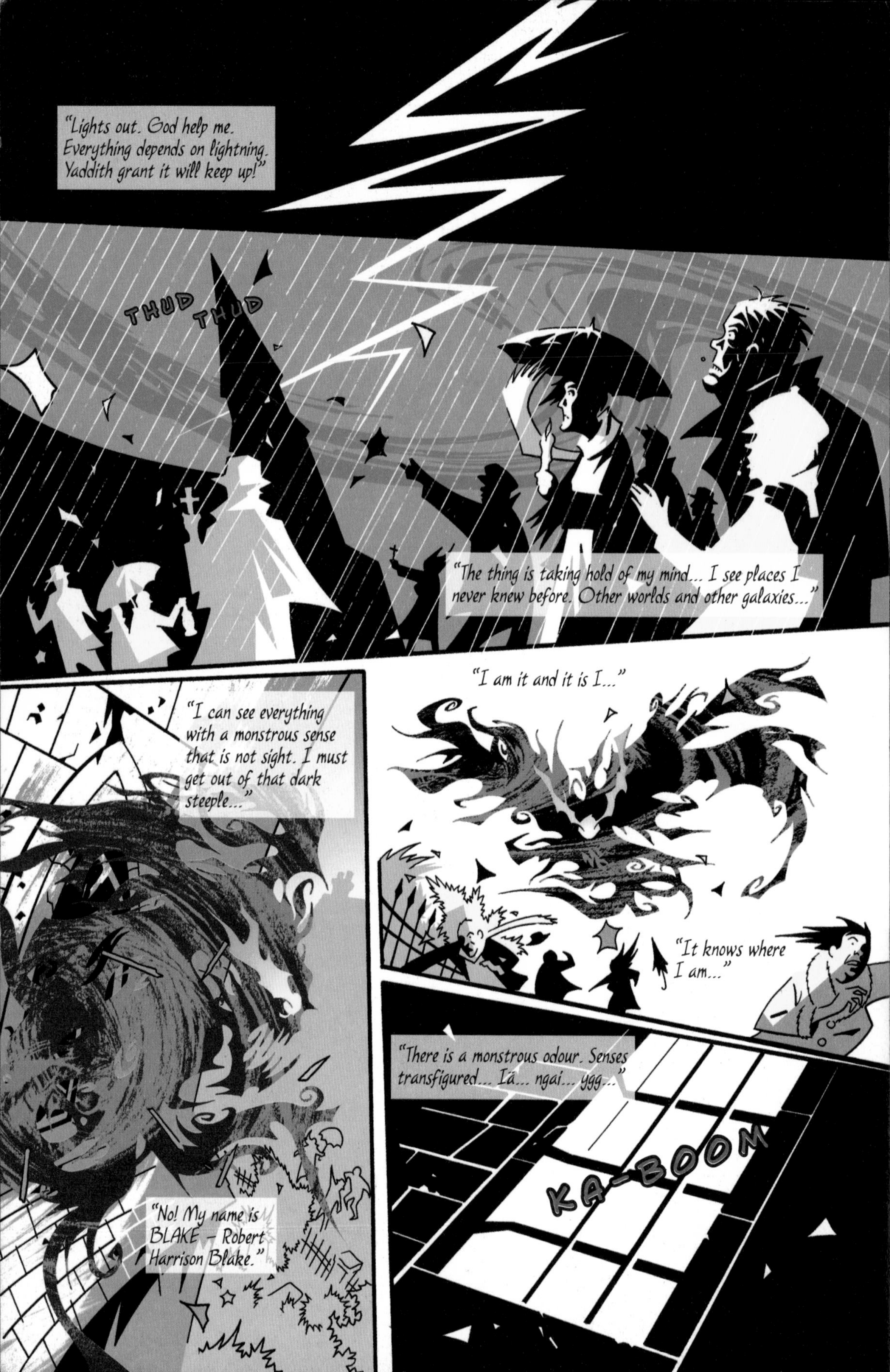
"Lights out. God help me. Everything depends on lightning. Yaddith grant it will keep up!"
THUD THUD
"The thing is taking hold of my mind... I see places I never knew before. Other worlds and other galaxies..."
"I can see everything with a monstrous sense that is not sight. I must get out of that dark steeple..."
"No! My name is BLAKE – Robert Harrison Blake."
"I am it and it is I..."
"It knows where I am..."
"There is a monstrous odour. Senses transfigured... Iä... ngai... ygg..."
KA-BOOM

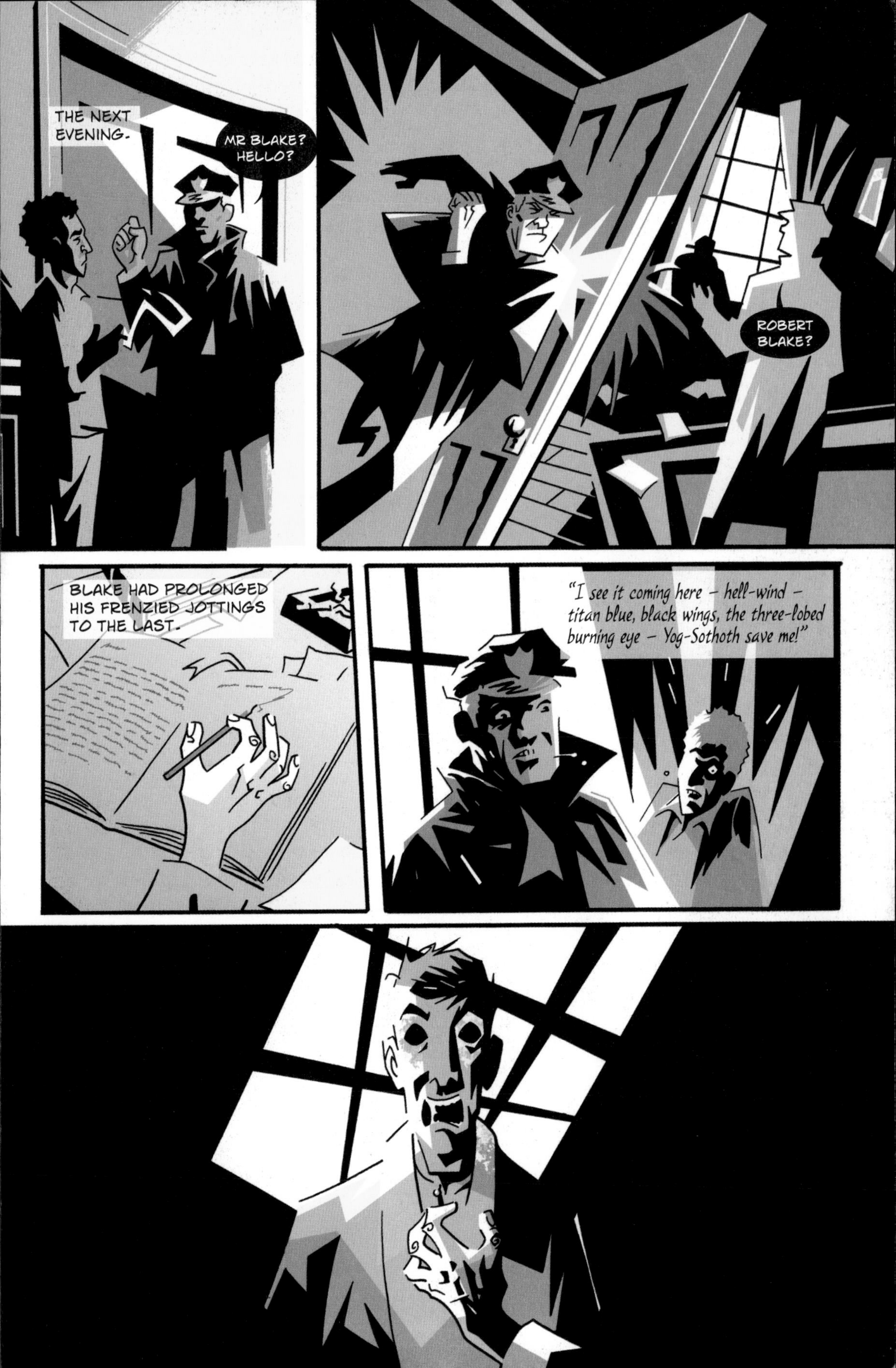
THE NEXT EVENING.
MR BLAKE? HELLO?
ROBERT BLAKE?
BLAKE HAD PROLONGED HIS FRENZIED JOTTINGS TO THE LAST.
"I see it coming here – hell-wind – titan blue, black wings, the three-lobed burning eye – Yog-Sothoth save me!"

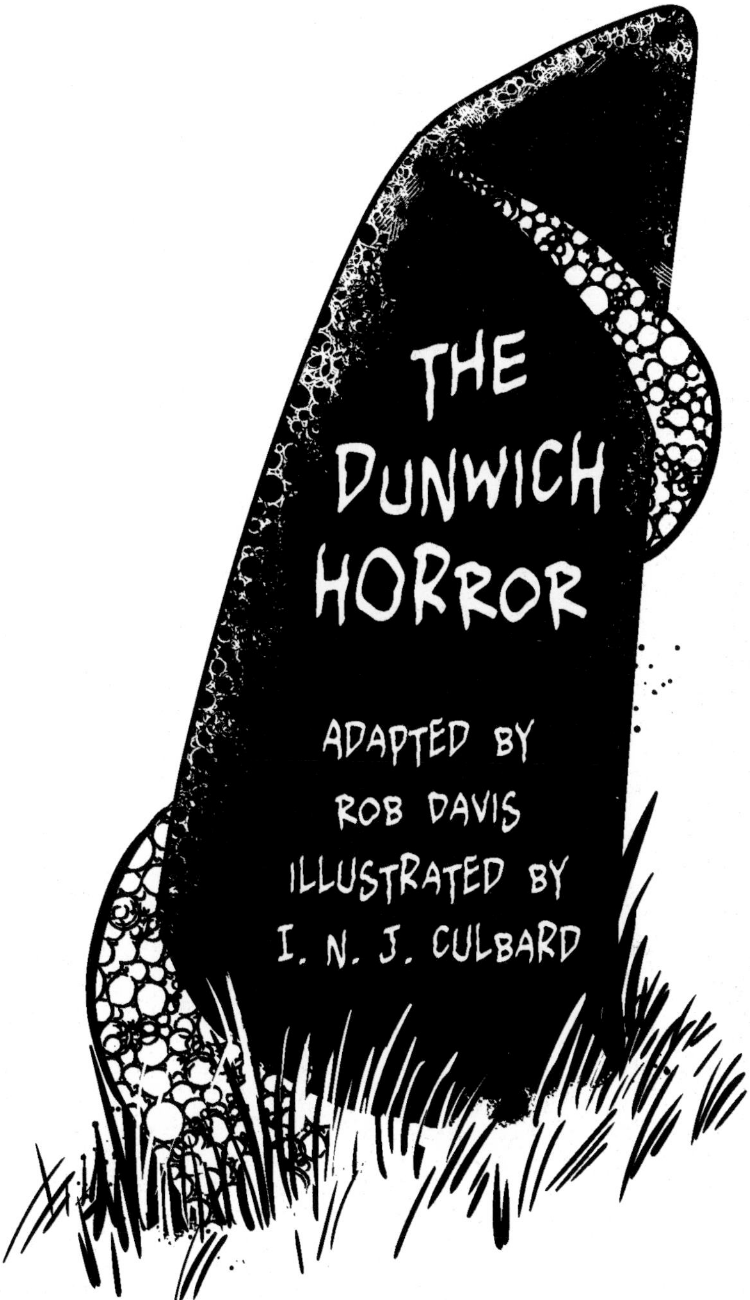
THE DUNWICH HORROR
ADAPTED BY ROB DAVIS
ILLUSTRATED BY I. N. J. CULBARD

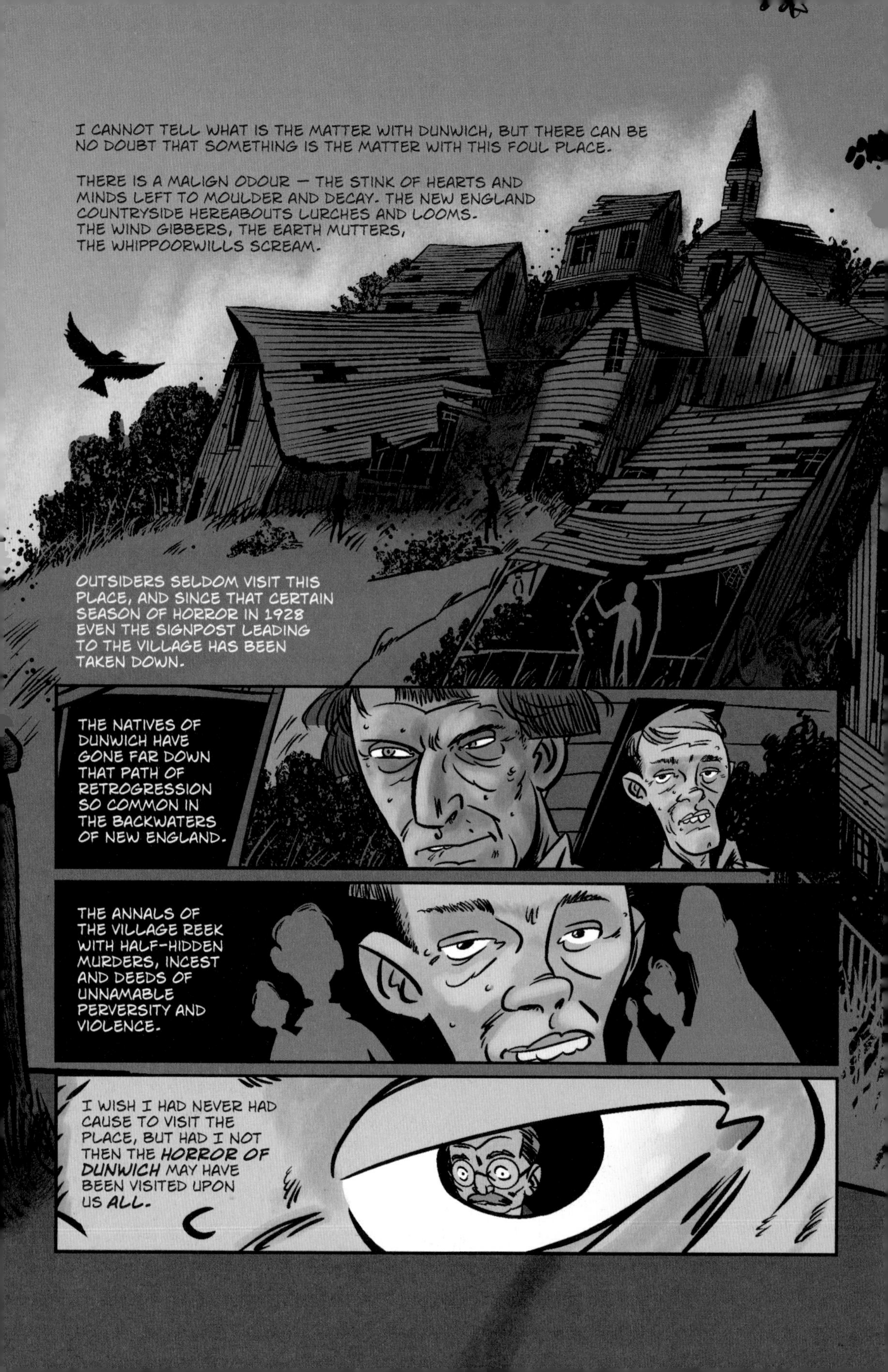
I CANNOT TELL WHAT IS THE MATTER WITH DUNWICH, BUT THERE CAN BE NO DOUBT THAT SOMETHING IS THE MATTER WITH THIS FOUL PLACE.
THERE IS A MALIGN ODOUR — THE STINK OF HEARTS AND MINDS LEFT TO MOULDER AND DECAY. THE NEW ENGLAND COUNTRYSIDE HEREABOUTS LURCHES AND LOOMS. THE WIND GIBBERS, THE EARTH MUTTERS, THE WHIPPOORWILLS SCREAM.
OUTSIDERS SELDOM VISIT THIS PLACE, AND SINCE THAT CERTAIN SEASON OF HORROR IN 1928 EVEN THE SIGNPOST LEADING TO THE VILLAGE HAS BEEN TAKEN DOWN.
THE NATIVES OF DUNWICH HAVE GONE FAR DOWN THAT PATH OF RETROGRESSION SO COMMON IN THE BACKWATERS OF NEW ENGLAND.
THE ANNALS OF THE VILLAGE REEK WITH HALF-HIDDEN MURDERS, INCEST AND DEEDS OF UNNAMABLE PERVERSITY AND VIOLENCE.
I WISH I HAD NEVER HAD CAUSE TO VISIT THE PLACE, BUT HAD I NOT THEN THE ***HORROR OF DUNWICH*** MAY HAVE BEEN VISITED UPON US ***ALL***.

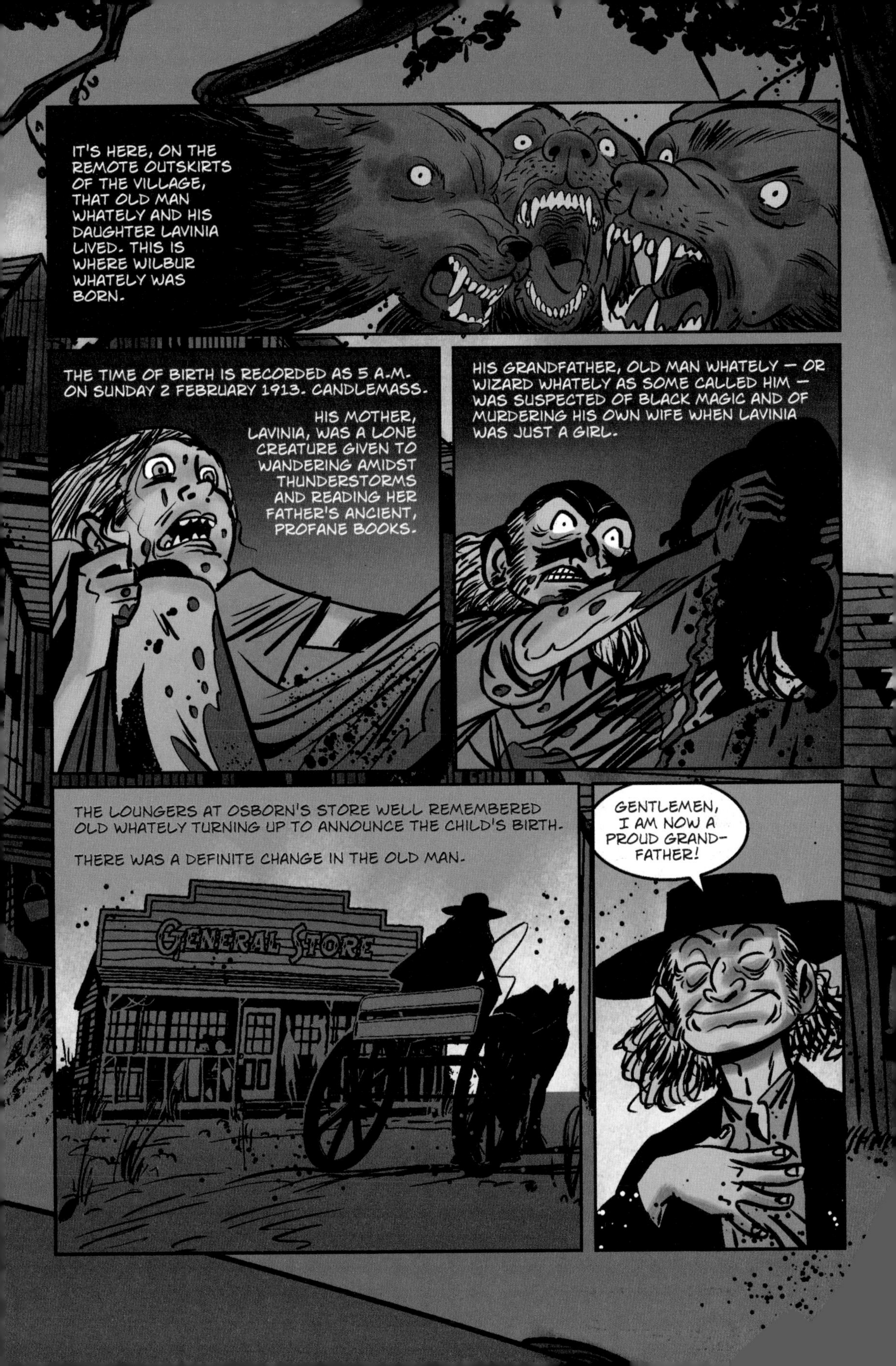
IT'S HERE, ON THE REMOTE OUTSKIRTS OF THE VILLAGE, THAT OLD MAN WHATELY AND HIS DAUGHTER LAVINIA LIVED. THIS IS WHERE WILBUR WHATELY WAS BORN.
THE TIME OF BIRTH IS RECORDED AS 5 A.M. ON SUNDAY 2 FEBRUARY 1913. CANDLEMASS.
HIS MOTHER, LAVINIA, WAS A LONE CREATURE GIVEN TO WANDERING AMIDST THUNDERSTORMS AND READING HER FATHER'S ANCIENT, PROFANE BOOKS.
HIS GRANDFATHER, OLD MAN WHATELY — OR WIZARD WHATELY AS SOME CALLED HIM — WAS SUSPECTED OF BLACK MAGIC AND OF MURDERING HIS OWN WIFE WHEN LAVINIA WAS JUST A GIRL.
THE LOUNGERS AT OSBORN'S STORE WELL REMEMBERED OLD WHATELY TURNING UP TO ANNOUNCE THE CHILD'S BIRTH.
THERE WAS A DEFINITE CHANGE IN THE OLD MAN.
GENERAL STORE
GENTLEMEN, I AM NOW A PROUD GRAND-FATHER!

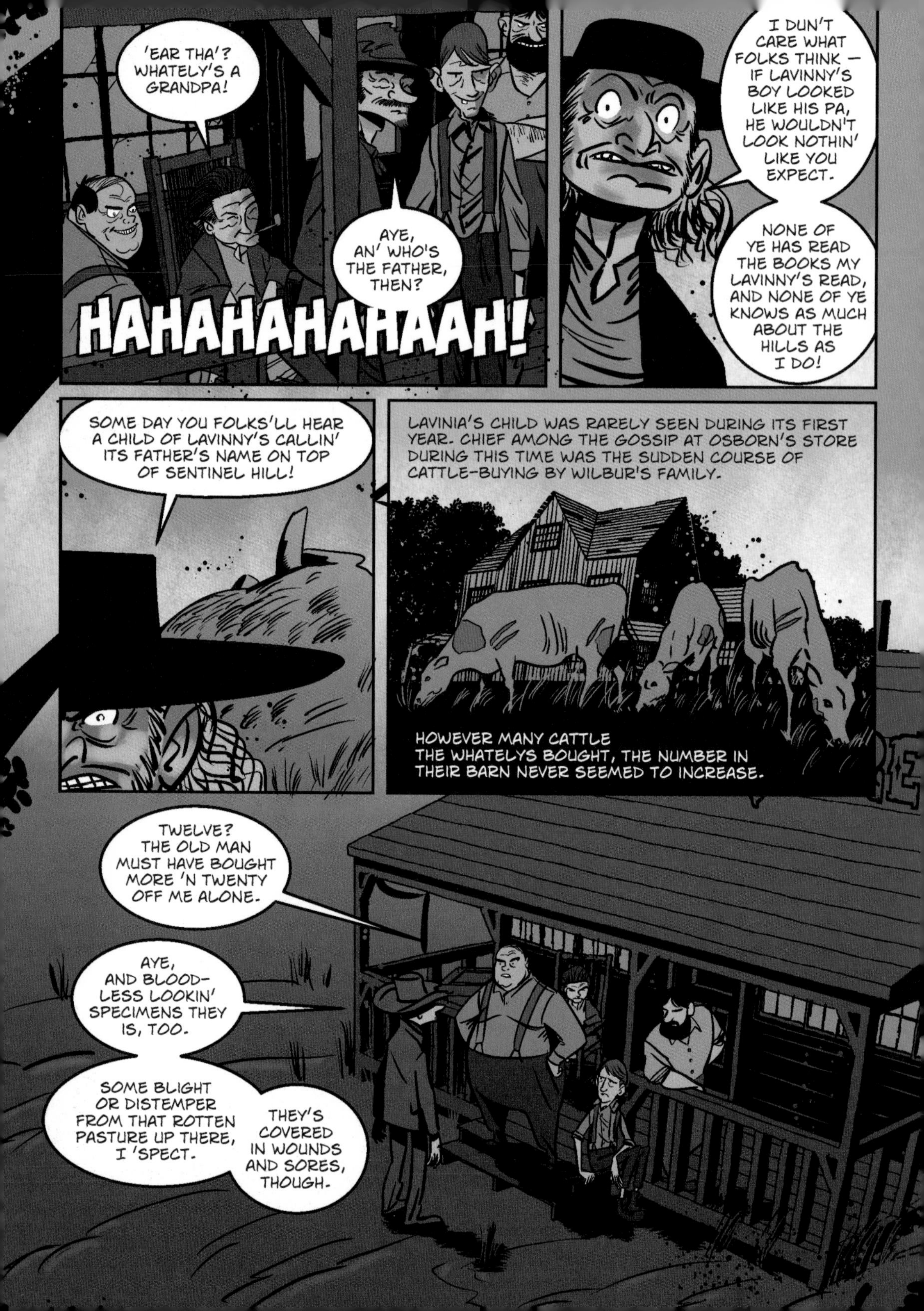
'EAR THA'? WHATELY'S A GRANDPA!
AYE, AN' WHO'S THE FATHER, THEN?
HAHAHAHAHAAAH!
I DUN'T CARE WHAT FOLKS THINK — IF LAVINNY'S BOY LOOKED LIKE HIS PA, HE WOULDN'T LOOK NOTHIN' LIKE YOU EXPECT.
NONE OF YE HAS READ THE BOOKS MY LAVINNY'S READ, AND NONE OF YE KNOWS AS MUCH ABOUT THE HILLS AS I DO!
SOME DAY YOU FOLKS'LL HEAR A CHILD OF LAVINNY'S CALLIN' ITS FATHER'S NAME ON TOP OF SENTINEL HILL!
LAVINIA'S CHILD WAS RARELY SEEN DURING ITS FIRST YEAR. CHIEF AMONG THE GOSSIP AT OSBORN'S STORE DURING THIS TIME WAS THE SUDDEN COURSE OF CATTLE-BUYING BY WILBUR'S FAMILY.
HOWEVER MANY CATTLE THE WHATELYS BOUGHT, THE NUMBER IN THEIR BARN NEVER SEEMED TO INCREASE.
TWELVE? THE OLD MAN MUST HAVE BOUGHT MORE 'N TWENTY OFF ME ALONE.
AYE, AND BLOOD-LESS LOOKIN' SPECIMENS THEY IS, TOO.
SOME BLIGHT OR DISTEMPER FROM THAT ROTTEN PASTURE UP THERE, I 'SPECT.
THEY'S COVERED IN WOUNDS AND SORES, THOUGH.

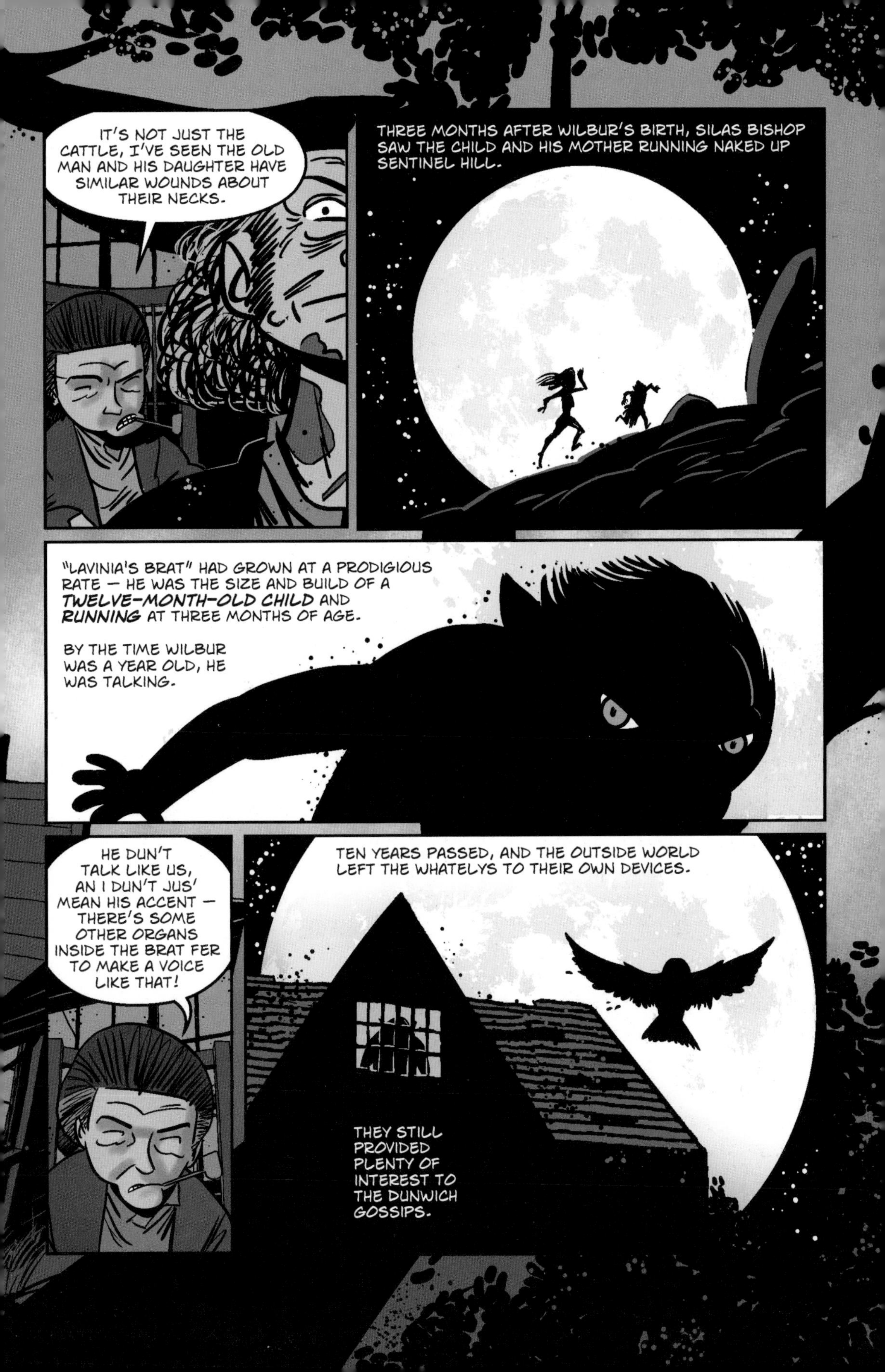
IT'S NOT JUST THE CATTLE, I'VE SEEN THE OLD MAN AND HIS DAUGHTER HAVE SIMILAR WOUNDS ABOUT THEIR NECKS.
THREE MONTHS AFTER WILBUR'S BIRTH, SILAS BISHOP SAW THE CHILD AND HIS MOTHER RUNNING NAKED UP SENTINEL HILL.
"LAVINIA'S BRAT" HAD GROWN AT A PRODIGIOUS RATE — HE WAS THE SIZE AND BUILD OF A TWELVE-MONTH-OLD CHILD AND RUNNING AT THREE MONTHS OF AGE.
BY THE TIME WILBUR WAS A YEAR OLD, HE WAS TALKING.
HE DUN'T TALK LIKE US, AN I DUN'T JUS' MEAN HIS ACCENT — THERE'S SOME OTHER ORGANS INSIDE THE BRAT FER TO MAKE A VOICE LIKE THAT!
TEN YEARS PASSED, AND THE OUTSIDE WORLD LEFT THE WHATELYS TO THEIR OWN DEVICES.
THEY STILL PROVIDED PLENTY OF INTEREST TO THE DUNWICH GOSSIPS.

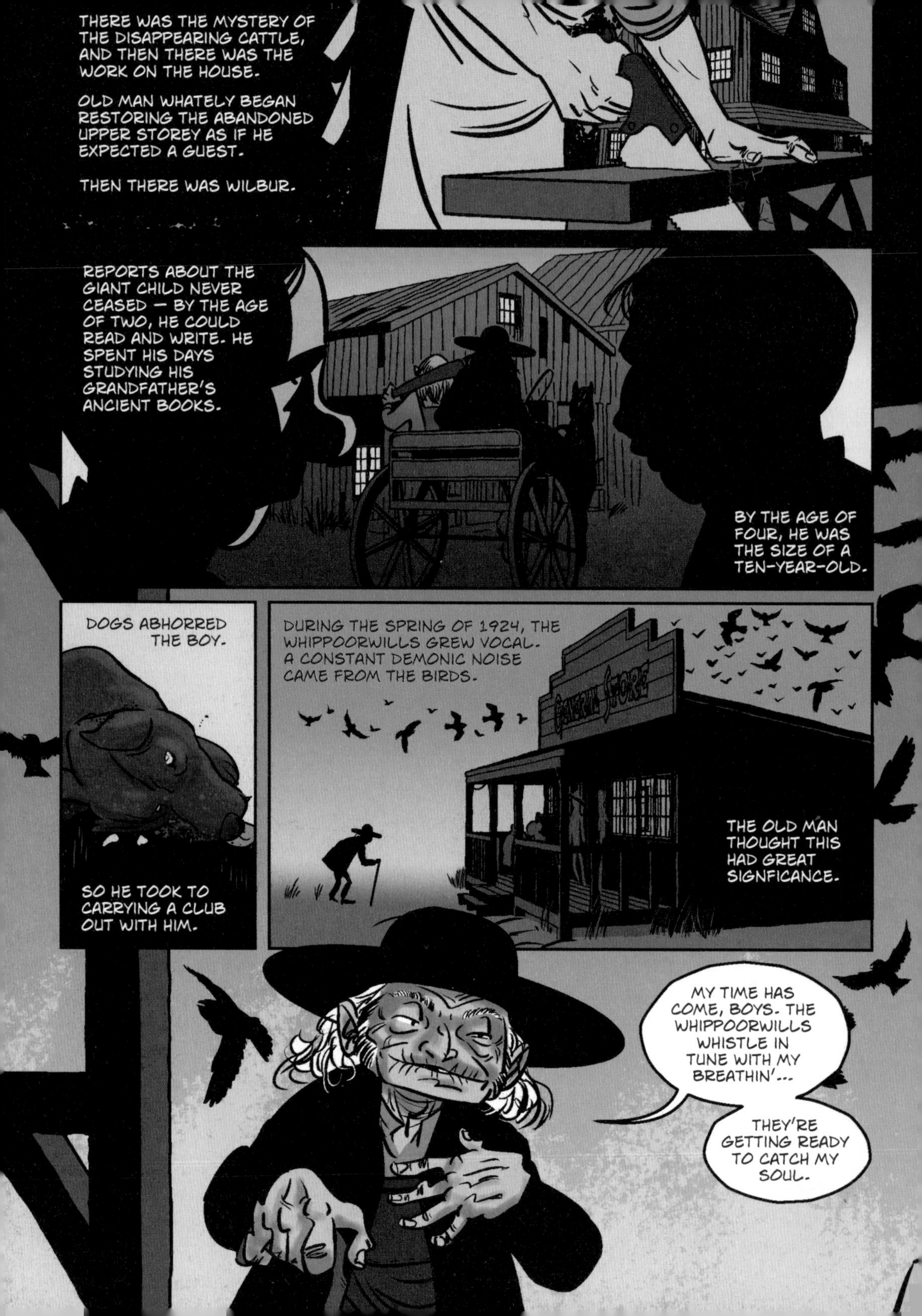
THERE WAS THE MYSTERY OF THE DISAPPEARING CATTLE, AND THEN THERE WAS THE WORK ON THE HOUSE.
OLD MAN WHATELY BEGAN RESTORING THE ABANDONED UPPER STOREY AS IF HE EXPECTED A GUEST.
THEN THERE WAS WILBUR.
REPORTS ABOUT THE GIANT CHILD NEVER CEASED — BY THE AGE OF TWO, HE COULD READ AND WRITE. HE SPENT HIS DAYS STUDYING HIS GRANDFATHER'S ANCIENT BOOKS.
BY THE AGE OF FOUR, HE WAS THE SIZE OF A TEN-YEAR-OLD.
DOGS ABHORRED THE BOY.
SO HE TOOK TO CARRYING A CLUB OUT WITH HIM.
DURING THE SPRING OF 1924, THE WHIPPOORWILLS GREW VOCAL. A CONSTANT DEMONIC NOISE CAME FROM THE BIRDS.
THE OLD MAN THOUGHT THIS HAD GREAT SIGNFICANCE.
MY TIME HAS COME, BOYS. THE WHIPPOORWILLS WHISTLE IN TUNE WITH MY BREATHIN'...
THEY'RE GETTING READY TO CATCH MY SOUL.

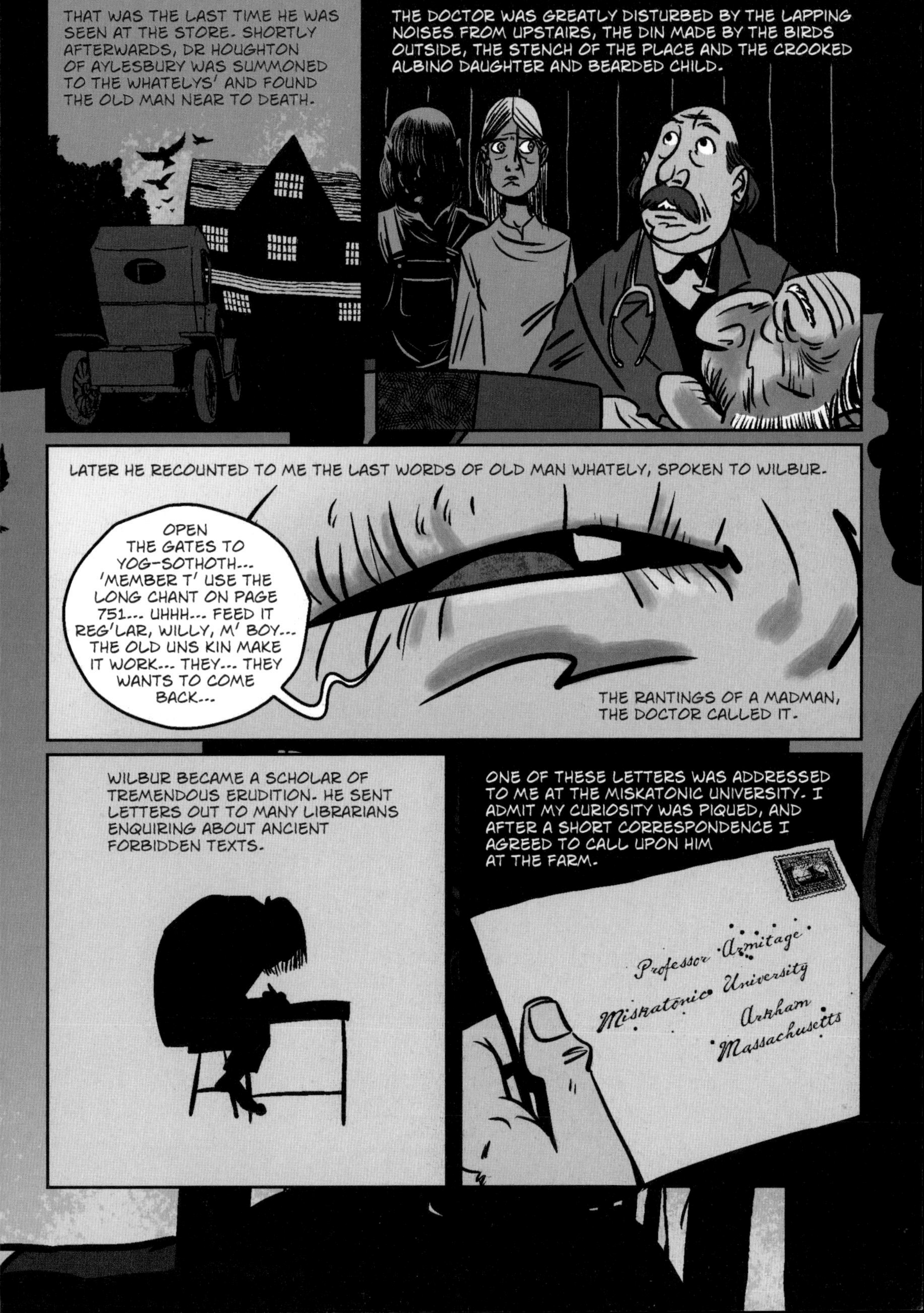
THAT WAS THE LAST TIME HE WAS SEEN AT THE STORE. SHORTLY AFTERWARDS, DR HOUGHTON OF AYLESBURY WAS SUMMONED TO THE WHATELYS' AND FOUND THE OLD MAN NEAR TO DEATH.
THE DOCTOR WAS GREATLY DISTURBED BY THE LAPPING NOISES FROM UPSTAIRS, THE DIN MADE BY THE BIRDS OUTSIDE, THE STENCH OF THE PLACE AND THE CROOKED ALBINO DAUGHTER AND BEARDED CHILD.
LATER HE RECOUNTED TO ME THE LAST WORDS OF OLD MAN WHATELY, SPOKEN TO WILBUR.
OPEN THE GATES TO YOG-SOTHOTH... 'MEMBER T' USE THE LONG CHANT ON PAGE 751... UHHH... FEED IT REG'LAR, WILLY, M' BOY... THE OLD UNS KIN MAKE IT WORK... THEY... THEY WANTS TO COME BACK...
THE RANTINGS OF A MADMAN, THE DOCTOR CALLED IT.
WILBUR BECAME A SCHOLAR OF TREMENDOUS ERUDITION. HE SENT LETTERS OUT TO MANY LIBRARIANS ENQUIRING ABOUT ANCIENT FORBIDDEN TEXTS.
ONE OF THESE LETTERS WAS ADDRESSED TO ME AT THE MISKATONIC UNIVERSITY. I ADMIT MY CURIOSITY WAS PIQUED, AND AFTER A SHORT CORRESPONDENCE I AGREED TO CALL UPON HIM AT THE FARM.
Professor Armitage
Miskatonic University
Arkham
Massachusetts

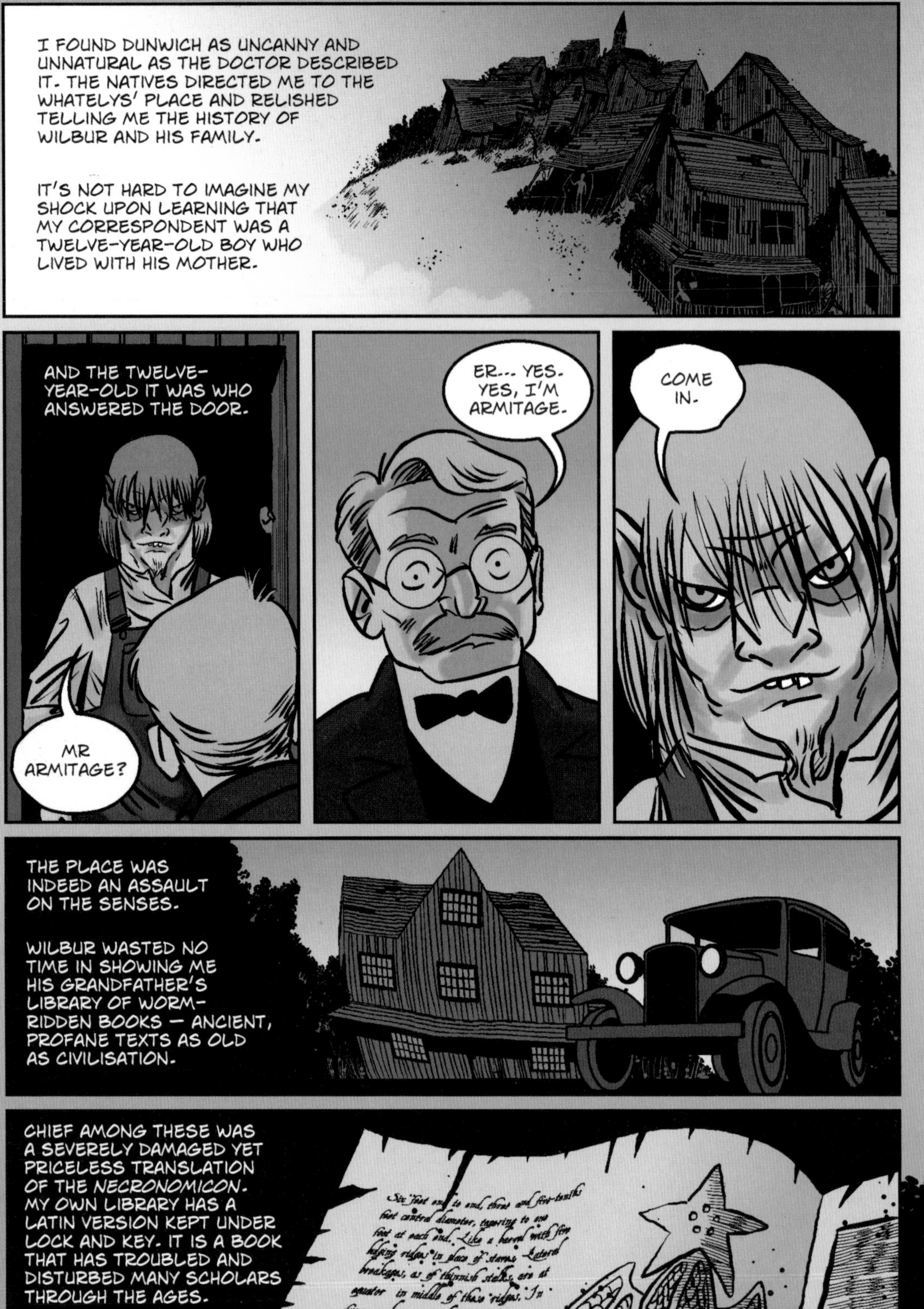

I FOUND DUNWICH AS UNCANNY AND UNNATURAL AS THE DOCTOR DESCRIBED IT. THE NATIVES DIRECTED ME TO THE WHATELYS' PLACE AND RELISHED TELLING ME THE HISTORY OF WILBUR AND HIS FAMILY.
IT'S NOT HARD TO IMAGINE MY SHOCK UPON LEARNING THAT MY CORRESPONDENT WAS A TWELVE-YEAR-OLD BOY WHO LIVED WITH HIS MOTHER.
AND THE TWELVE-YEAR-OLD IT WAS WHO ANSWERED THE DOOR.
MR ARMITAGE?
ER... YES. YES, I'M ARMITAGE.
COME IN.
THE PLACE WAS INDEED AN ASSAULT ON THE SENSES.
WILBUR WASTED NO TIME IN SHOWING ME HIS GRANDFATHER'S LIBRARY OF WORM-RIDDEN BOOKS — ANCIENT, PROFANE TEXTS AS OLD AS CIVILISATION.
CHIEF AMONG THESE WAS A SEVERELY DAMAGED YET PRICELESS TRANSLATION OF THE *NECRONOMICON*. MY OWN LIBRARY HAS A LATIN VERSION KEPT UNDER LOCK AND KEY. IT IS A BOOK THAT HAS TROUBLED AND DISTURBED MANY SCHOLARS THROUGH THE AGES.
Six feet end to end, three and five-tenths
feet central diameter, tapering to one
foot at each end. Like a barrel with five
bulging ridges in place of staves. Lateral
breakages, as of thinnish stalks, are at
equator in middle of these ridges. In

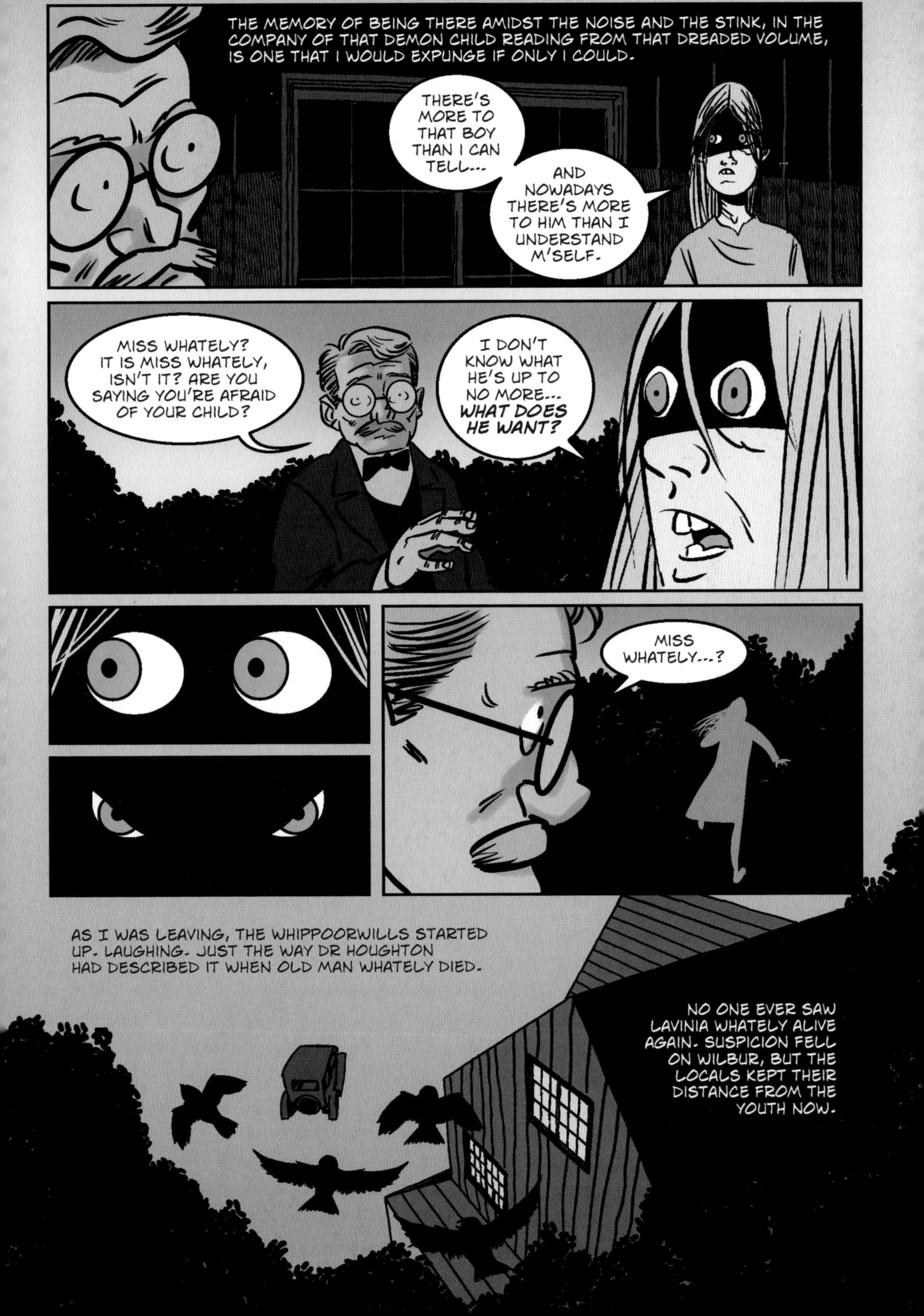

THE MEMORY OF BEING THERE AMIDST THE NOISE AND THE STINK, IN THE COMPANY OF THAT DEMON CHILD READING FROM THAT DREADED VOLUME, IS ONE THAT I WOULD EXPUNGE IF ONLY I COULD.
THERE'S MORE TO THAT BOY THAN I CAN TELL...
AND NOWADAYS THERE'S MORE TO HIM THAN I UNDERSTAND M'SELF.
MISS WHATELY? IT IS MISS WHATELY, ISN'T IT? ARE YOU SAYING YOU'RE AFRAID OF YOUR CHILD?
I DON'T KNOW WHAT HE'S UP TO NO MORE... ***WHAT DOES HE WANT?***
MISS WHATELY...?
AS I WAS LEAVING, THE WHIPPOORWILLS STARTED UP. LAUGHING. JUST THE WAY DR HOUGHTON HAD DESCRIBED IT WHEN OLD MAN WHATELY DIED.
NO ONE EVER SAW LAVINIA WHATELY ALIVE AGAIN. SUSPICION FELL ON WILBUR, BUT THE LOCALS KEPT THEIR DISTANCE FROM THE YOUTH NOW.

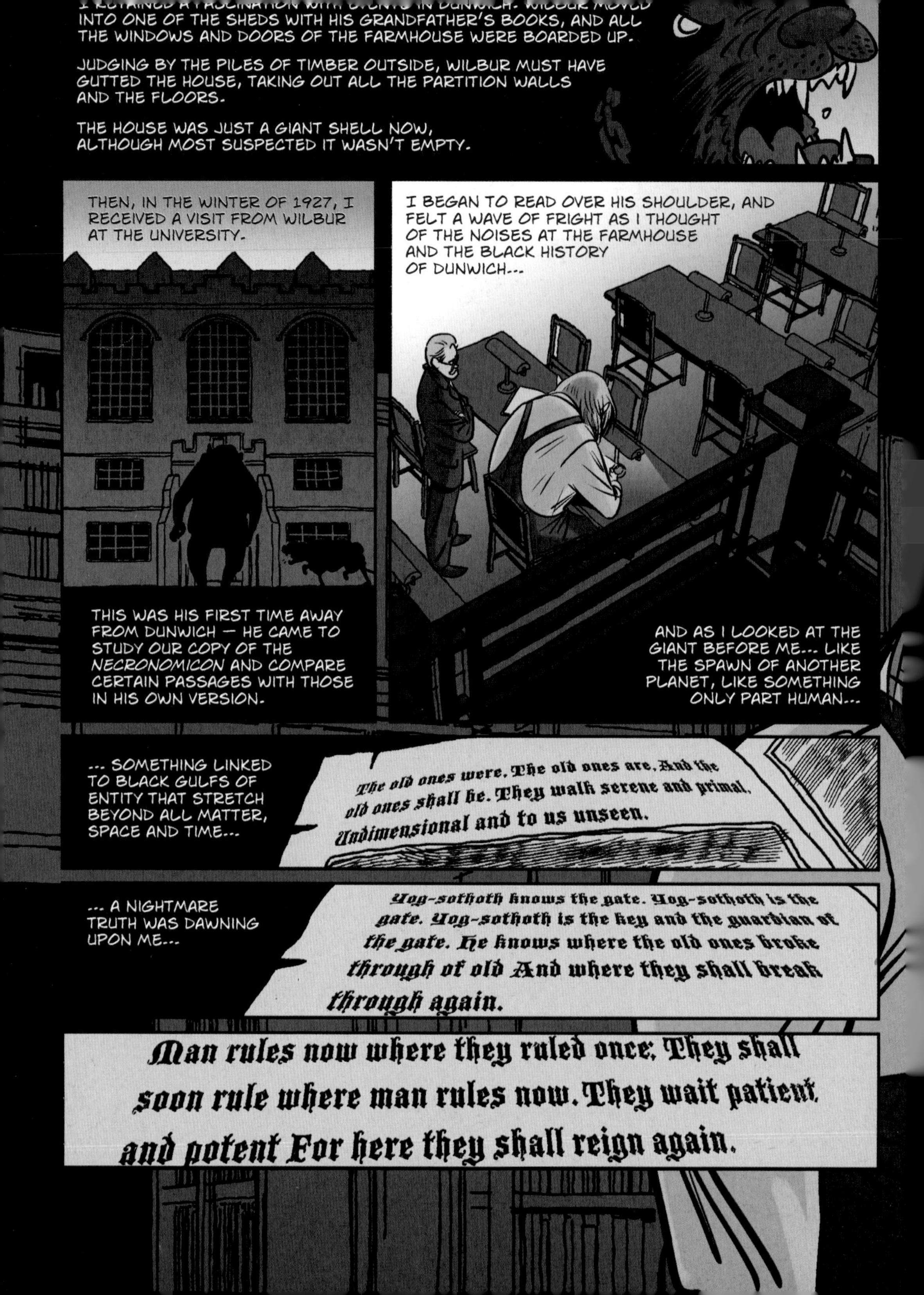
INTO ONE OF THE SHEDS WITH HIS GRANDFATHER'S BOOKS, AND ALL THE WINDOWS AND DOORS OF THE FARMHOUSE WERE BOARDED UP.
JUDGING BY THE PILES OF TIMBER OUTSIDE, WILBUR MUST HAVE GUTTED THE HOUSE, TAKING OUT ALL THE PARTITION WALLS AND THE FLOORS.
THE HOUSE WAS JUST A GIANT SHELL NOW, ALTHOUGH MOST SUSPECTED IT WASN'T EMPTY.
THEN, IN THE WINTER OF 1927, I RECEIVED A VISIT FROM WILBUR AT THE UNIVERSITY.
THIS WAS HIS FIRST TIME AWAY FROM DUNWICH — HE CAME TO STUDY OUR COPY OF THE *NECRONOMICON* AND COMPARE CERTAIN PASSAGES WITH THOSE IN HIS OWN VERSION.
I BEGAN TO READ OVER HIS SHOULDER, AND FELT A WAVE OF FRIGHT AS I THOUGHT OF THE NOISES AT THE FARMHOUSE AND THE BLACK HISTORY OF DUNWICH...
AND AS I LOOKED AT THE GIANT BEFORE ME... LIKE THE SPAWN OF ANOTHER PLANET, LIKE SOMETHING ONLY PART HUMAN...
... SOMETHING LINKED TO BLACK GULFS OF ENTITY THAT STRETCH BEYOND ALL MATTER, SPACE AND TIME...
The old ones were, The old ones are, And the old ones shall be. They walk serene and primal, Undimensional and to us unseen.
... A NIGHTMARE TRUTH WAS DAWNING UPON ME...
Yog-sothoth knows the gate. Yog-sothoth is the gate. Yog-sothoth is the key and the guardian of the gate. He knows where the old ones broke through of old And where they shall break through again.
Man rules now where they ruled once; They shall soon rule where man rules now. They wait patient, and potent For here they shall reign again.

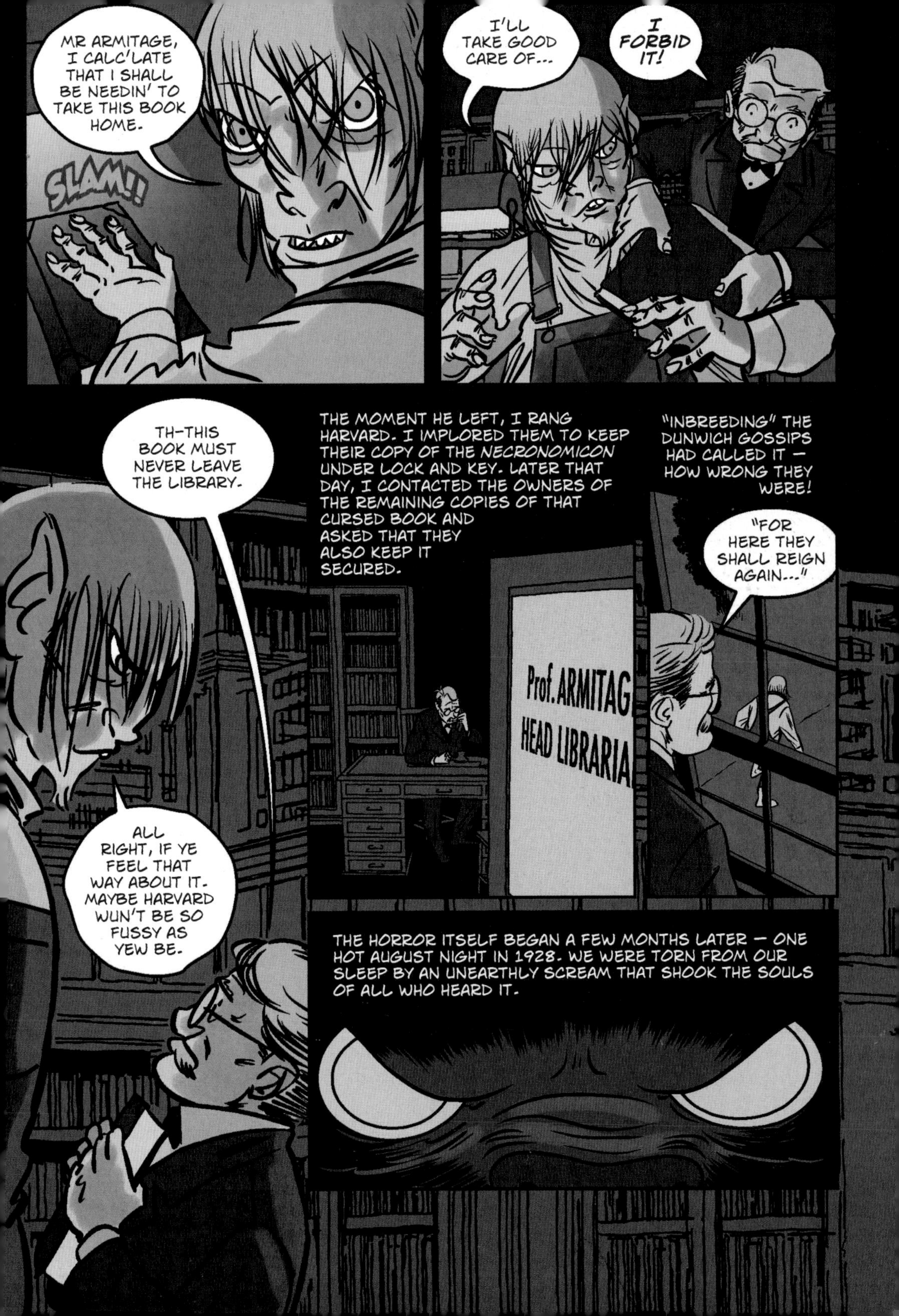

MR ARMITAGE, I CALC'LATE THAT I SHALL BE NEEDIN' TO TAKE THIS BOOK HOME.
SLAM!!
I'LL TAKE GOOD CARE OF...
I FORBID IT!
TH-THIS BOOK MUST NEVER LEAVE THE LIBRARY.
ALL RIGHT, IF YE FEEL THAT WAY ABOUT IT. MAYBE HARVARD WUN'T BE SO FUSSY AS YEW BE.
THE MOMENT HE LEFT, I RANG HARVARD. I IMPLORED THEM TO KEEP THEIR COPY OF THE *NECRONOMICON* UNDER LOCK AND KEY. LATER THAT DAY, I CONTACTED THE OWNERS OF THE REMAINING COPIES OF THAT CURSED BOOK AND ASKED THAT THEY ALSO KEEP IT SECURED.
Prof. ARMITAG
HEAD LIBRARIA
"INBREEDING" THE DUNWICH GOSSIPS HAD CALLED IT — HOW WRONG THEY WERE!
"FOR HERE THEY SHALL REIGN AGAIN..."
THE HORROR ITSELF BEGAN A FEW MONTHS LATER — ONE HOT AUGUST NIGHT IN 1928. WE WERE TORN FROM OUR SLEEP BY AN UNEARTHLY SCREAM THAT SHOOK THE SOULS OF ALL WHO HEARD IT.

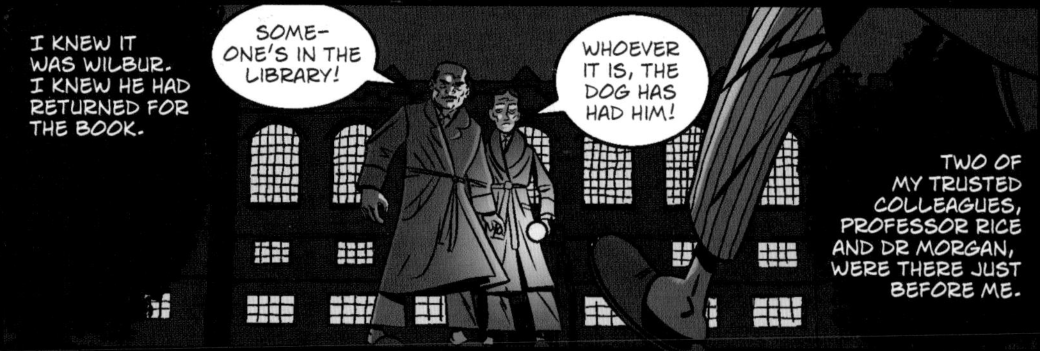
I KNEW IT WAS WILBUR. I KNEW HE HAD RETURNED FOR THE BOOK.
SOME-ONE'S IN THE LIBRARY!
WHOEVER IT IS, THE DOG HAS HAD HIM!
TWO OF MY TRUSTED COLLEAGUES, PROFESSOR RICE AND DR MORGAN, WERE THERE JUST BEFORE ME.

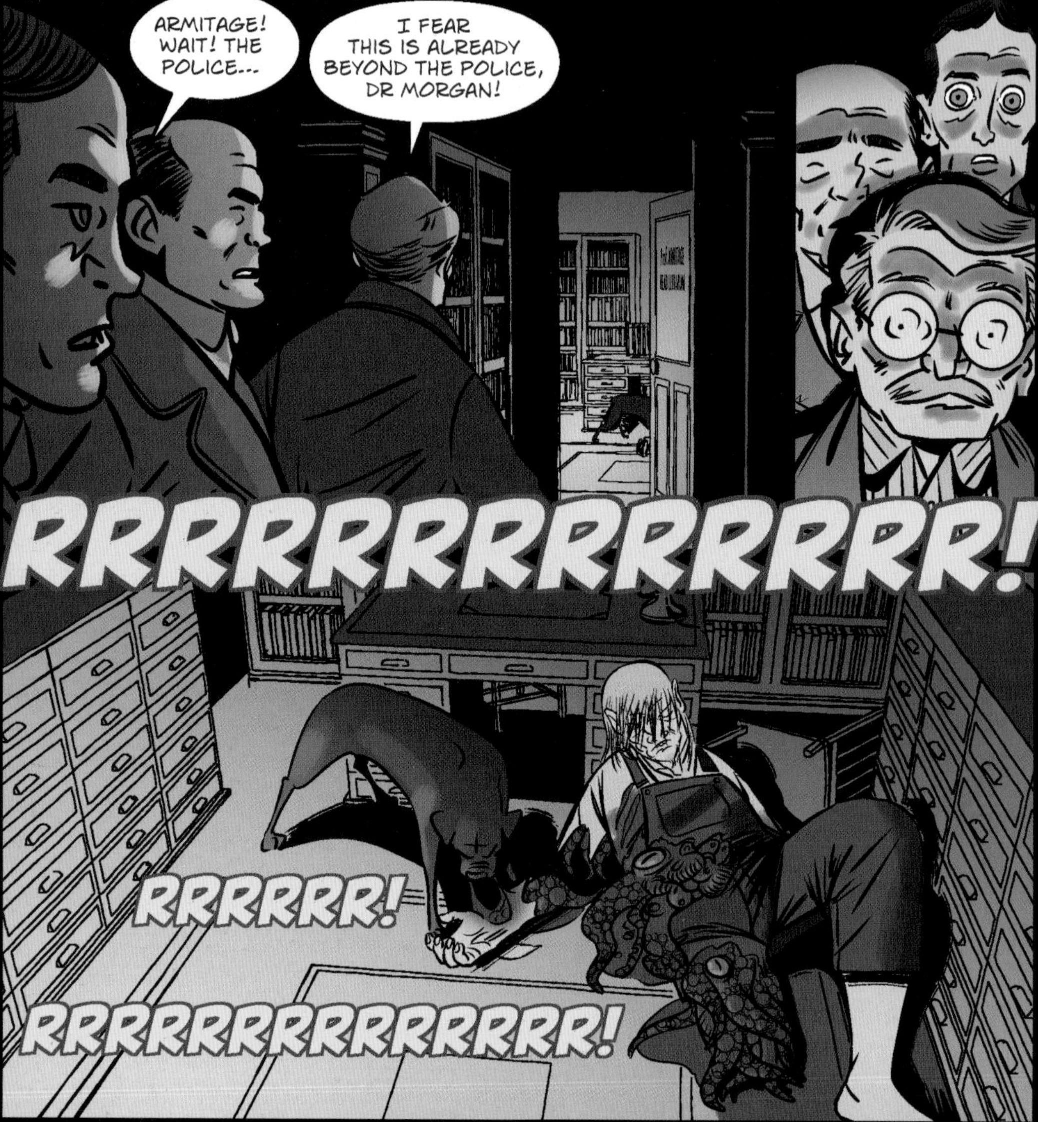
ARMITAGE! WAIT! THE POLICE...
I FEAR THIS IS ALREADY BEYOND THE POLICE, DR MORGAN!
RRRRRRRRRRRRRR!
RRRRRR!
RRRRRRRRRRRRRRR!

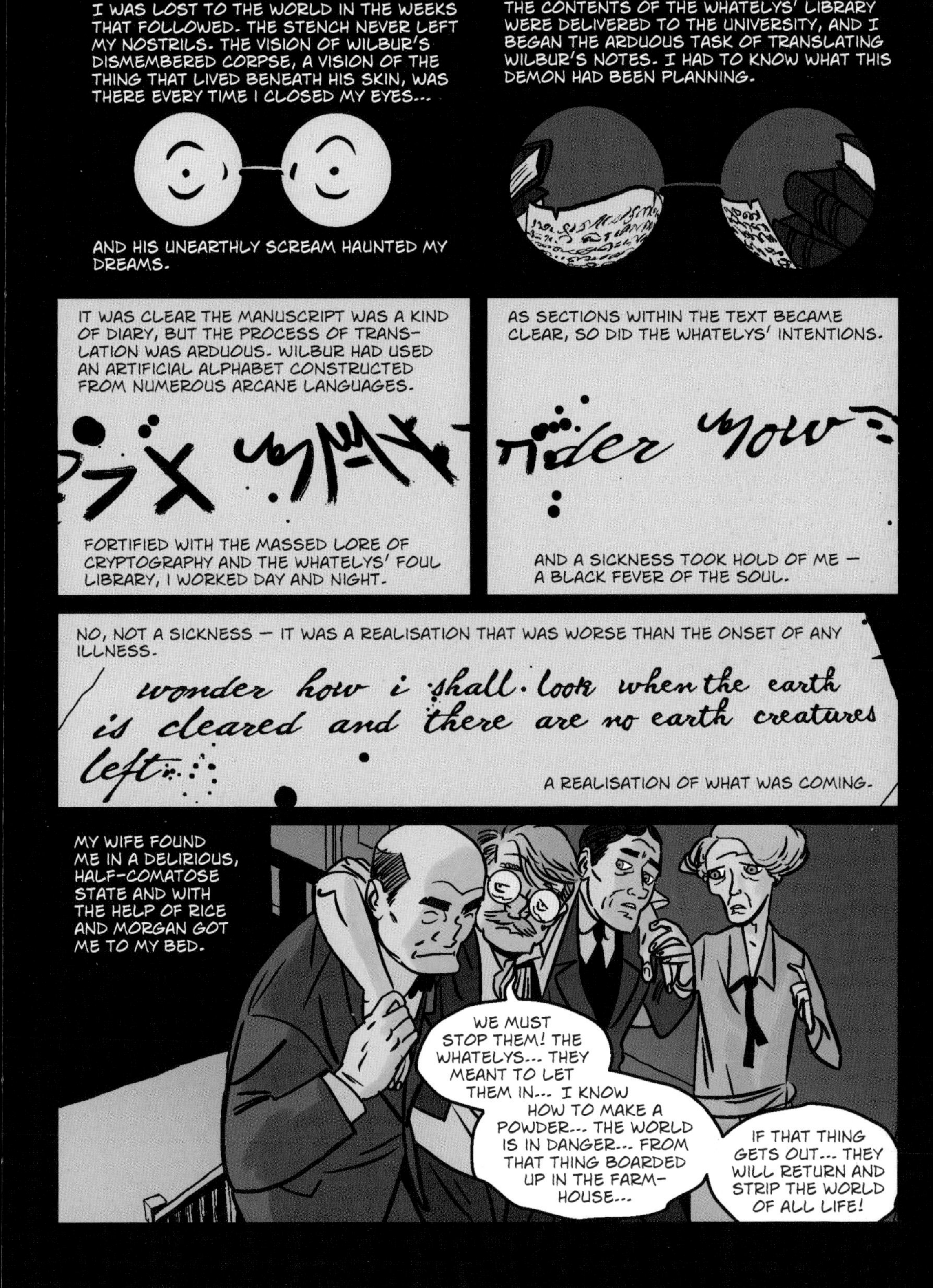
I WAS LOST TO THE WORLD IN THE WEEKS THAT FOLLOWED. THE STENCH NEVER LEFT MY NOSTRILS. THE VISION OF WILBUR'S DISMEMBERED CORPSE, A VISION OF THE THING THAT LIVED BENEATH HIS SKIN, WAS THERE EVERY TIME I CLOSED MY EYES...
AND HIS UNEARTHLY SCREAM HAUNTED MY DREAMS.
THE CONTENTS OF THE WHATELYS' LIBRARY WERE DELIVERED TO THE UNIVERSITY, AND I BEGAN THE ARDUOUS TASK OF TRANSLATING WILBUR'S NOTES. I HAD TO KNOW WHAT THIS DEMON HAD BEEN PLANNING.
IT WAS CLEAR THE MANUSCRIPT WAS A KIND OF DIARY, BUT THE PROCESS OF TRANS-LATION WAS ARDUOUS. WILBUR HAD USED AN ARTIFICIAL ALPHABET CONSTRUCTED FROM NUMEROUS ARCANE LANGUAGES.
FORTIFIED WITH THE MASSED LORE OF CRYPTOGRAPHY AND THE WHATELYS' FOUL LIBRARY, I WORKED DAY AND NIGHT.
AS SECTIONS WITHIN THE TEXT BECAME CLEAR, SO DID THE WHATELYS' INTENTIONS.
nder now
AND A SICKNESS TOOK HOLD OF ME — A BLACK FEVER OF THE SOUL.
NO, NOT A SICKNESS — IT WAS A REALISATION THAT WAS WORSE THAN THE ONSET OF ANY ILLNESS.
wonder how i shall look when the earth is cleared and there are no earth creatures left
A REALISATION OF WHAT WAS COMING.
MY WIFE FOUND ME IN A DELIRIOUS, HALF-COMATOSE STATE AND WITH THE HELP OF RICE AND MORGAN GOT ME TO MY BED.
WE MUST STOP THEM! THE WHATELYS... THEY MEANT TO LET THEM IN... I KNOW HOW TO MAKE A POWDER... THE WORLD IS IN DANGER... FROM THAT THING BOARDED UP IN THE FARM-HOUSE...
IF THAT THING GETS OUT... THEY WILL RETURN AND STRIP THE WORLD OF ALL LIFE!

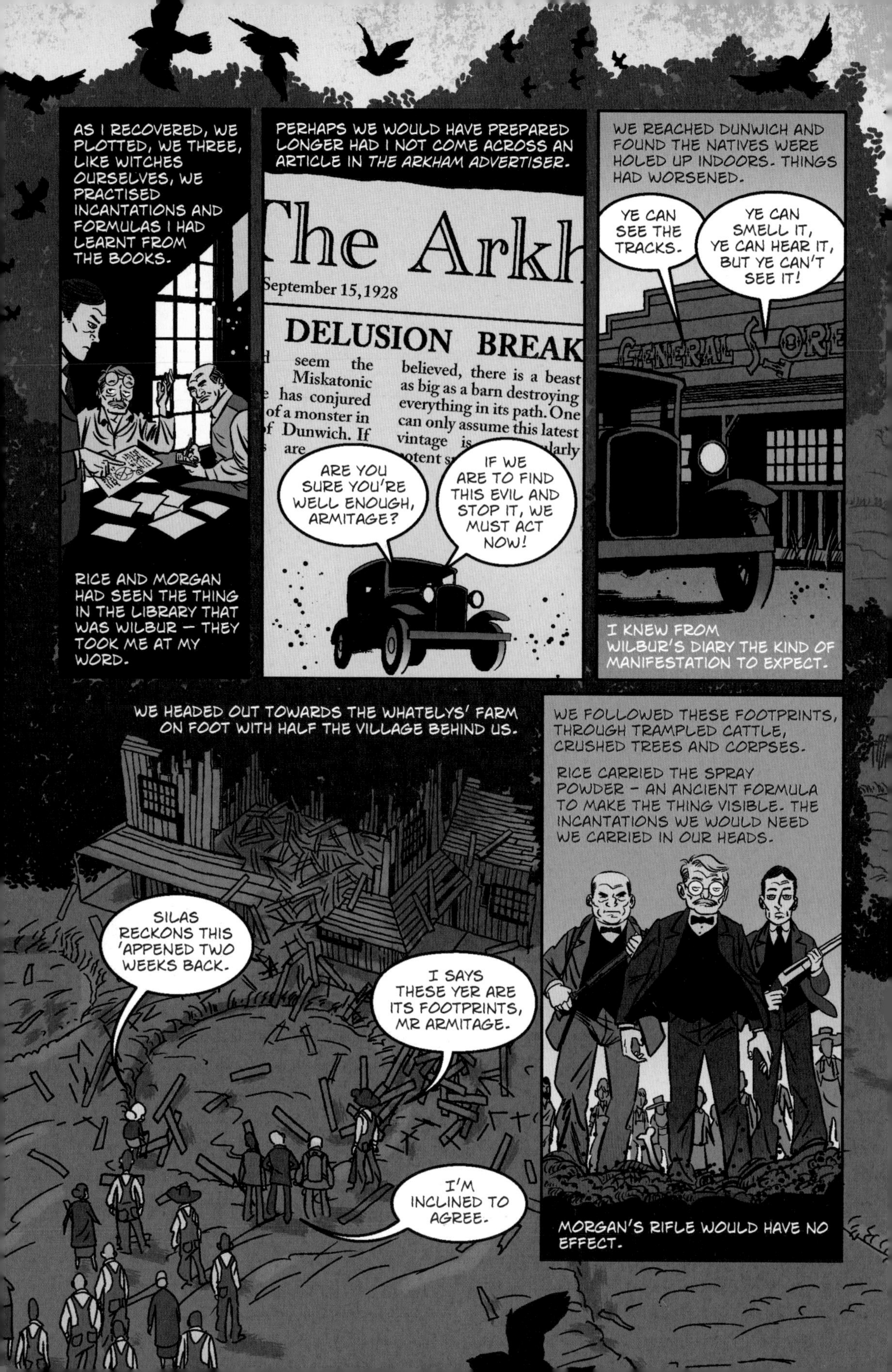

AS I RECOVERED, WE PLOTTED, WE THREE, LIKE WITCHES OURSELVES, WE PRACTISED INCANTATIONS AND FORMULAS I HAD LEARNT FROM THE BOOKS.
RICE AND MORGAN HAD SEEN THE THING IN THE LIBRARY THAT WAS WILBUR — THEY TOOK ME AT MY WORD.
PERHAPS WE WOULD HAVE PREPARED LONGER HAD I NOT COME ACROSS AN ARTICLE IN THE ARKHAM ADVERTISER.
The Arkh
September 15, 1928
DELUSION BREAK
seem the Miskatonic has conjured of a monster in f Dunwich. If are
believed, there is a beast as big as a barn destroying everything in its path. One can only assume this latest vintage is
ARE YOU SURE YOU'RE WELL ENOUGH, ARMITAGE?
IF WE ARE TO FIND THIS EVIL AND STOP IT, WE MUST ACT NOW!
WE REACHED DUNWICH AND FOUND THE NATIVES WERE HOLED UP INDOORS. THINGS HAD WORSENED.
YE CAN SEE THE TRACKS.
YE CAN SMELL IT, YE CAN HEAR IT, BUT YE CAN'T SEE IT!
GENERAL STORE
I KNEW FROM WILBUR'S DIARY THE KIND OF MANIFESTATION TO EXPECT.
WE HEADED OUT TOWARDS THE WHATELYS' FARM ON FOOT WITH HALF THE VILLAGE BEHIND US.
SILAS RECKONS THIS 'APPENED TWO WEEKS BACK.
I SAYS THESE YER ARE ITS FOOTPRINTS, MR ARMITAGE.
I'M INCLINED TO AGREE.
WE FOLLOWED THESE FOOTPRINTS, THROUGH TRAMPLED CATTLE, CRUSHED TREES AND CORPSES.
RICE CARRIED THE SPRAY POWDER – AN ANCIENT FORMULA TO MAKE THE THING VISIBLE. THE INCANTATIONS WE WOULD NEED WE CARRIED IN OUR HEADS.
MORGAN'S RIFLE WOULD HAVE NO EFFECT.

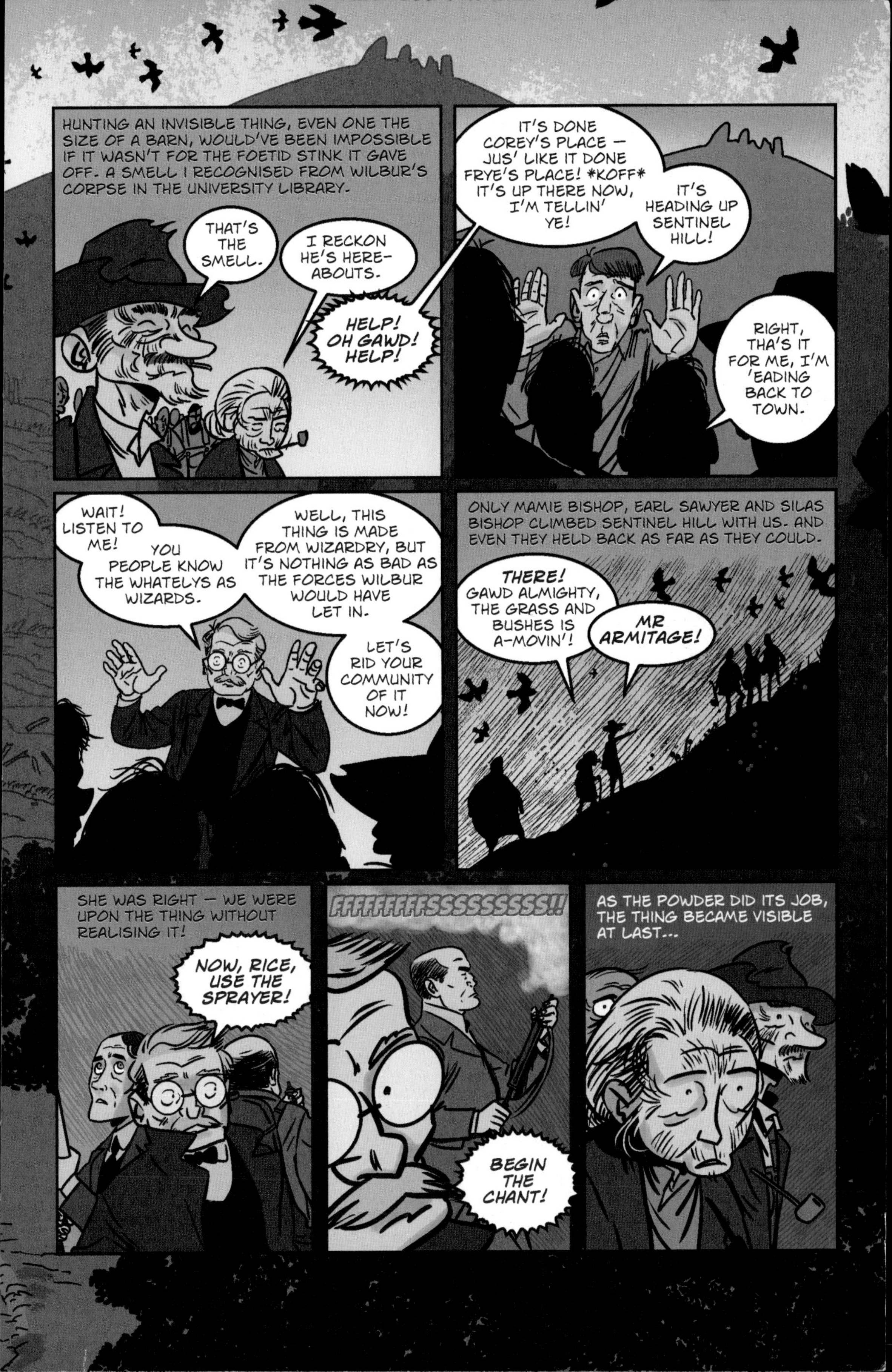

HUNTING AN INVISIBLE THING, EVEN ONE THE SIZE OF A BARN, WOULD'VE BEEN IMPOSSIBLE IF IT WASN'T FOR THE FOETID STINK IT GAVE OFF. A SMELL I RECOGNISED FROM WILBUR'S CORPSE IN THE UNIVERSITY LIBRARY.
THAT'S THE SMELL.
I RECKON HE'S HERE-ABOUTS.
HELP! OH GAWD! HELP!
IT'S DONE COREY'S PLACE — JUS' LIKE IT DONE FRYE'S PLACE! *KOFF* IT'S UP THERE NOW, I'M TELLIN' YE!
IT'S HEADING UP SENTINEL HILL!
RIGHT, THA'S IT FOR ME, I'M 'EADING BACK TO TOWN.
WAIT! LISTEN TO ME!
YOU PEOPLE KNOW THE WHATELYS AS WIZARDS.
WELL, THIS THING IS MADE FROM WIZARDRY, BUT IT'S NOTHING AS BAD AS THE FORCES WILBUR WOULD HAVE LET IN.
LET'S RID YOUR COMMUNITY OF IT NOW!
ONLY MAMIE BISHOP, EARL SAWYER AND SILAS BISHOP CLIMBED SENTINEL HILL WITH US. AND EVEN THEY HELD BACK AS FAR AS THEY COULD.
THERE! GAWD ALMIGHTY, THE GRASS AND BUSHES IS A-MOVIN'!
MR ARMITAGE!
SHE WAS RIGHT — WE WERE UPON THE THING WITHOUT REALISING IT!
NOW, RICE, USE THE SPRAYER!
FFFFFFFFFSSSSSSSSS!!
BEGIN THE CHANT!
AS THE POWDER DID ITS JOB, THE THING BECAME VISIBLE AT LAST...

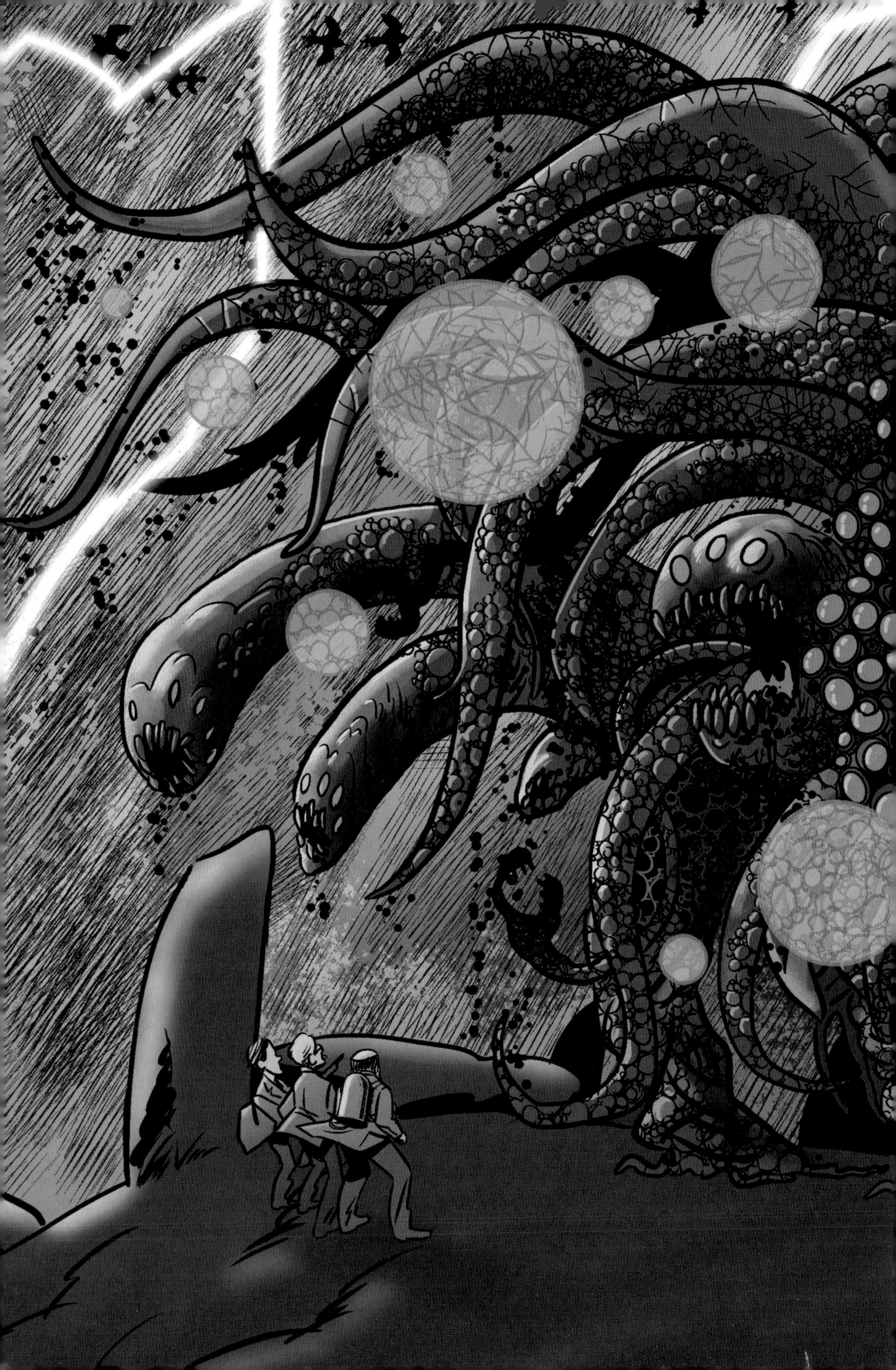

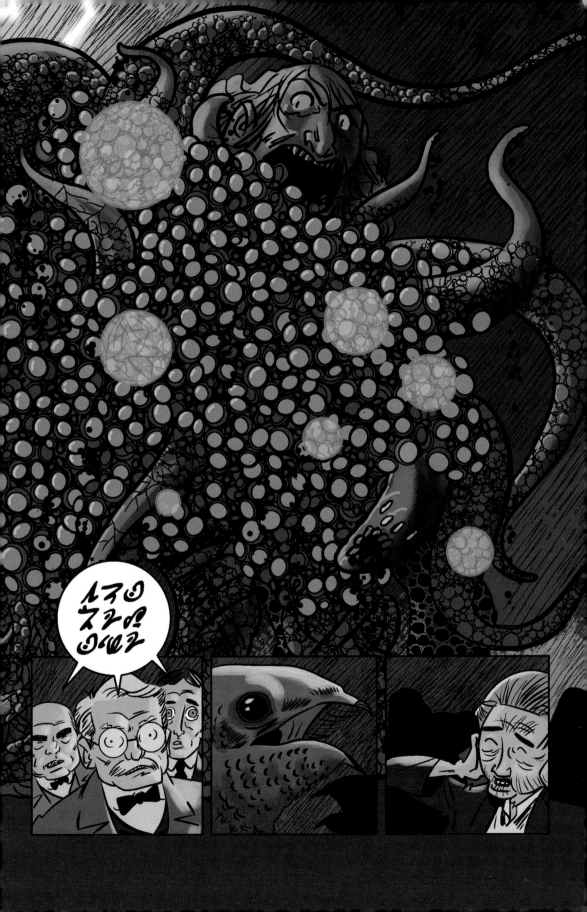

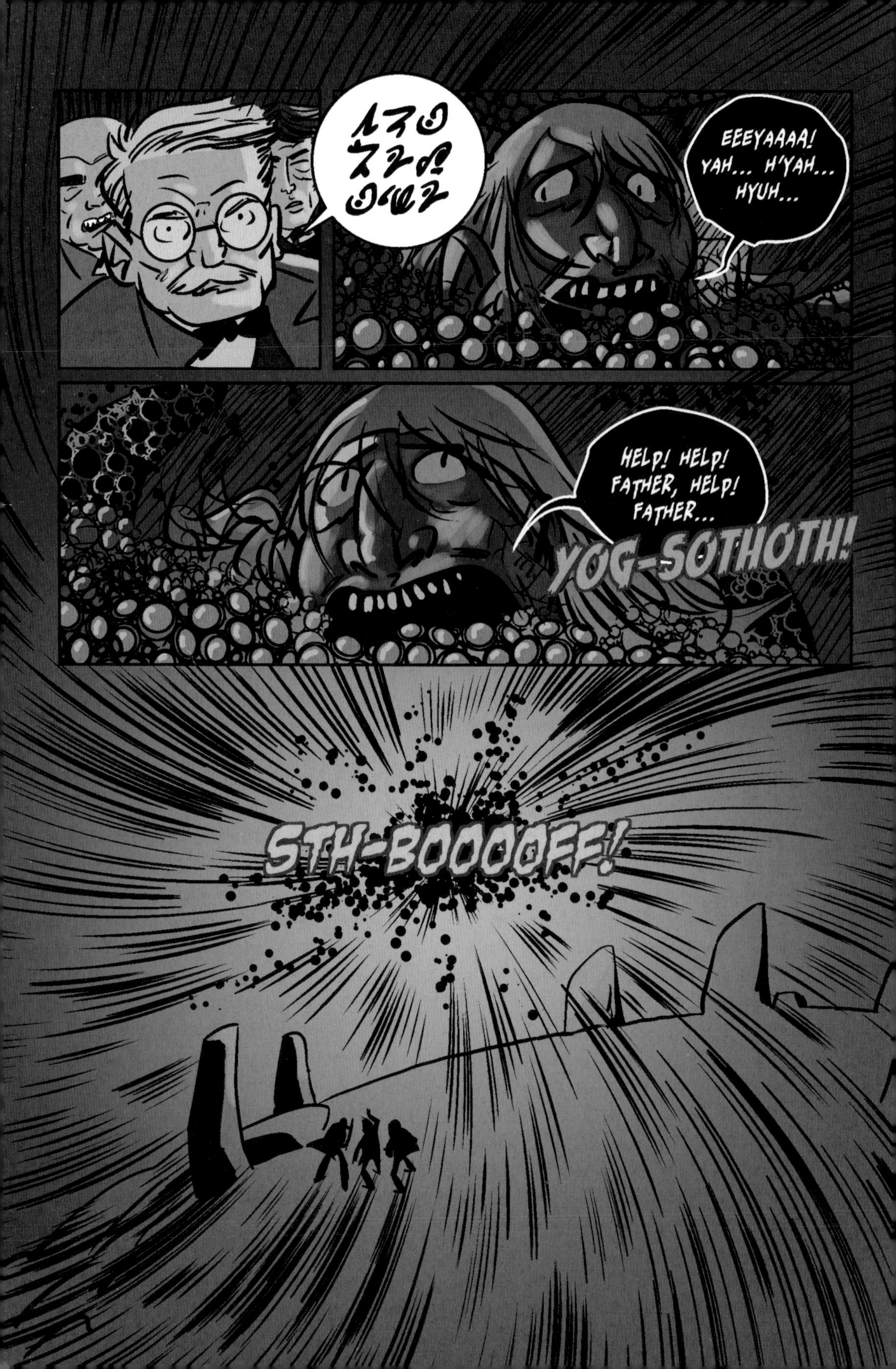
EEEYAAAA! YAH... H'YAH... HYUH...
HELP! HELP! FATHER, HELP! FATHER...
YOG-SOTHOTH!
STH-BOOOOOFF!

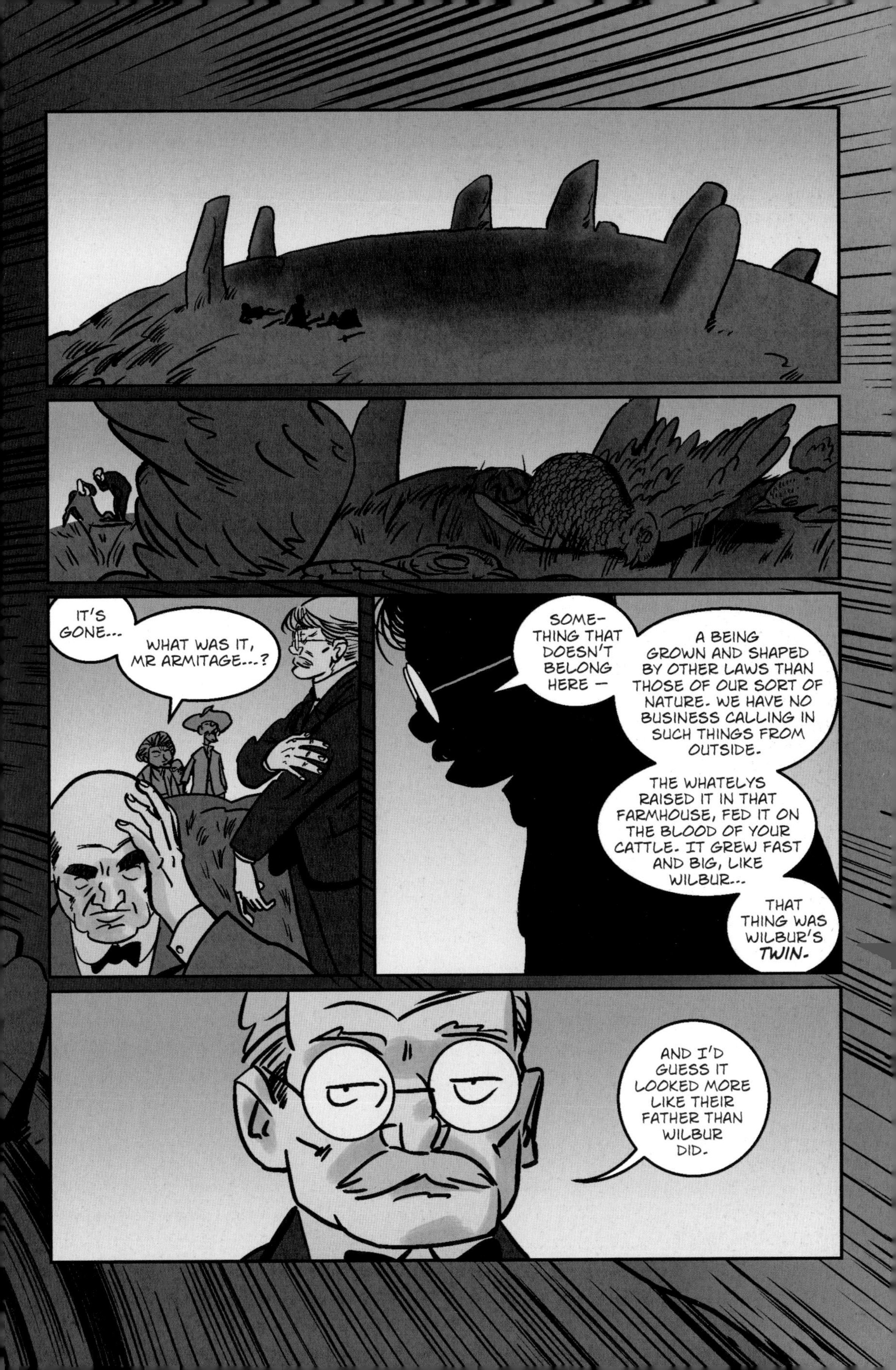
IT'S GONE...
WHAT WAS IT, MR ARMITAGE...?
SOME-THING THAT DOESN'T BELONG HERE —
A BEING GROWN AND SHAPED BY OTHER LAWS THAN THOSE OF OUR SORT OF NATURE. WE HAVE NO BUSINESS CALLING IN SUCH THINGS FROM OUTSIDE.
THE WHATELYS RAISED IT IN THAT FARMHOUSE, FED IT ON THE BLOOD OF YOUR CATTLE. IT GREW FAST AND BIG, LIKE WILBUR...
THAT THING WAS WILBUR'S TWIN.
AND I'D GUESS IT LOOKED MORE LIKE THEIR FATHER THAN WILBUR DID.

THE COLOUR OUT OF SPACE

Adapted by David Hine • Illustrated by Mark Stafford

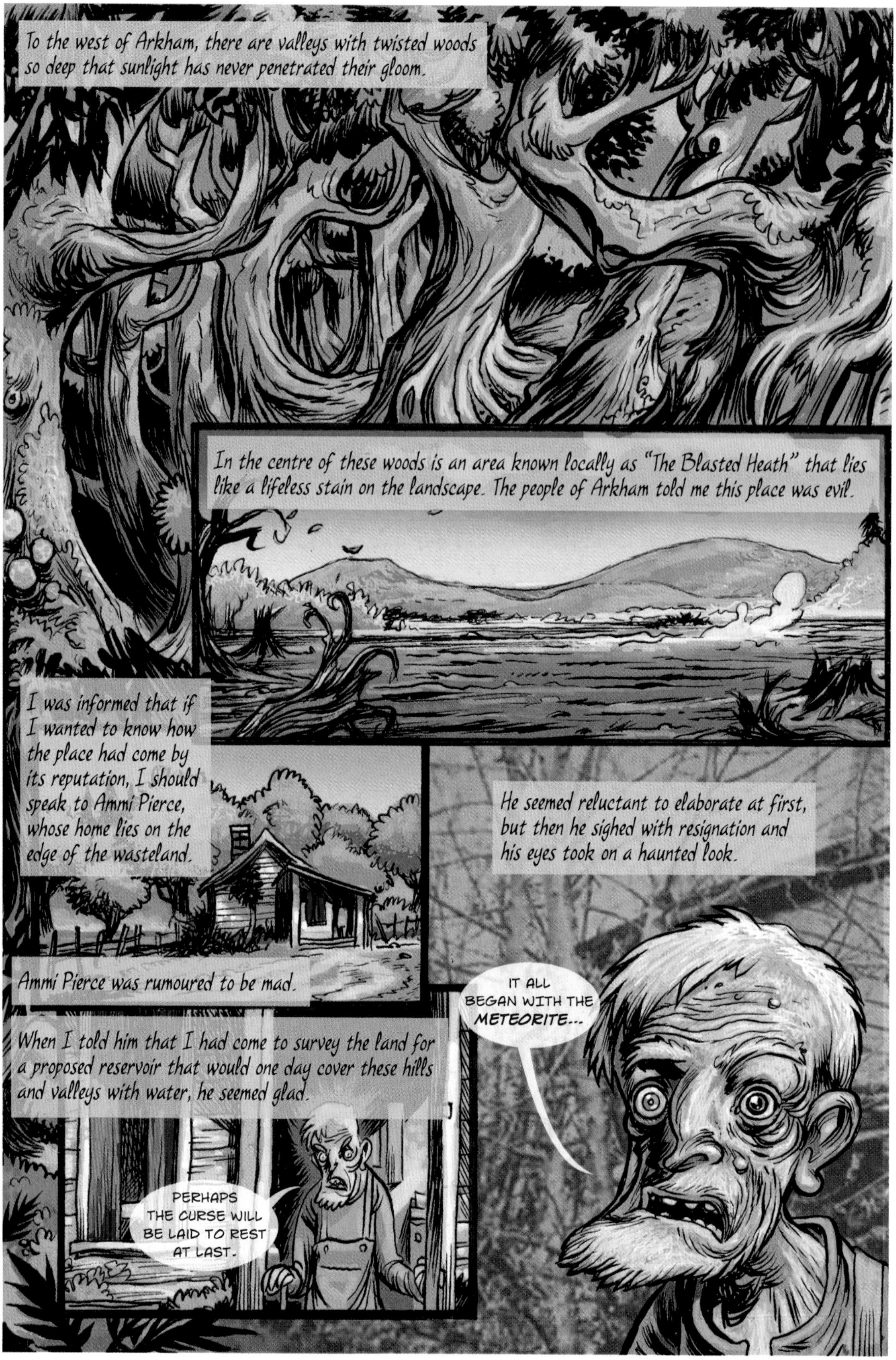
To the west of Arkham, there are valleys with twisted woods so deep that sunlight has never penetrated their gloom.
In the centre of these woods is an area known locally as "The Blasted Heath" that lies like a lifeless stain on the landscape. The people of Arkham told me this place was evil.
I was informed that if I wanted to know how the place had come by its reputation, I should speak to Ammi Pierce, whose home lies on the edge of the wasteland.
Ammi Pierce was rumoured to be mad.
When I told him that I had come to survey the land for a proposed reservoir that would one day cover these hills and valleys with water, he seemed glad.
PERHAPS THE CURSE WILL BE LAID TO REST AT LAST.
He seemed reluctant to elaborate at first, but then he sighed with resignation and his eyes took on a haunted look.
IT ALL BEGAN WITH THE METEORITE...

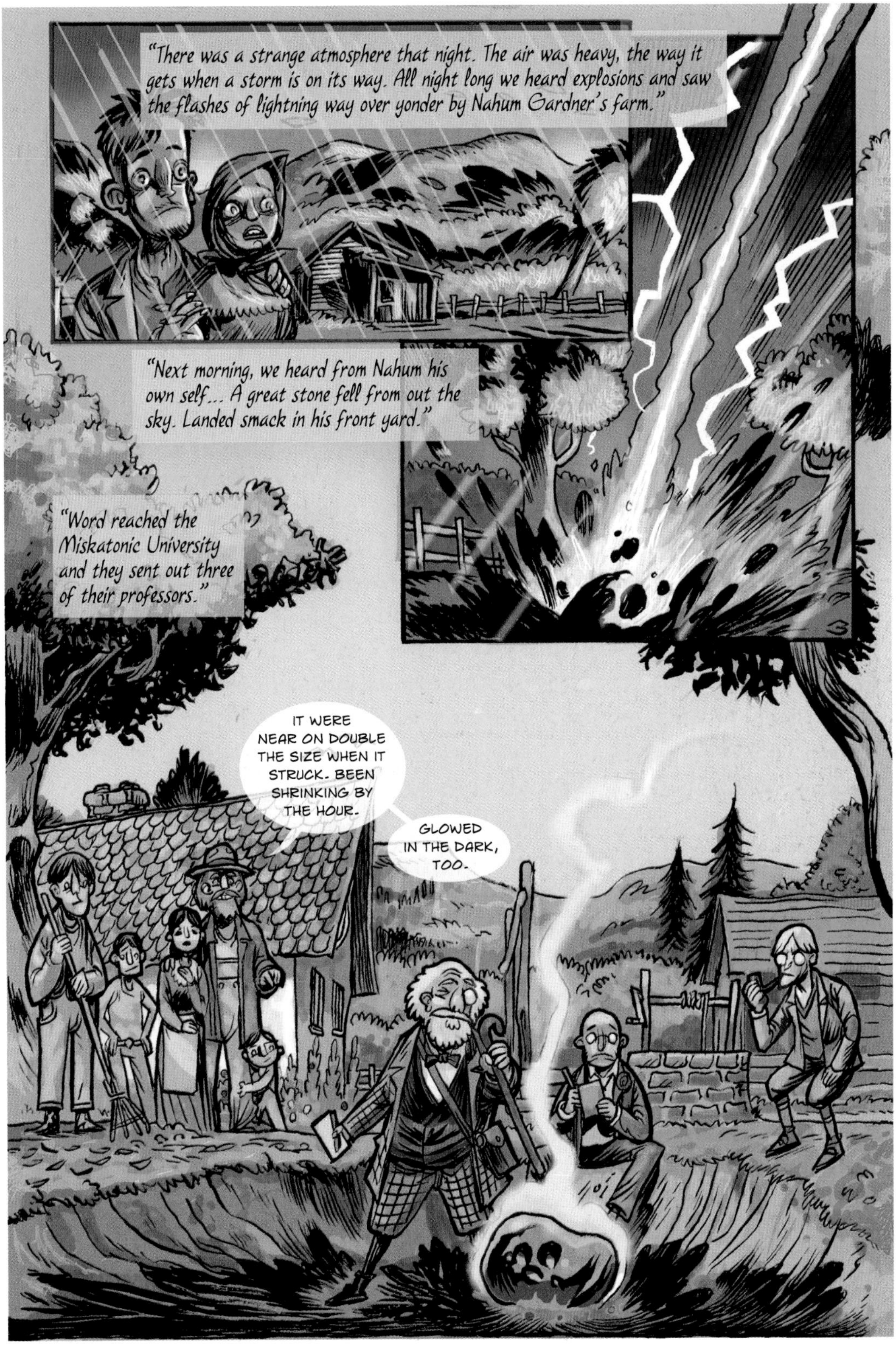
"There was a strange atmosphere that night. The air was heavy, the way it gets when a storm is on its way. All night long we heard explosions and saw the flashes of lightning way over yonder by Nahum Gardner's farm."
"Next morning, we heard from Nahum his own self... A great stone fell from out the sky. Landed smack in his front yard."
"Word reached the Miskatonic University and they sent out three of their professors."
IT WERE NEAR ON DOUBLE THE SIZE WHEN IT STRUCK. BEEN SHRINKING BY THE HOUR.
GLOWED IN THE DARK, TOO.

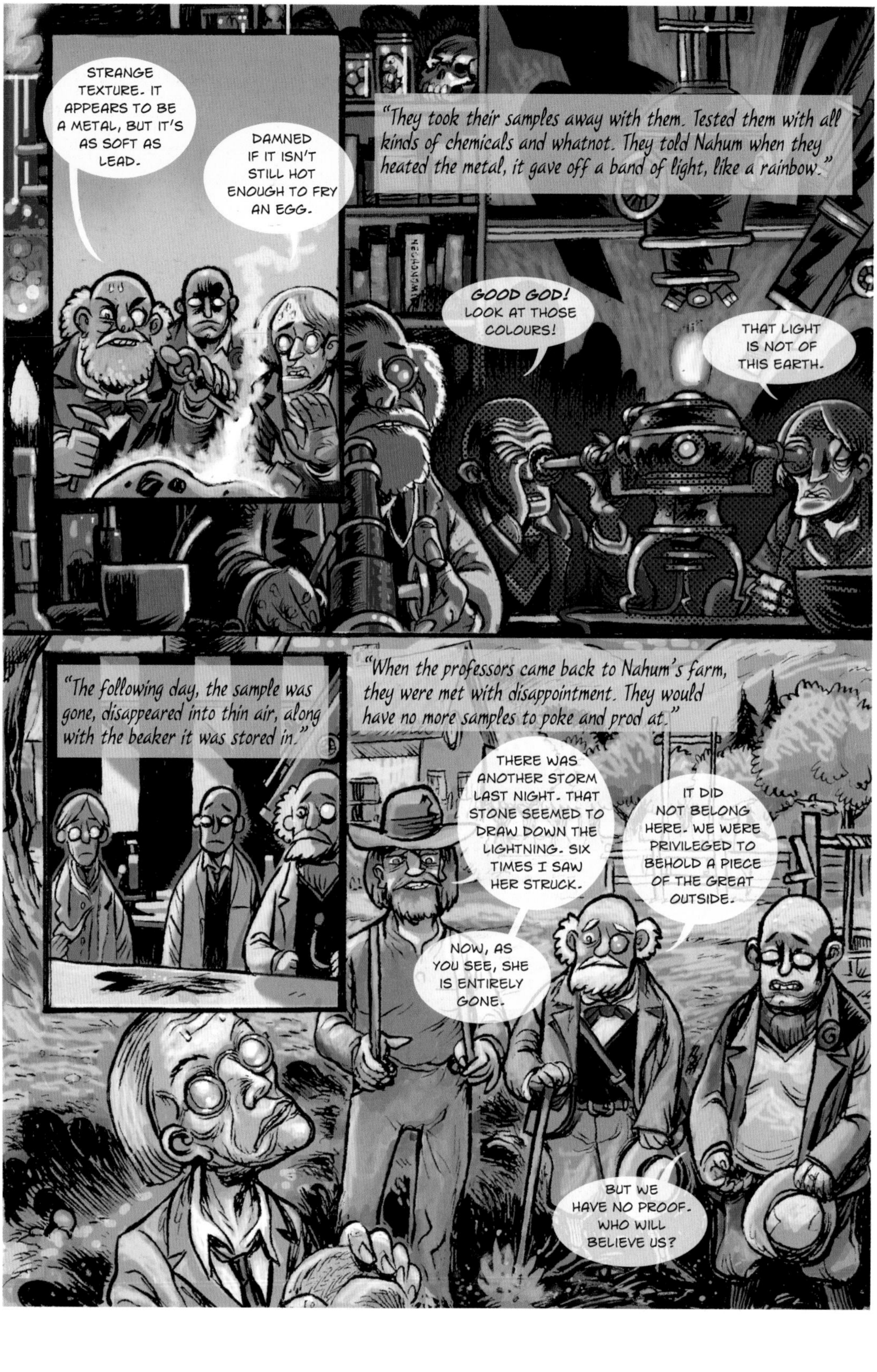
STRANGE TEXTURE. IT APPEARS TO BE A METAL, BUT IT'S AS SOFT AS LEAD.
DAMNED IF IT ISN'T STILL HOT ENOUGH TO FRY AN EGG.
"They took their samples away with them. Tested them with all kinds of chemicals and whatnot. They told Nahum when they heated the metal, it gave off a band of light, like a rainbow."
GOOD GOD! LOOK AT THOSE COLOURS!
THAT LIGHT IS NOT OF THIS EARTH.
"The following day, the sample was gone, disappeared into thin air, along with the beaker it was stored in."
"When the professors came back to Nahum's farm, they were met with disappointment. They would have no more samples to poke and prod at."
THERE WAS ANOTHER STORM LAST NIGHT. THAT STONE SEEMED TO DRAW DOWN THE LIGHTNING. SIX TIMES I SAW HER STRUCK.
NOW, AS YOU SEE, SHE IS ENTIRELY GONE.
IT DID NOT BELONG HERE. WE WERE PRIVILEGED TO BEHOLD A PIECE OF THE GREAT OUTSIDE.
BUT WE HAVE NO PROOF. WHO WILL BELIEVE US?

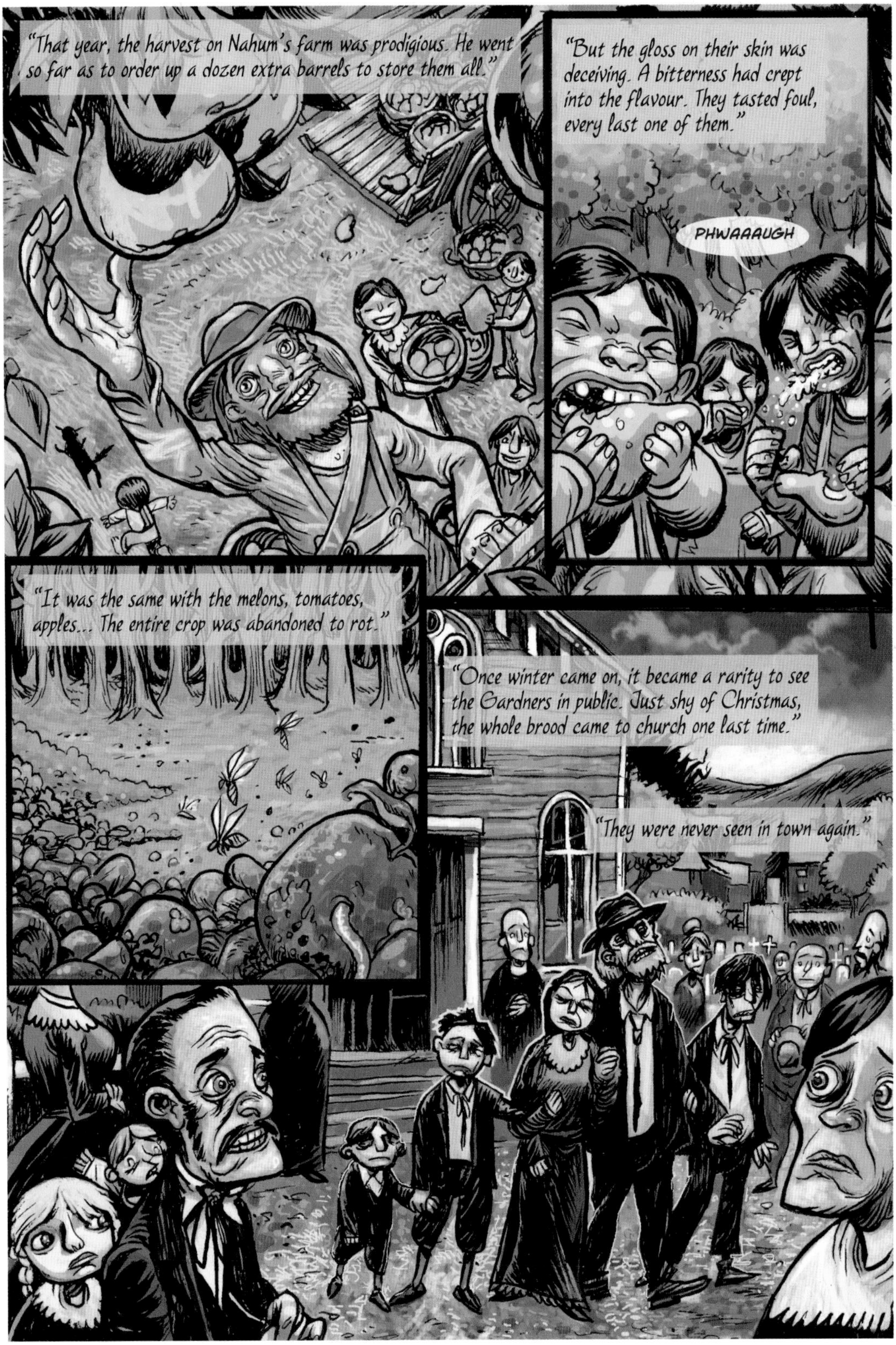
"That year, the harvest on Nahum's farm was prodigious. He went so far as to order up a dozen extra barrels to store them all."
"But the gloss on their skin was deceiving. A bitterness had crept into the flavour. They tasted foul, every last one of them."
PHWAAAUGH
"It was the same with the melons, tomatoes, apples... The entire crop was abandoned to rot."
"Once winter came on, it became a rarity to see the Gardners in public. Just shy of Christmas, the whole brood came to church one last time."
"They were never seen in town again."

"It was February when the McGregor boys went hunting jackrabbit near the Gardner place."

"They came back jabbering about a monstrous freak of nature. Most folk didn't pay any mind to their story, for they could present no carcass in evidence."

"Fact is, those boys were so afeared of that rabbit, they couldn't bear to touch it and left it where it lay."

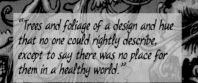

"Spring brought an abundance of new growth to Nahum's farm. Foul-smelling skunk cabbages the like of which had never been seen."

"Trees and foliage of a design and hue that no one could rightly describe, except to say there was no place for them in a healthy world."

"And then there were the insects...."

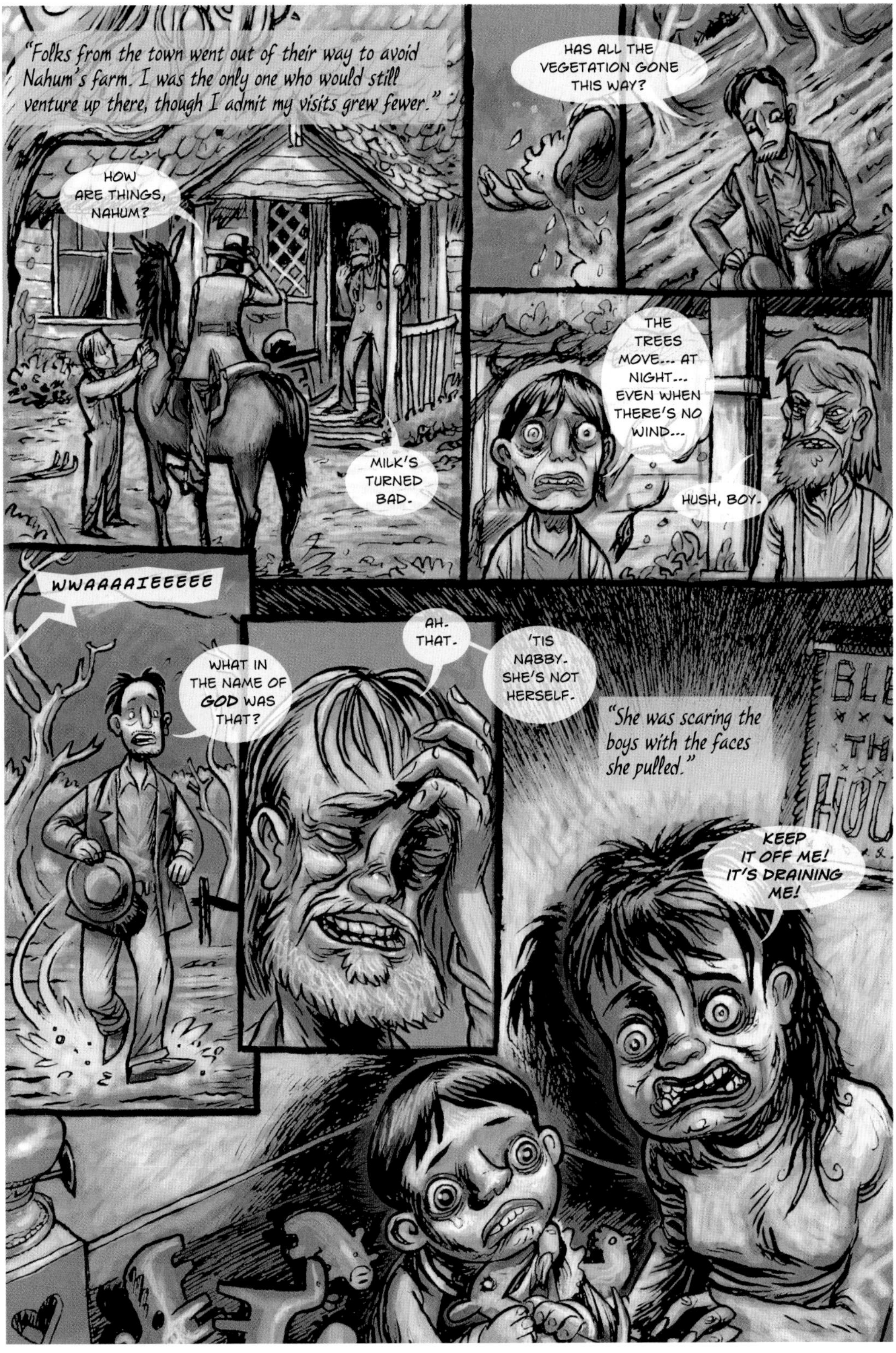
"Folks from the town went out of their way to avoid Nahum's farm. I was the only one who would still venture up there, though I admit my visits grew fewer."
HOW ARE THINGS, NAHUM?
MILK'S TURNED BAD.
HAS ALL THE VEGETATION GONE THIS WAY?
THE TREES MOVE... AT NIGHT... EVEN WHEN THERE'S NO WIND...
HUSH, BOY.
WWAAAAAIEEEEE
WHAT IN THE NAME OF **GOD** WAS THAT?
AH. THAT.
'TIS NABBY. SHE'S NOT HERSELF.
"She was scaring the boys with the faces she pulled."
KEEP IT OFF ME! IT'S DRAINING ME!

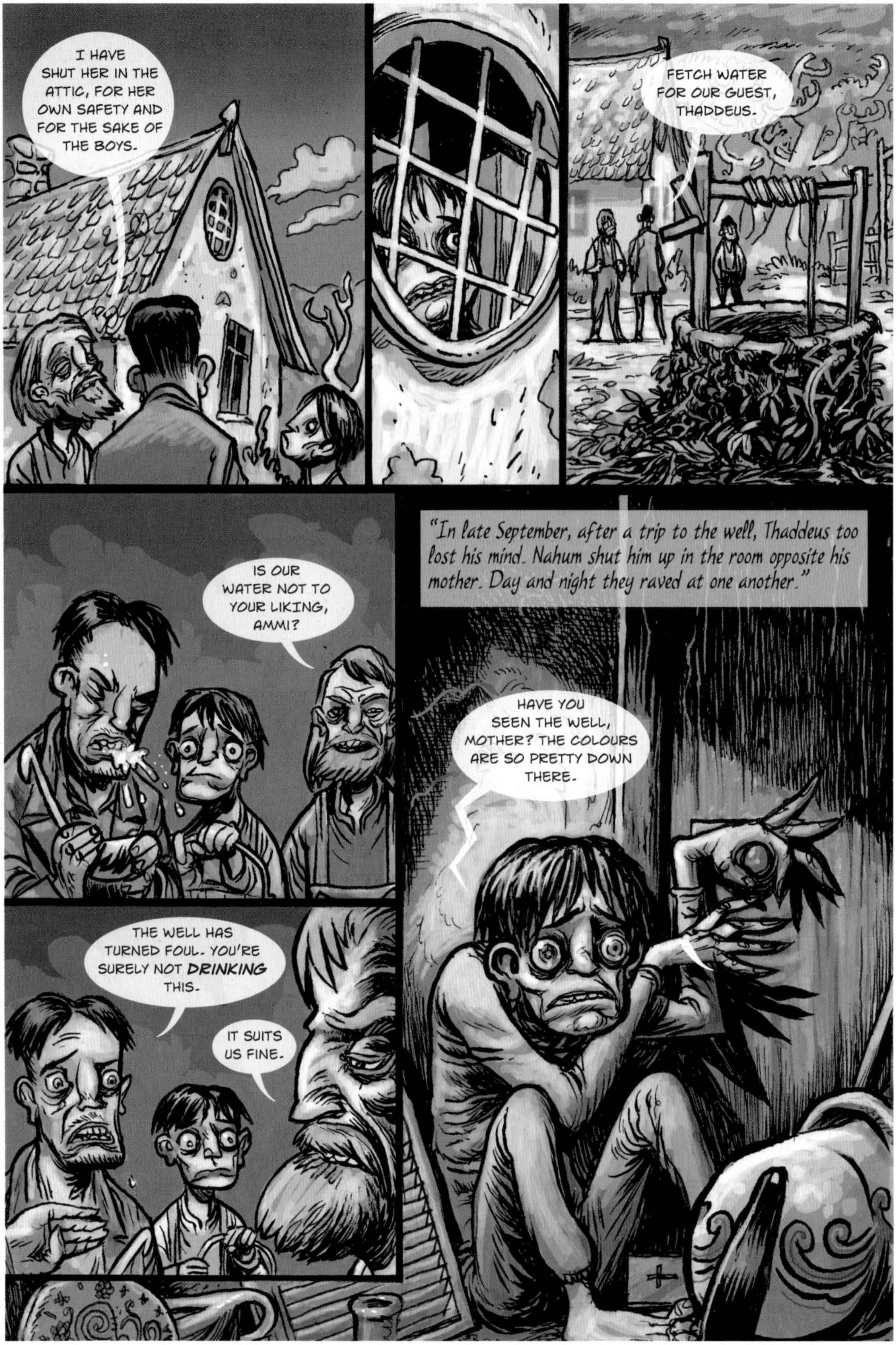
I HAVE SHUT HER IN THE ATTIC, FOR HER OWN SAFETY AND FOR THE SAKE OF THE BOYS.
FETCH WATER FOR OUR GUEST, THADDEUS.
IS OUR WATER NOT TO YOUR LIKING, AMMI?
THE WELL HAS TURNED FOUL. YOU'RE SURELY NOT DRINKING THIS.
IT SUITS US FINE.
"In late September, after a trip to the well, Thaddeus too lost his mind. Nahum shut him up in the room opposite his mother. Day and night they raved at one another."
HAVE YOU SEEN THE WELL, MOTHER? THE COLOURS ARE SO PRETTY DOWN THERE.

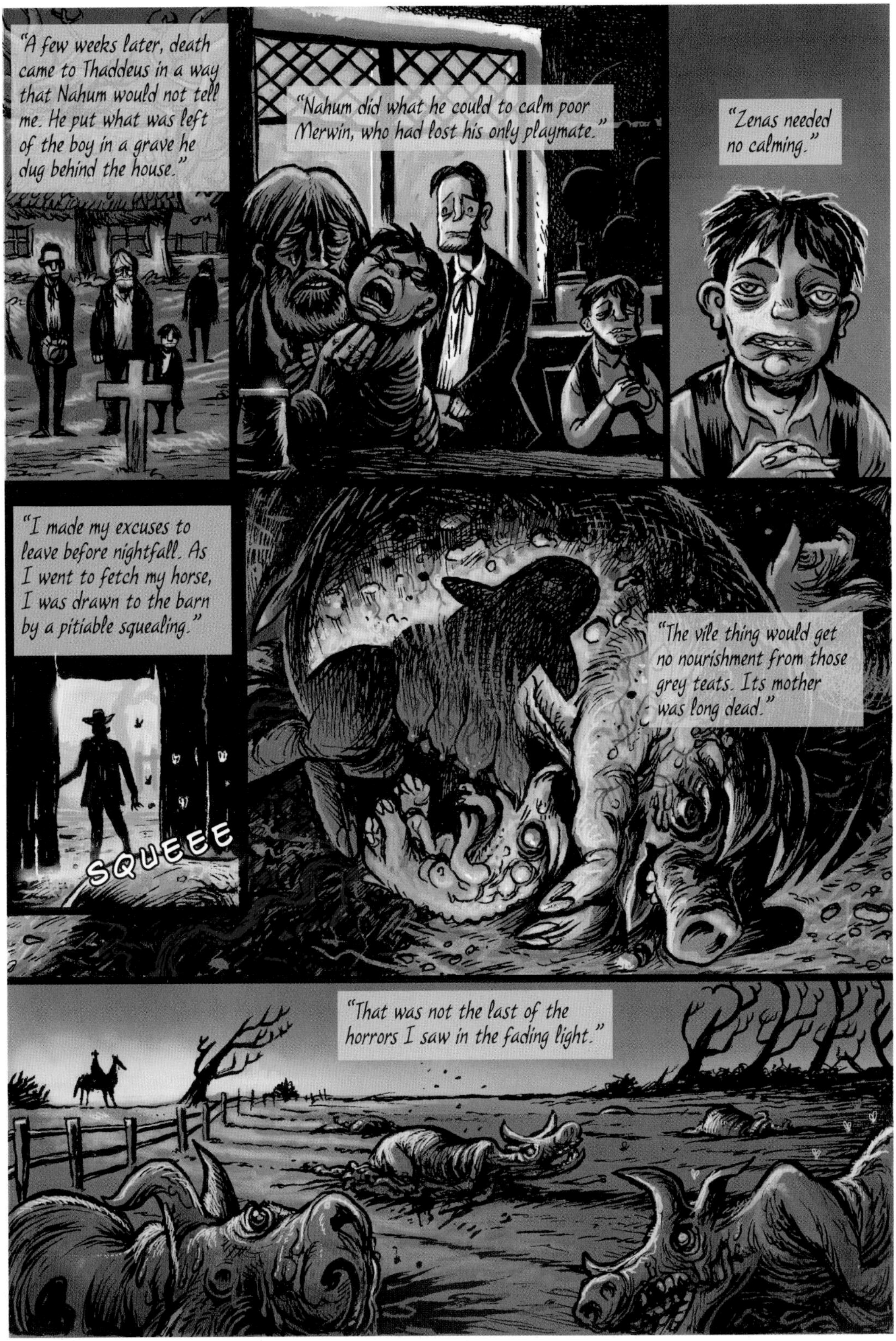
"A few weeks later, death came to Thaddeus in a way that Nahum would not tell me. He put what was left of the boy in a grave he dug behind the house."
"Nahum did what he could to calm poor Merwin, who had lost his only playmate."
"Zenas needed no calming."
"I made my excuses to leave before nightfall. As I went to fetch my horse, I was drawn to the barn by a pitiable squealing."
SQUEEE
"The vile thing would get no nourishment from those grey teats. Its mother was long dead."
"That was not the last of the horrors I saw in the fading light."

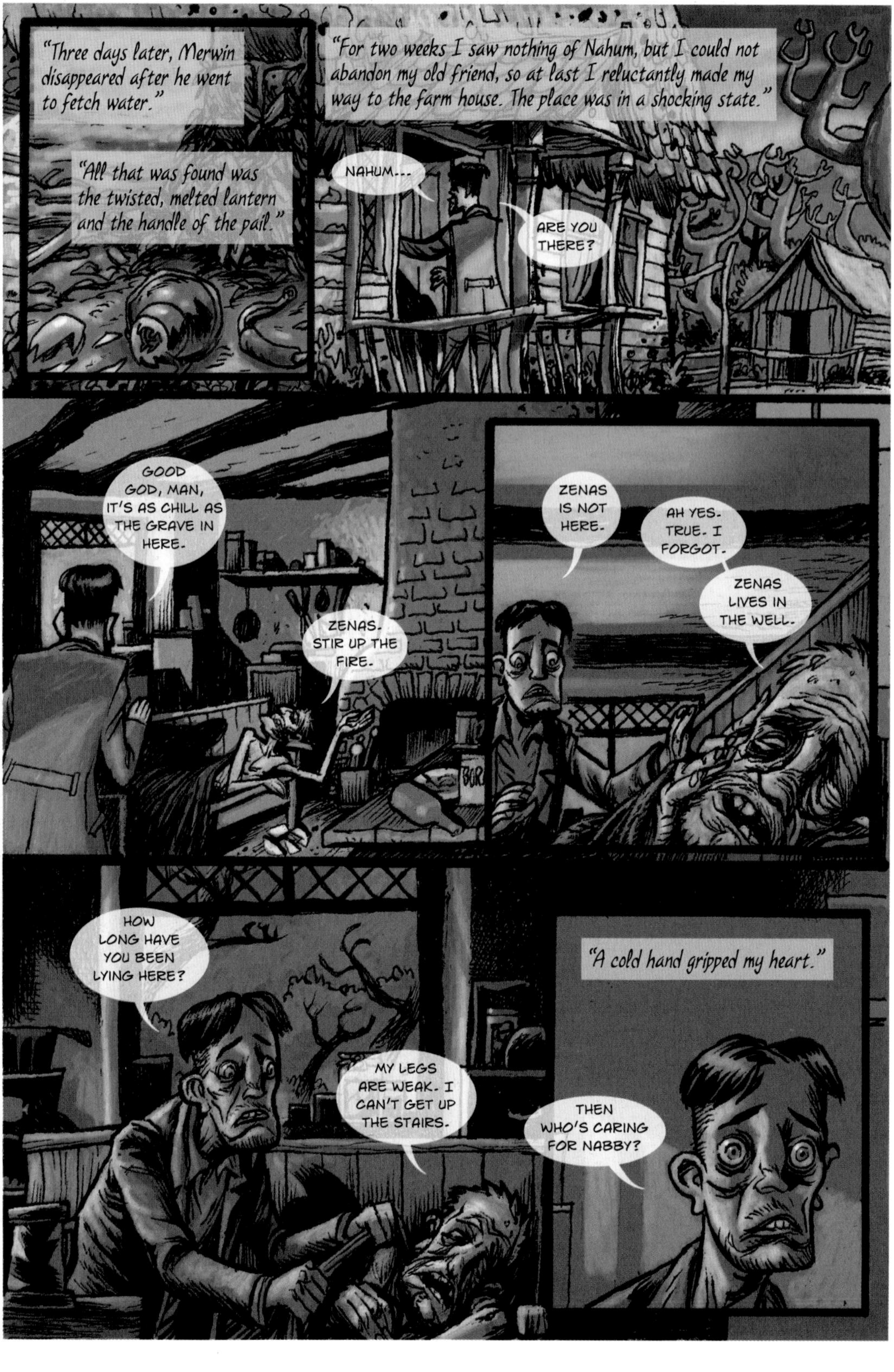
"Three days later, Merwin disappeared after he went to fetch water."
"All that was found was the twisted, melted lantern and the handle of the pail."
"For two weeks I saw nothing of Nahum, but I could not abandon my old friend, so at last I reluctantly made my way to the farm house. The place was in a shocking state."
NAHUM...
ARE YOU THERE?
GOOD GOD, MAN, IT'S AS CHILL AS THE GRAVE IN HERE.
ZENAS. STIR UP THE FIRE.
ZENAS IS NOT HERE.
AH YES. TRUE. I FORGOT.
ZENAS LIVES IN THE WELL.
HOW LONG HAVE YOU BEEN LYING HERE?
MY LEGS ARE WEAK. I CAN'T GET UP THE STAIRS.
"A cold hand gripped my heart."
THEN WHO'S CARING FOR NABBY?

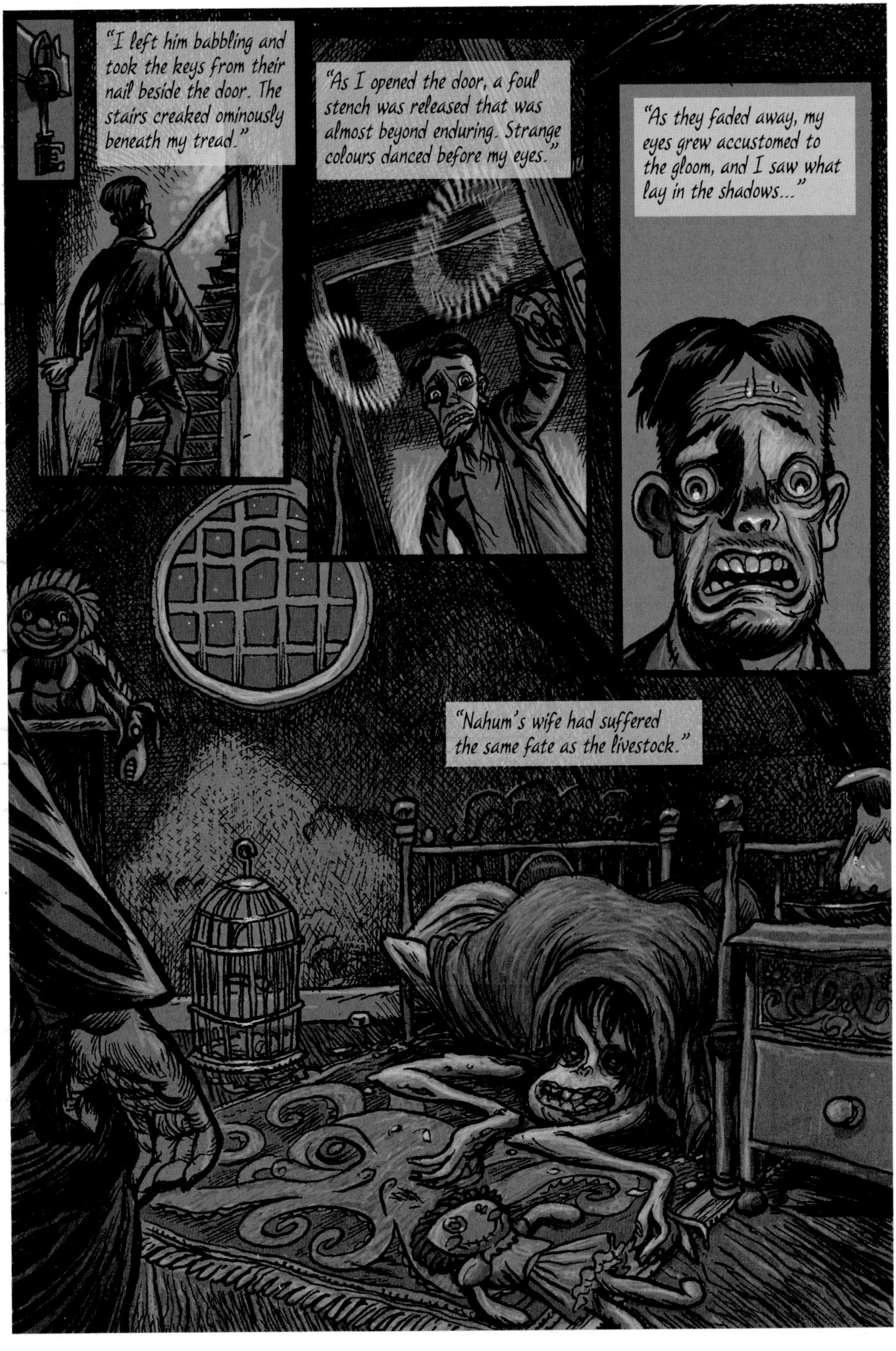
"I left him babbling and took the keys from their nail beside the door. The stairs creaked ominously beneath my tread."
"As I opened the door, a foul stench was released that was almost beyond enduring. Strange colours danced before my eyes."
"As they faded away, my eyes grew accustomed to the gloom, and I saw what lay in the shadows..."
"Nahum's wife had suffered the same fate as the livestock."

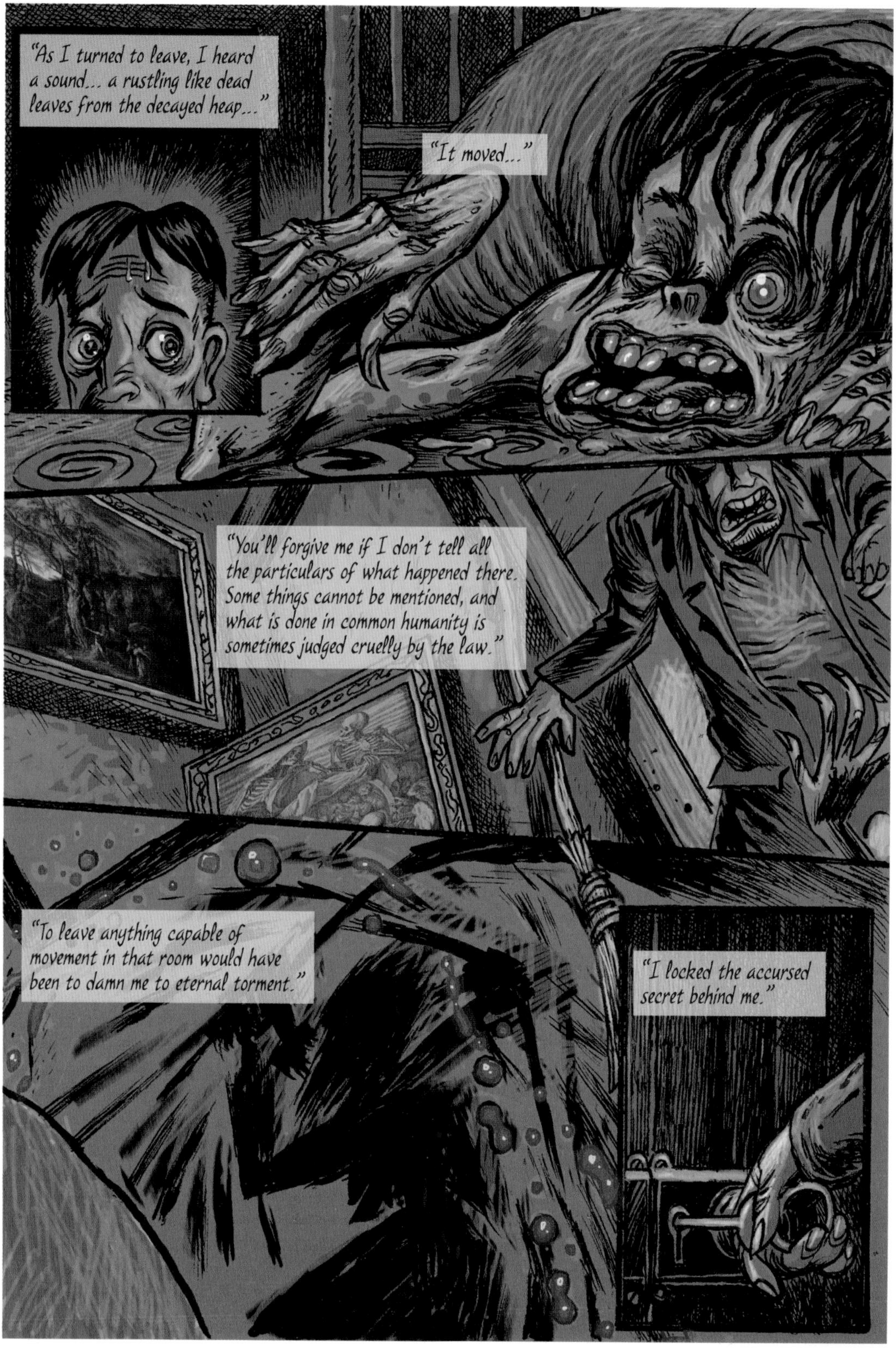
"As I turned to leave, I heard a sound... a rustling like dead leaves from the decayed heap..."
"It moved..."
"You'll forgive me if I don't tell all the particulars of what happened there. Some things cannot be mentioned, and what is done in common humanity is sometimes judged cruelly by the law."
"To leave anything capable of movement in that room would have been to damn me to eternal torment."
"I locked the accursed secret behind me."

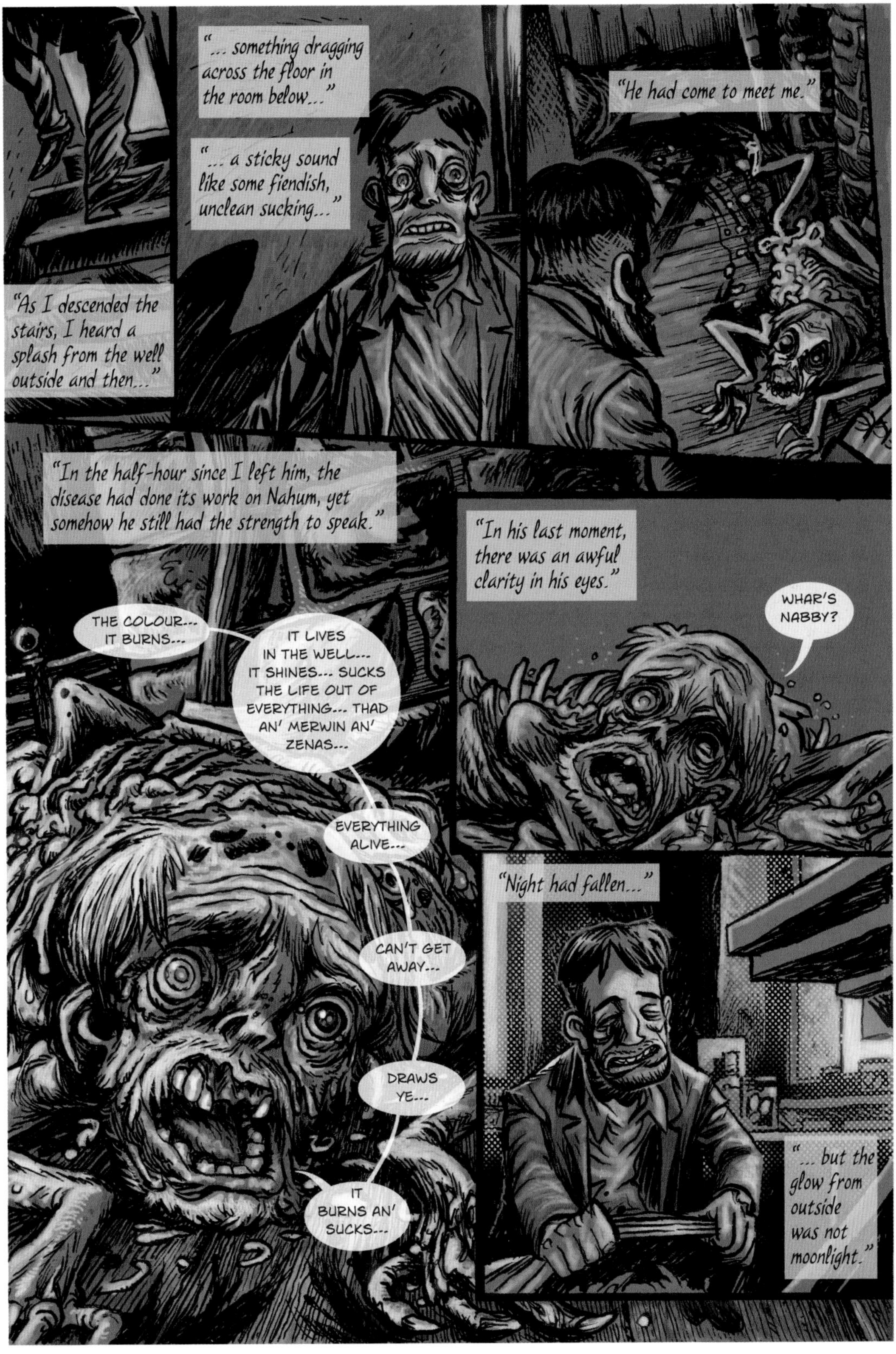
"As I descended the stairs, I heard a splash from the well outside and then..."
"... something dragging across the floor in the room below..."
"... a sticky sound like some fiendish, unclean sucking..."
"He had come to meet me."
"In the half-hour since I left him, the disease had done its work on Nahum, yet somehow he still had the strength to speak."
THE COLOUR... IT BURNS...
IT LIVES IN THE WELL... IT SHINES... SUCKS THE LIFE OUT OF EVERYTHING... THAD AN' MERWIN AN' ZENAS...
EVERYTHING ALIVE...
CAN'T GET AWAY...
DRAWS YE...
IT BURNS AN' SUCKS...
"In his last moment, there was an awful clarity in his eyes."
WHAR'S NABBY?
"Night had fallen..."
"... but the glow from outside was not moonlight."

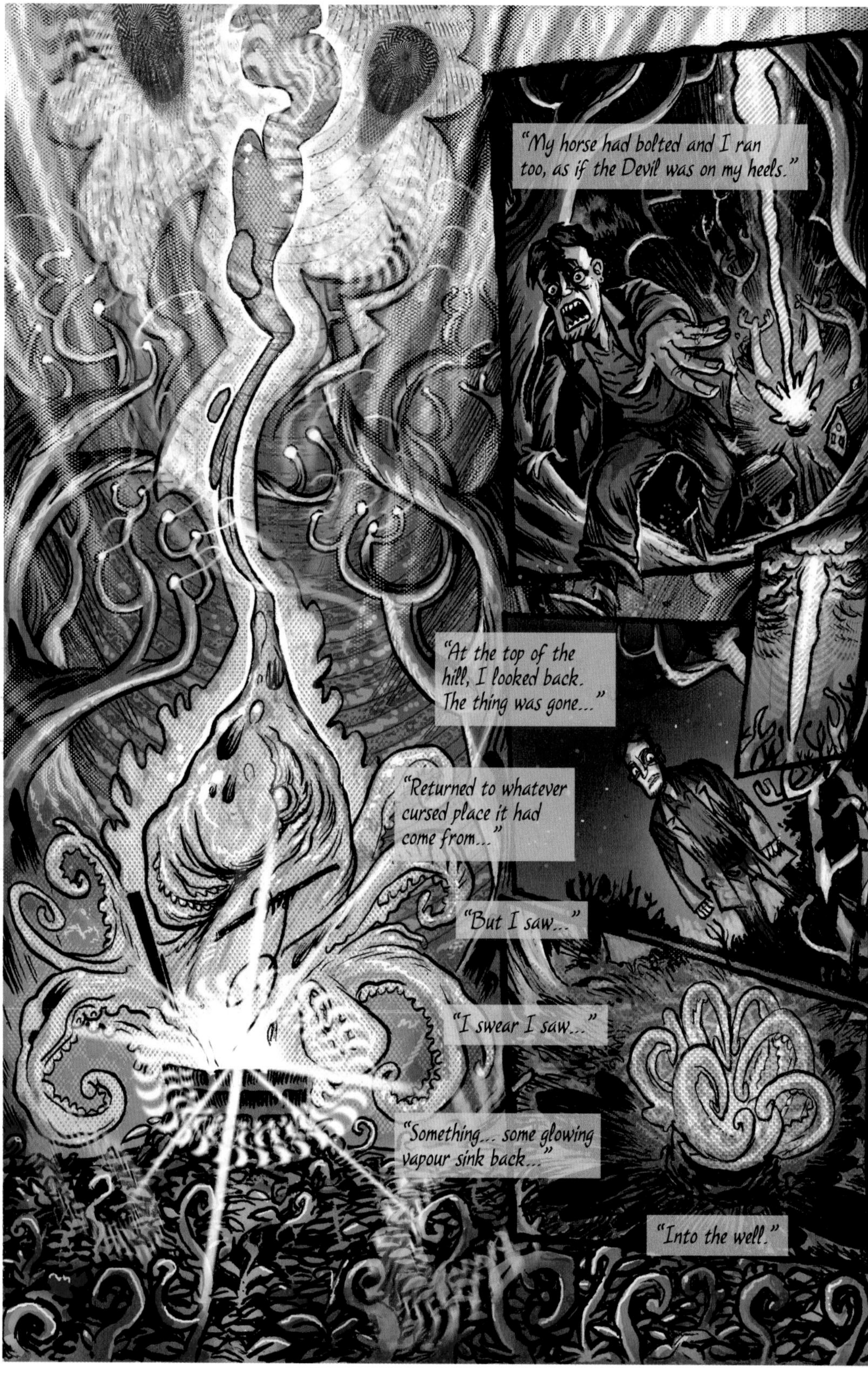
"My horse had bolted and I ran too, as if the Devil was on my heels."
"At the top of the hill, I looked back. The thing was gone..."
"Returned to whatever cursed place it had come from..."
"But I saw..."
"I swear I saw..."
"Something... some glowing vapour sink back..."
"Into the well."

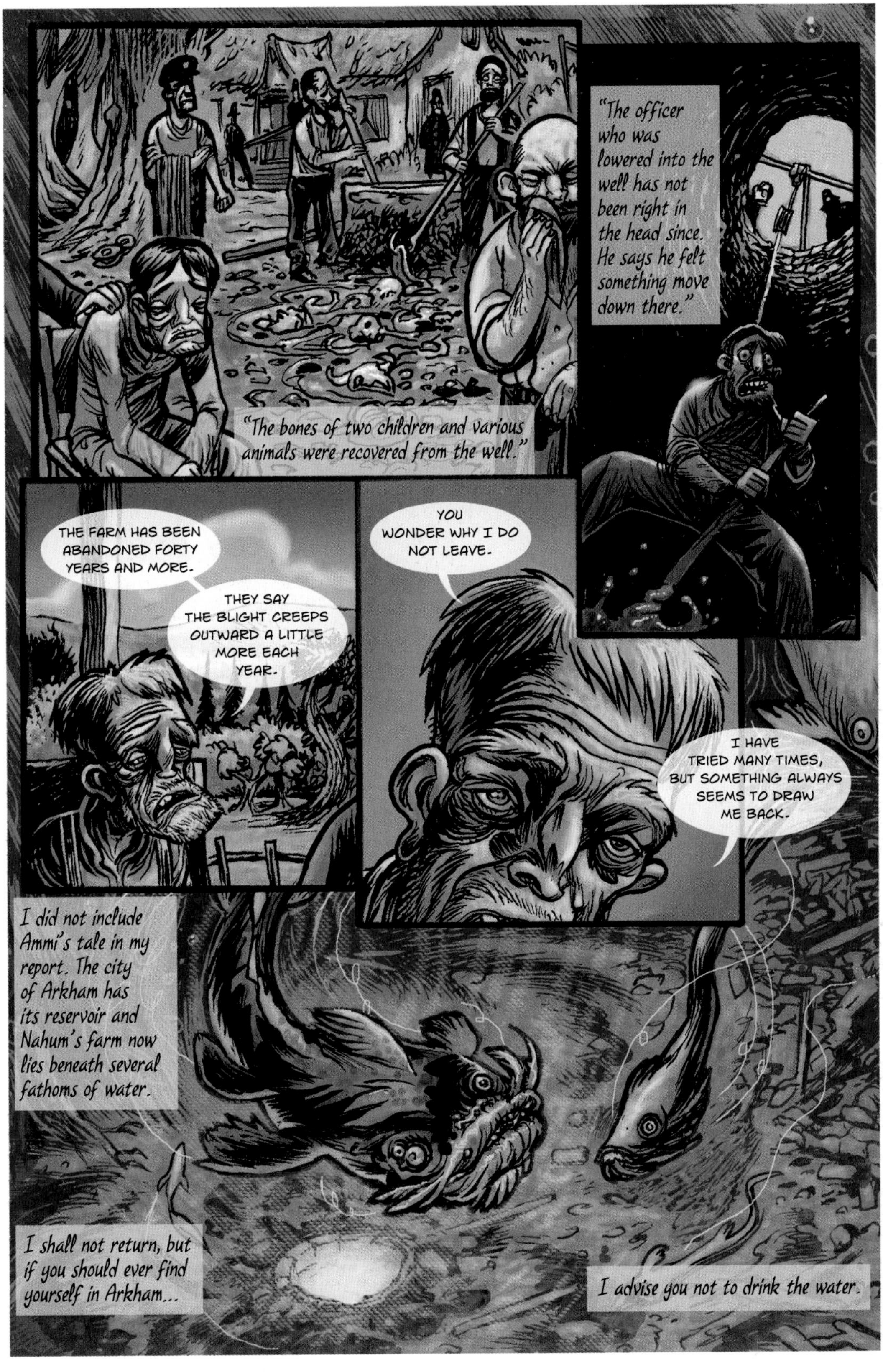
"The bones of two children and various animals were recovered from the well."
"The officer who was lowered into the well has not been right in the head since. He says he felt something move down there."
THE FARM HAS BEEN ABANDONED FORTY YEARS AND MORE.
THEY SAY THE BLIGHT CREEPS OUTWARD A LITTLE MORE EACH YEAR.
YOU WONDER WHY I DO NOT LEAVE.
I HAVE TRIED MANY TIMES, BUT SOMETHING ALWAYS SEEMS TO DRAW ME BACK.
I did not include Ammi's tale in my report. The city of Arkham has its reservoir and Nahum's farm now lies beneath several fathoms of water.
I shall not return, but if you should ever find yourself in Arkham...
I advise you not to drink the water.

THE
SHADOW
OVER
INNSMOUTH

Adapted by Leah Moore & John Reppion
Illustrated by Leigh Gallagher

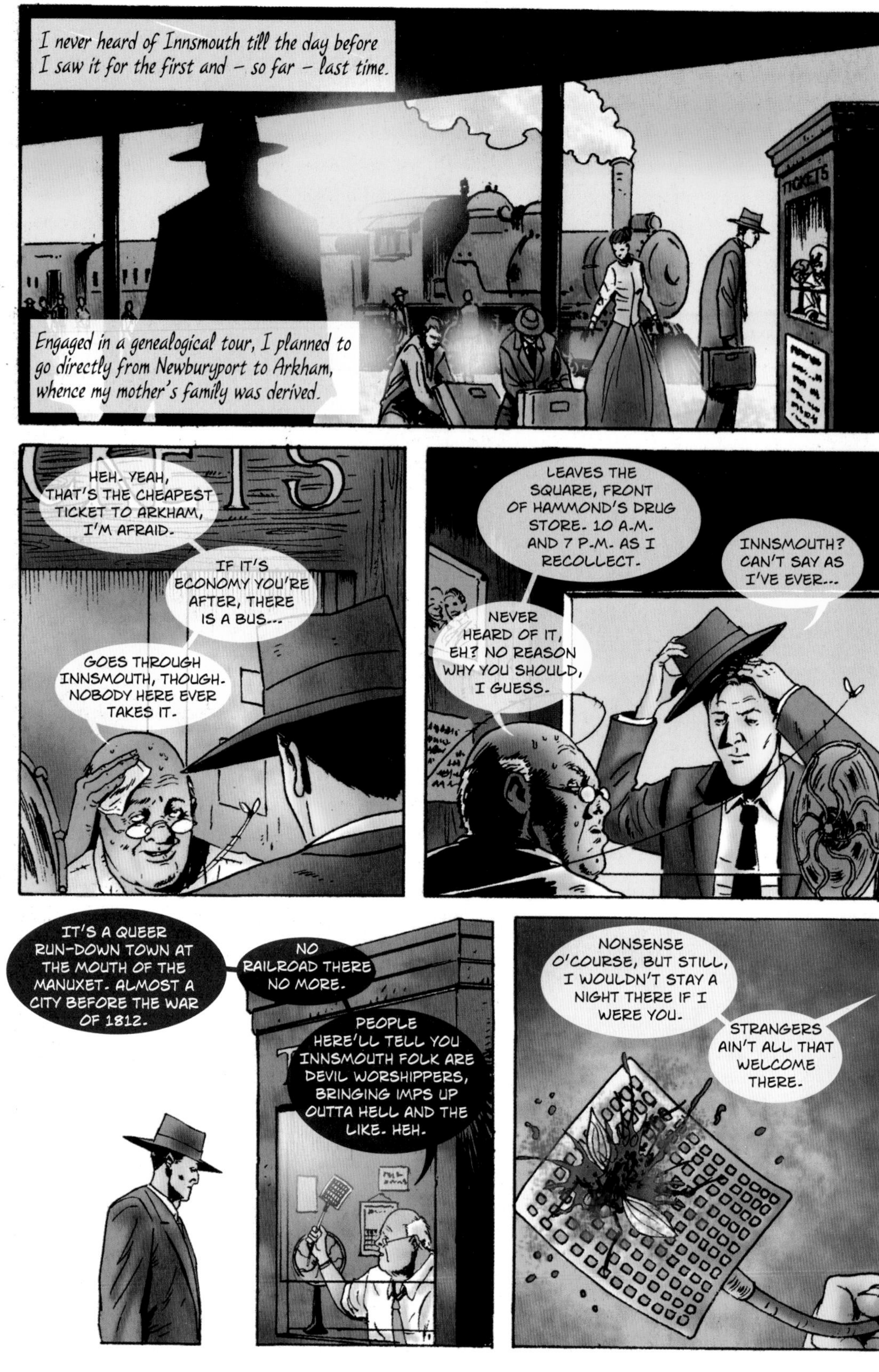
I never heard of Innsmouth till the day before I saw it for the first and – so far – last time.
Engaged in a genealogical tour, I planned to go directly from Newburyport to Arkham, whence my mother's family was derived.
TICKETS
HEH. YEAH, THAT'S THE CHEAPEST TICKET TO ARKHAM, I'M AFRAID.
IF IT'S ECONOMY YOU'RE AFTER, THERE IS A BUS...
GOES THROUGH INNSMOUTH, THOUGH. NOBODY HERE EVER TAKES IT.
INNSMOUTH? CAN'T SAY AS I'VE EVER...
NEVER HEARD OF IT, EH? NO REASON WHY YOU SHOULD, I GUESS.
LEAVES THE SQUARE, FRONT OF HAMMOND'S DRUG STORE. 10 A.M. AND 7 P.M. AS I RECOLLECT.
IT'S A QUEER RUN-DOWN TOWN AT THE MOUTH OF THE MANUXET. ALMOST A CITY BEFORE THE WAR OF 1812.
NO RAILROAD THERE NO MORE.
PEOPLE HERE'LL TELL YOU INNSMOUTH FOLK ARE DEVIL WORSHIPPERS, BRINGING IMPS UP OUTTA HELL AND THE LIKE. HEH.
NONSENSE O'COURSE, BUT STILL, I WOULDN'T STAY A NIGHT THERE IF I WERE YOU.
STRANGERS AIN'T ALL THAT WELCOME THERE.

The ticket agent told me a foolish yarn about a factory inspector supposedly driven to insanity by an overnight stay in the town.

My curiosity had been aroused, however, and that evening I visited Newburyport Public Library seeking details of Innsmouth's history.

The information was largely unremarkable, though cryptic references to a curious epidemic of 1846 intrigued me somewhat. Most interesting of all was mention of the strange jewellery vaguely associated with Innsmouth, a specimen of which was kept at the Newburyport Historical Society.

The librarian kindly gave me a note of introduction to the curator of the society, a Miss Anna Tilton, who lived nearby.

After a brief explanation, that ancient gentlewoman charitably piloted me into the closed building, since the hour was not outrageously late.

IT WAS ACQUIRED BY THE SOCIETY FROM A PAWNBROKER IN 1873. MAN WHO PAWNED IT WAS KILLED... FIGHTING, I SEEM TO RECALL.

INNSMOUTH FOLKS HAVE BEEN TRYING TO BUY IT BACK EVER SINCE, OFFERING ALL KINDS OF MONEY.

PIRATE LOOT IS WHAT MOST PEOPLE SAY.

SUPPOSED TO BE A HOARD OUT ON THAT BLACK REEF OF THEIRS.

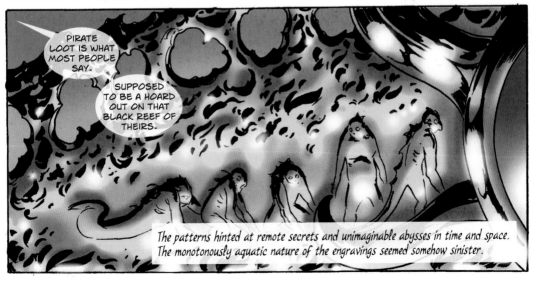

The patterns hinted at remote secrets and unimaginable abysses in time and space. The monotonously aquatic nature of the engravings seemed somehow sinister.

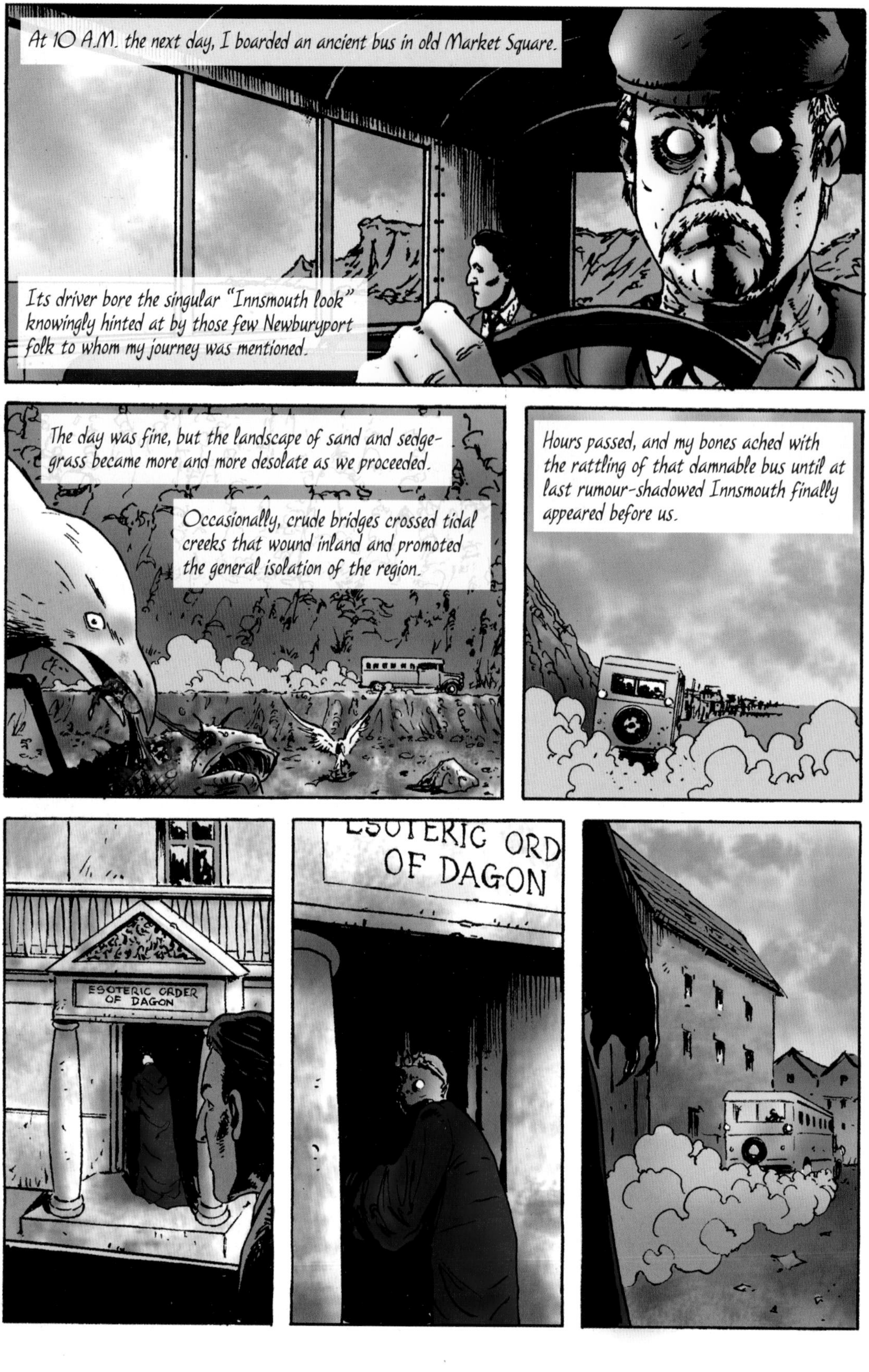
At 10 A.M. the next day, I boarded an ancient bus in old Market Square.
Its driver bore the singular "Innsmouth look" knowingly hinted at by those few Newburyport folk to whom my journey was mentioned.
The day was fine, but the landscape of sand and sedge-grass became more and more desolate as we proceeded.
Occasionally, crude bridges crossed tidal creeks that wound inland and promoted the general isolation of the region.
Hours passed, and my bones ached with the rattling of that damnable bus until at last rumour-shadowed Innsmouth finally appeared before us.
ESOTERIC ORDER OF DAGON
ESOTERIC ORD OF DAGON

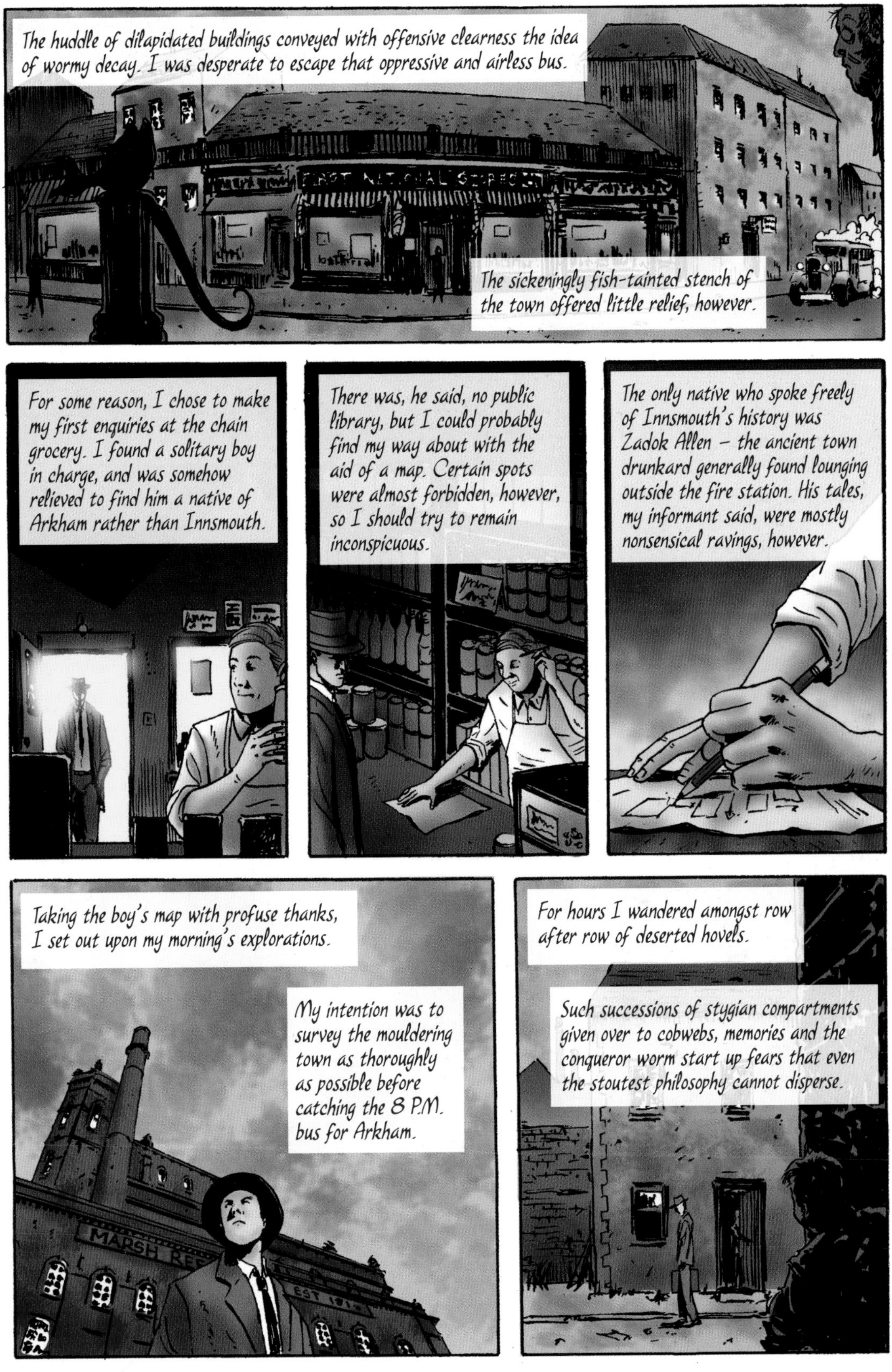

The huddle of dilapidated buildings conveyed with offensive clearness the idea of wormy decay. I was desperate to escape that oppressive and airless bus.
The sickeningly fish-tainted stench of the town offered little relief, however.
For some reason, I chose to make my first enquiries at the chain grocery. I found a solitary boy in charge, and was somehow relieved to find him a native of Arkham rather than Innsmouth.
There was, he said, no public library, but I could probably find my way about with the aid of a map. Certain spots were almost forbidden, however, so I should try to remain inconspicuous.
The only native who spoke freely of Innsmouth's history was Zadok Allen – the ancient town drunkard generally found lounging outside the fire station. His tales, my informant said, were mostly nonsensical ravings, however.
Taking the boy's map with profuse thanks, I set out upon my morning's explorations.
My intention was to survey the mouldering town as thoroughly as possible before catching the 8 P.M. bus for Arkham.
For hours I wandered amongst row after row of deserted hovels.
Such successions of stygian compartments given over to cobwebs, memories and the conqueror worm start up fears that even the stoutest philosophy cannot disperse.

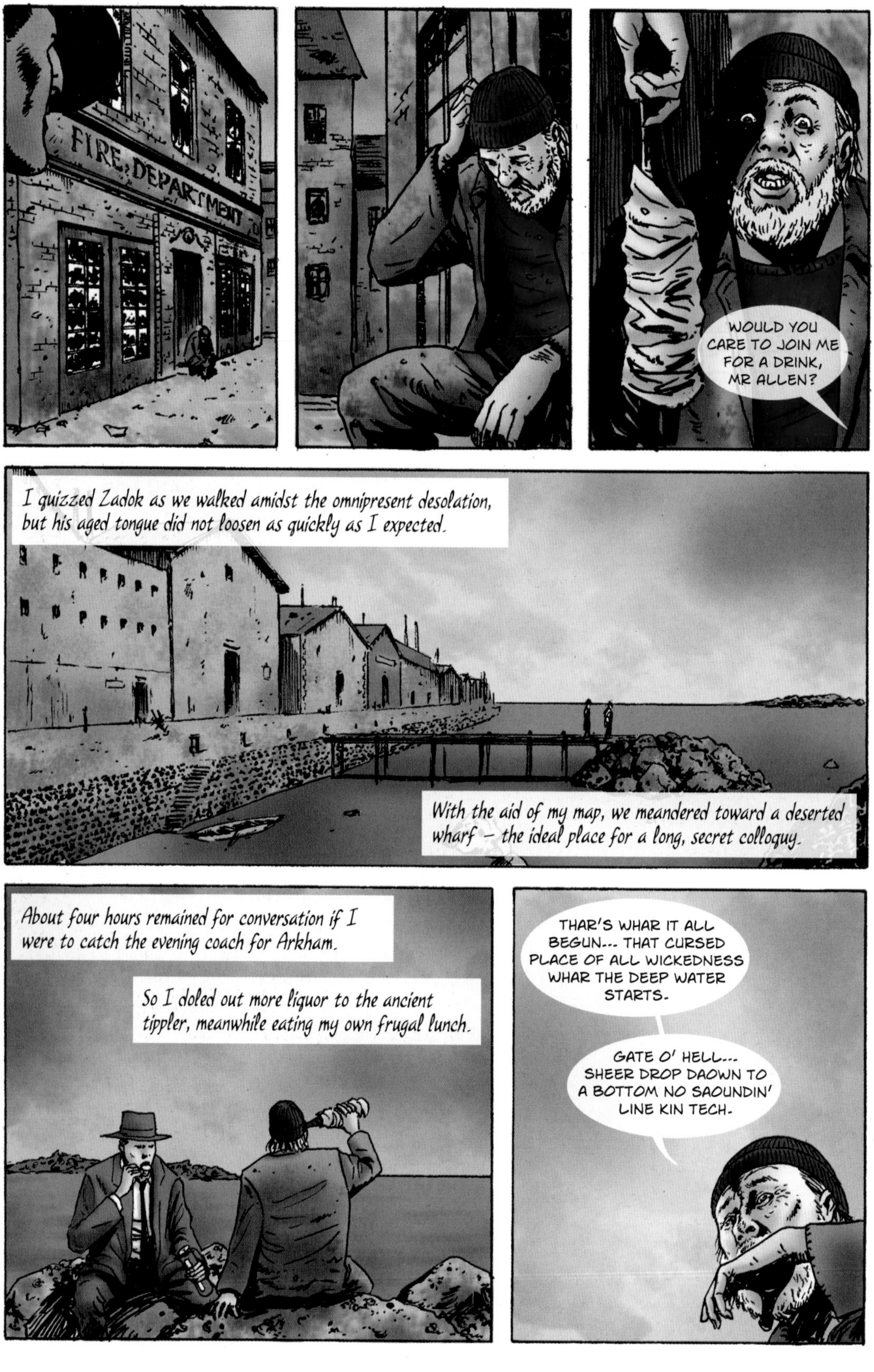
FIRE DEPARTMENT
WOULD YOU CARE TO JOIN ME FOR A DRINK, MR ALLEN?
I quizzed Zadok as we walked amidst the omnipresent desolation, but his aged tongue did not loosen as quickly as I expected.
With the aid of my map, we meandered toward a deserted wharf – the ideal place for a long, secret colloquy.
About four hours remained for conversation if I were to catch the evening coach for Arkham.
So I doled out more liquor to the ancient tippler, meanwhile eating my own frugal lunch.
THAR'S WHAR IT ALL BEGUN... THAT CURSED PLACE OF ALL WICKEDNESS WHAR THE DEEP WATER STARTS.
GATE O' HELL... SHEER DROP DAOWN TO A BOTTOM NO SAOUNDIN' LINE KIN TECH.

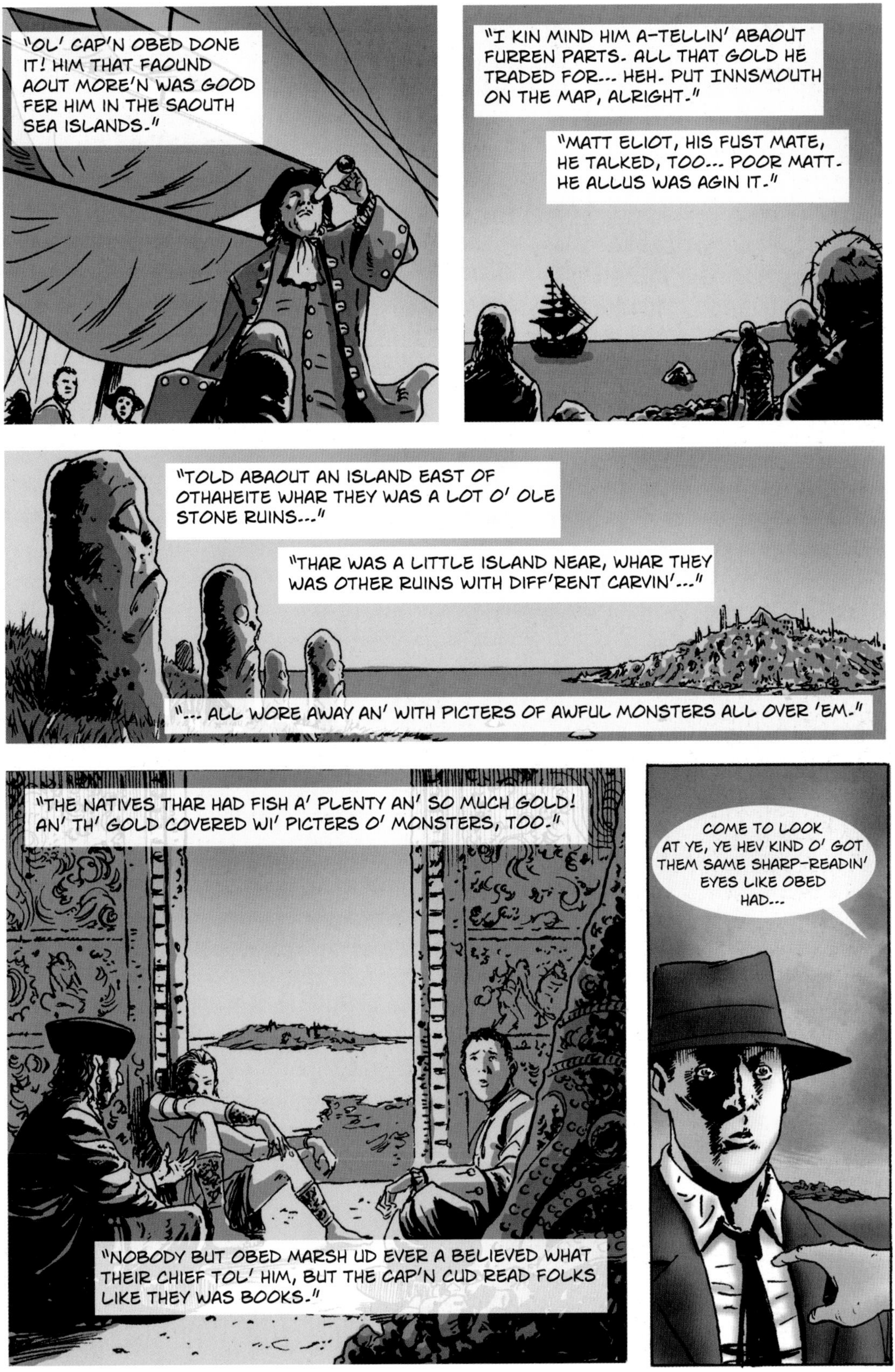
"OL' CAP'N OBED DONE IT! HIM THAT FAOUND AOUT MORE'N WAS GOOD FER HIM IN THE SAOUTH SEA ISLANDS."
"I KIN MIND HIM A-TELLIN' ABAOUT FURREN PARTS. ALL THAT GOLD HE TRADED FOR... HEH. PUT INNSMOUTH ON THE MAP, ALRIGHT."
"MATT ELIOT, HIS FUST MATE, HE TALKED, TOO... POOR MATT. HE ALLUS WAS AGIN IT."
"TOLD ABAOUT AN ISLAND EAST OF OTHAHEITE WHAR THEY WAS A LOT O' OLE STONE RUINS..."
"THAR WAS A LITTLE ISLAND NEAR, WHAR THEY WAS OTHER RUINS WITH DIFF'RENT CARVIN'..."
"... ALL WORE AWAY AN' WITH PICTERS OF AWFUL MONSTERS ALL OVER 'EM."
"THE NATIVES THAR HAD FISH A' PLENTY AN' SO MUCH GOLD! AN' TH' GOLD COVERED WI' PICTERS O' MONSTERS, TOO."
"NOBODY BUT OBED MARSH UD EVER A BELIEVED WHAT THEIR CHIEF TOL' HIM, BUT THE CAP'N CUD READ FOLKS LIKE THEY WAS BOOKS."
COME TO LOOK AT YE, YE HEV KIND O' GOT THEM SAME SHARP-READIN' EYES LIKE OBED HAD...

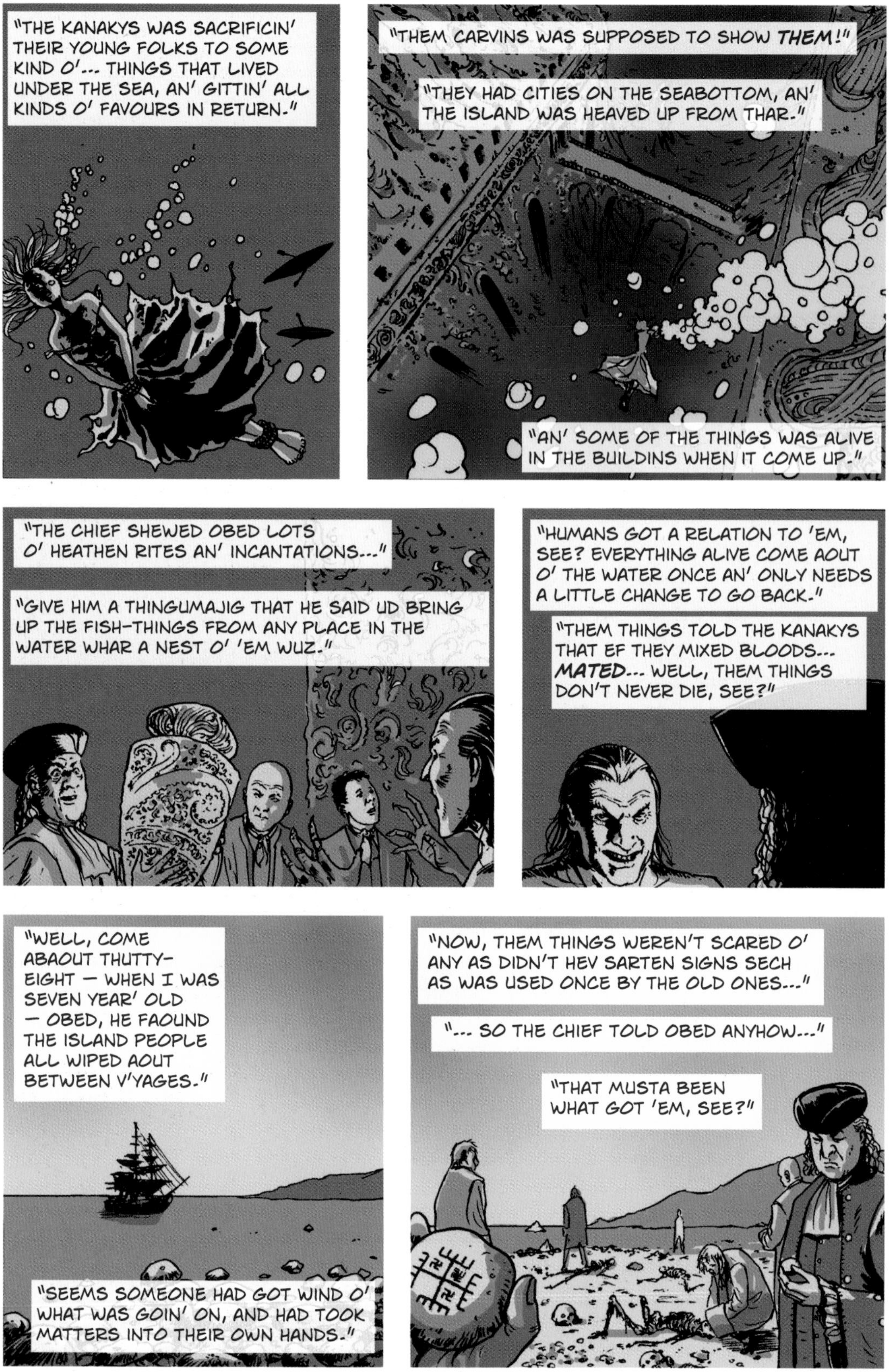
"THE KANAKYS WAS SACRIFICIN' THEIR YOUNG FOLKS TO SOME KIND O'... THINGS THAT LIVED UNDER THE SEA, AN' GITTIN' ALL KINDS O' FAVOURS IN RETURN."
"THEM CARVINS WAS SUPPOSED TO SHOW *THEM!*"
"THEY HAD CITIES ON THE SEABOTTOM, AN' THE ISLAND WAS HEAVED UP FROM THAR."
"AN' SOME OF THE THINGS WAS ALIVE IN THE BUILDINS WHEN IT COME UP."
"THE CHIEF SHEWED OBED LOTS O' HEATHEN RITES AN' INCANTATIONS..."
"GIVE HIM A THINGUMAJIG THAT HE SAID UD BRING UP THE FISH-THINGS FROM ANY PLACE IN THE WATER WHAR A NEST O' 'EM WUZ."
"HUMANS GOT A RELATION TO 'EM, SEE? EVERYTHING ALIVE COME AOUT O' THE WATER ONCE AN' ONLY NEEDS A LITTLE CHANGE TO GO BACK."
"THEM THINGS TOLD THE KANAKYS THAT EF THEY MIXED BLOODS... *MATED*... WELL, THEM THINGS DON'T NEVER DIE, SEE?"
"WELL, COME ABAOUT THUTTY-EIGHT — WHEN I WAS SEVEN YEAR' OLD — OBED, HE FAOUND THE ISLAND PEOPLE ALL WIPED AOUT BETWEEN V'YAGES."
"SEEMS SOMEONE HAD GOT WIND O' WHAT WAS GOIN' ON, AND HAD TOOK MATTERS INTO THEIR OWN HANDS."
"NOW, THEM THINGS WEREN'T SCARED O' ANY AS DIDN'T HEV SARTEN SIGNS SECH AS WAS USED ONCE BY THE OLD ONES..."
"... SO THE CHIEF TOLD OBED ANYHOW..."
"THAT MUSTA BEEN WHAT GOT 'EM, SEE?"

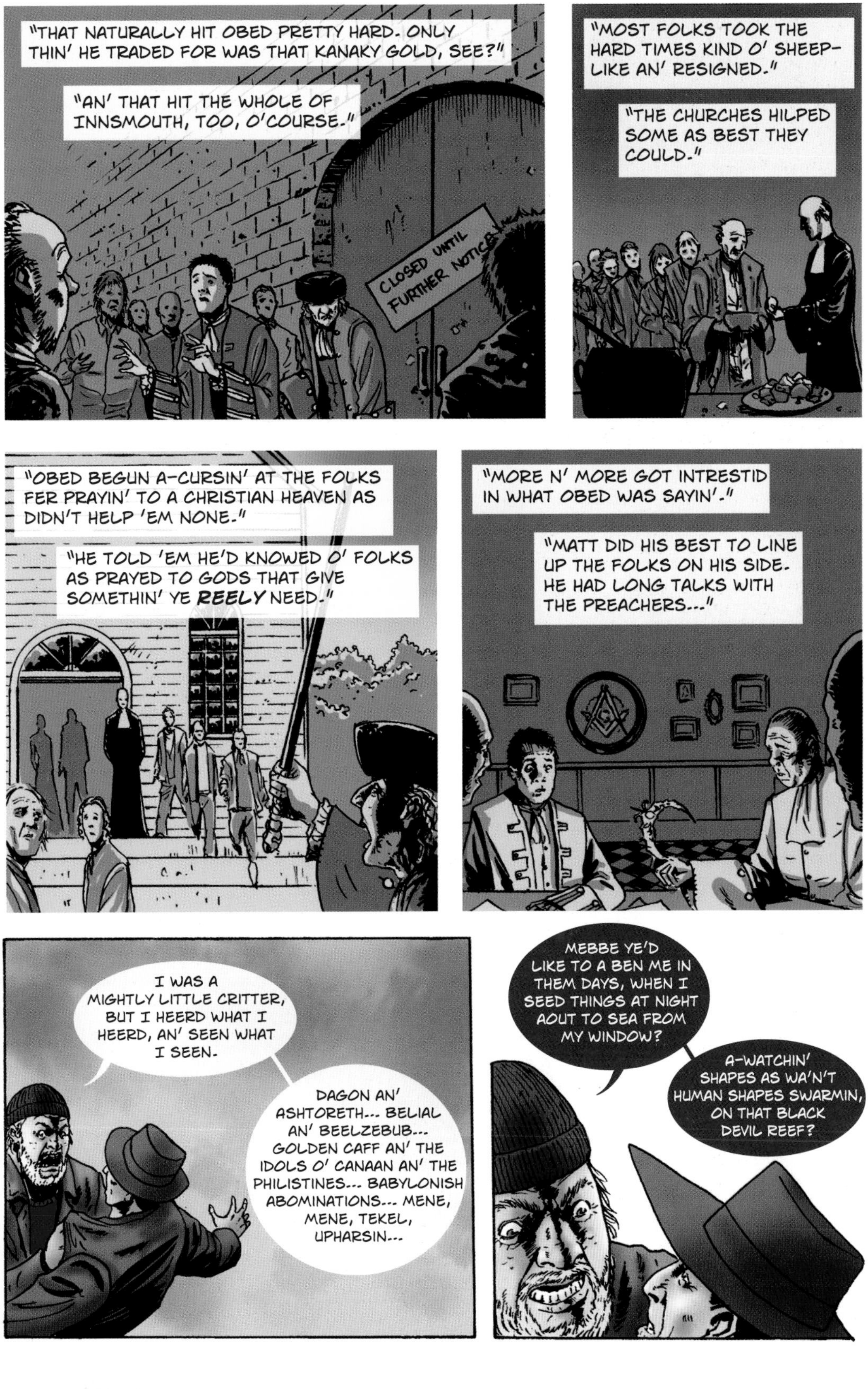
"THAT NATURALLY HIT OBED PRETTY HARD. ONLY THIN' HE TRADED FOR WAS THAT KANAKY GOLD, SEE?"
"AN' THAT HIT THE WHOLE OF INNSMOUTH, TOO, O'COURSE."
CLOSED UNTIL FURTHER NOTICE
"MOST FOLKS TOOK THE HARD TIMES KIND O' SHEEP-LIKE AN' RESIGNED."
"THE CHURCHES HILPED SOME AS BEST THEY COULD."
"OBED BEGUN A-CURSIN' AT THE FOLKS FER PRAYIN' TO A CHRISTIAN HEAVEN AS DIDN'T HELP 'EM NONE."
"HE TOLD 'EM HE'D KNOWED O' FOLKS AS PRAYED TO GODS THAT GIVE SOMETHIN' YE REELY NEED."
"MORE N' MORE GOT INTRESTID IN WHAT OBED WAS SAYIN'."
"MATT DID HIS BEST TO LINE UP THE FOLKS ON HIS SIDE. HE HAD LONG TALKS WITH THE PREACHERS..."
I WAS A MIGHTLY LITTLE CRITTER, BUT I HEERD WHAT I HEERD, AN' SEEN WHAT I SEEN.
DAGON AN' ASHTORETH... BELIAL AN' BEELZEBUB... GOLDEN CAFF AN' THE IDOLS O' CANAAN AN' THE PHILISTINES... BABYLONISH ABOMINATIONS... MENE, MENE, TEKEL, UPHARSIN...
MEBBE YE'D LIKE TO A BEN ME IN THEM DAYS, WHEN I SEED THINGS AT NIGHT AOUT TO SEA FROM MY WINDOW?
A-WATCHIN' SHAPES AS WA'N'T HUMAN SHAPES SWARMIN, ON THAT BLACK DEVIL REEF?

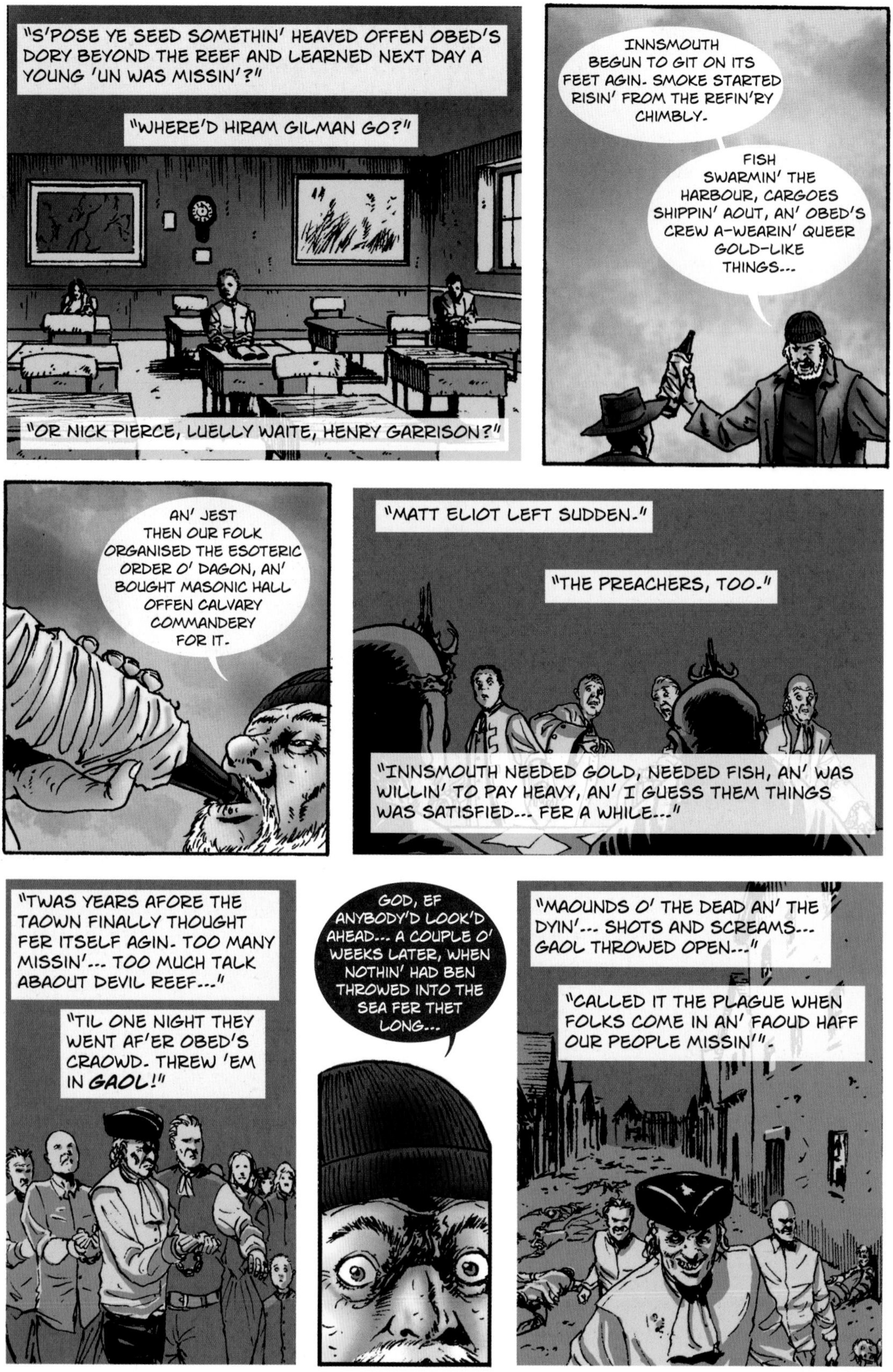
"S'POSE YE SEED SOMETHIN' HEAVED OFFEN OBED'S DORY BEYOND THE REEF AND LEARNED NEXT DAY A YOUNG 'UN WAS MISSIN'?"
"WHERE'D HIRAM GILMAN GO?"
"OR NICK PIERCE, LUELLY WAITE, HENRY GARRISON?"
INNSMOUTH BEGUN TO GIT ON ITS FEET AGIN. SMOKE STARTED RISIN' FROM THE REFIN'RY CHIMBLY.
FISH SWARMIN' THE HARBOUR, CARGOES SHIPPIN' AOUT, AN' OBED'S CREW A-WEARIN' QUEER GOLD-LIKE THINGS...
AN' JEST THEN OUR FOLK ORGANISED THE ESOTERIC ORDER O' DAGON, AN' BOUGHT MASONIC HALL OFFEN CALVARY COMMANDERY FOR IT.
"MATT ELIOT LEFT SUDDEN."
"THE PREACHERS, TOO."
"INNSMOUTH NEEDED GOLD, NEEDED FISH, AN' WAS WILLIN' TO PAY HEAVY, AN' I GUESS THEM THINGS WAS SATISFIED... FER A WHILE..."
"TWAS YEARS AFORE THE TAOWN FINALLY THOUGHT FER ITSELF AGIN. TOO MANY MISSIN'... TOO MUCH TALK ABAOUT DEVIL REEF..."
"TIL ONE NIGHT THEY WENT AF'ER OBED'S CRAOWD. THREW 'EM IN GAOL!"
GOD, EF ANYBODY'D LOOK'D AHEAD... A COUPLE O' WEEKS LATER, WHEN NOTHIN' HAD BEN THROWED INTO THE SEA FER THET LONG...
"MAOUNDS O' THE DEAD AN' THE DYIN'... SHOTS AND SCREAMS... GAOL THROWED OPEN..."
"CALLED IT THE PLAGUE WHEN FOLKS COME IN AN' FAOUD HAFF OUR PEOPLE MISSIN'".

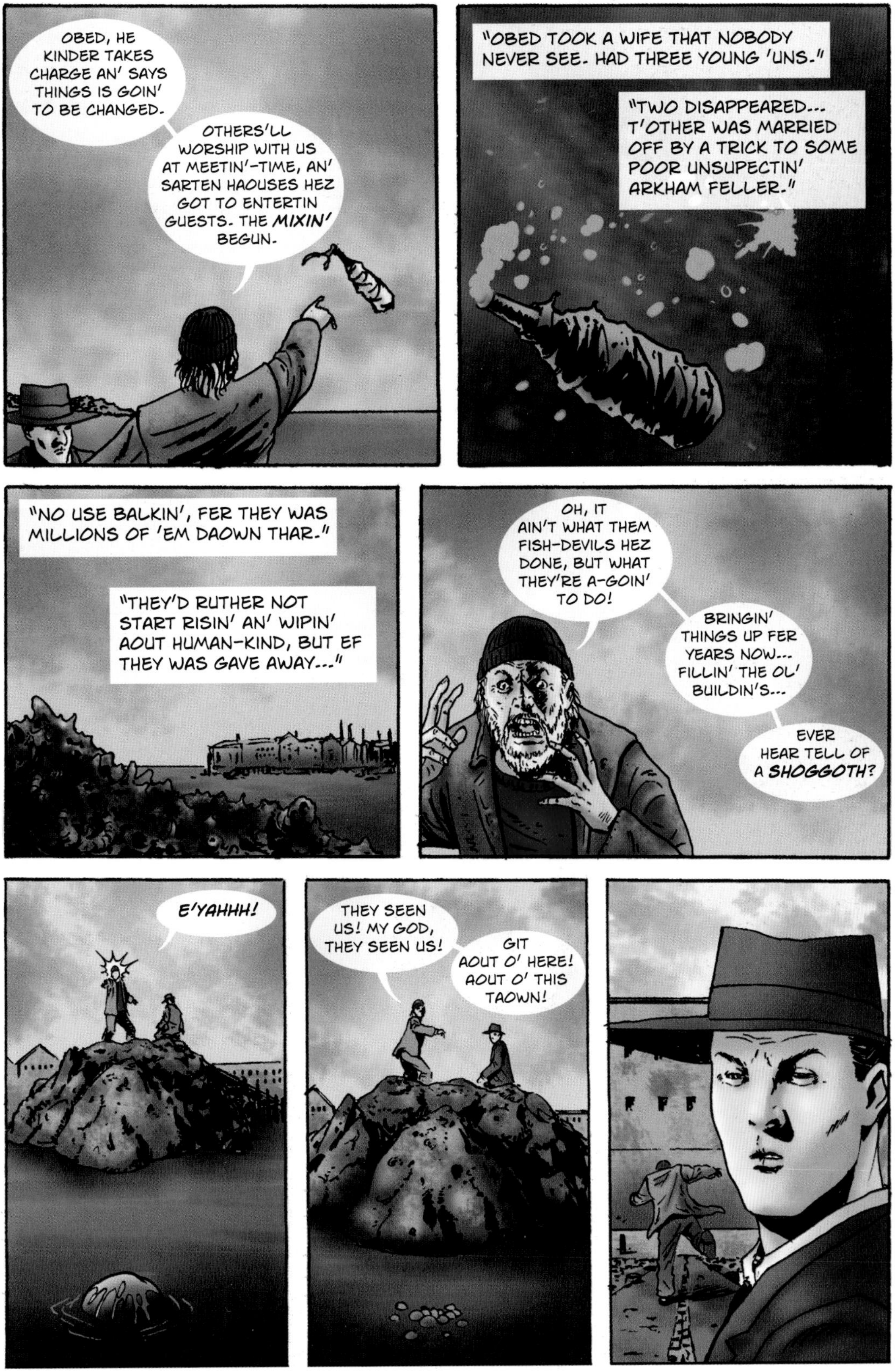
OBED, HE KINDER TAKES CHARGE AN' SAYS THINGS IS GOIN' TO BE CHANGED.
OTHERS'LL WORSHIP WITH US AT MEETIN'-TIME, AN' SARTEN HAOUSES HEZ GOT TO ENTERTIN GUESTS. THE MIXIN' BEGUN.
"OBED TOOK A WIFE THAT NOBODY NEVER SEE. HAD THREE YOUNG 'UNS."
"TWO DISAPPEARED... T'OTHER WAS MARRIED OFF BY A TRICK TO SOME POOR UNSUPECTIN' ARKHAM FELLER."
"NO USE BALKIN', FER THEY WAS MILLIONS OF 'EM DAOWN THAR."
"THEY'D RUTHER NOT START RISIN' AN' WIPIN' AOUT HUMAN-KIND, BUT EF THEY WAS GAVE AWAY..."
OH, IT AIN'T WHAT THEM FISH-DEVILS HEZ DONE, BUT WHAT THEY'RE A-GOIN' TO DO!
BRINGIN' THINGS UP FER YEARS NOW... FILLIN' THE OL' BUILDIN'S...
EVER HEAR TELL OF A SHOGGOTH?
E'YAHHH!
THEY SEEN US! MY GOD, THEY SEEN US!
GIT AOUT O' HERE! AOUT O' THIS TAOWN!

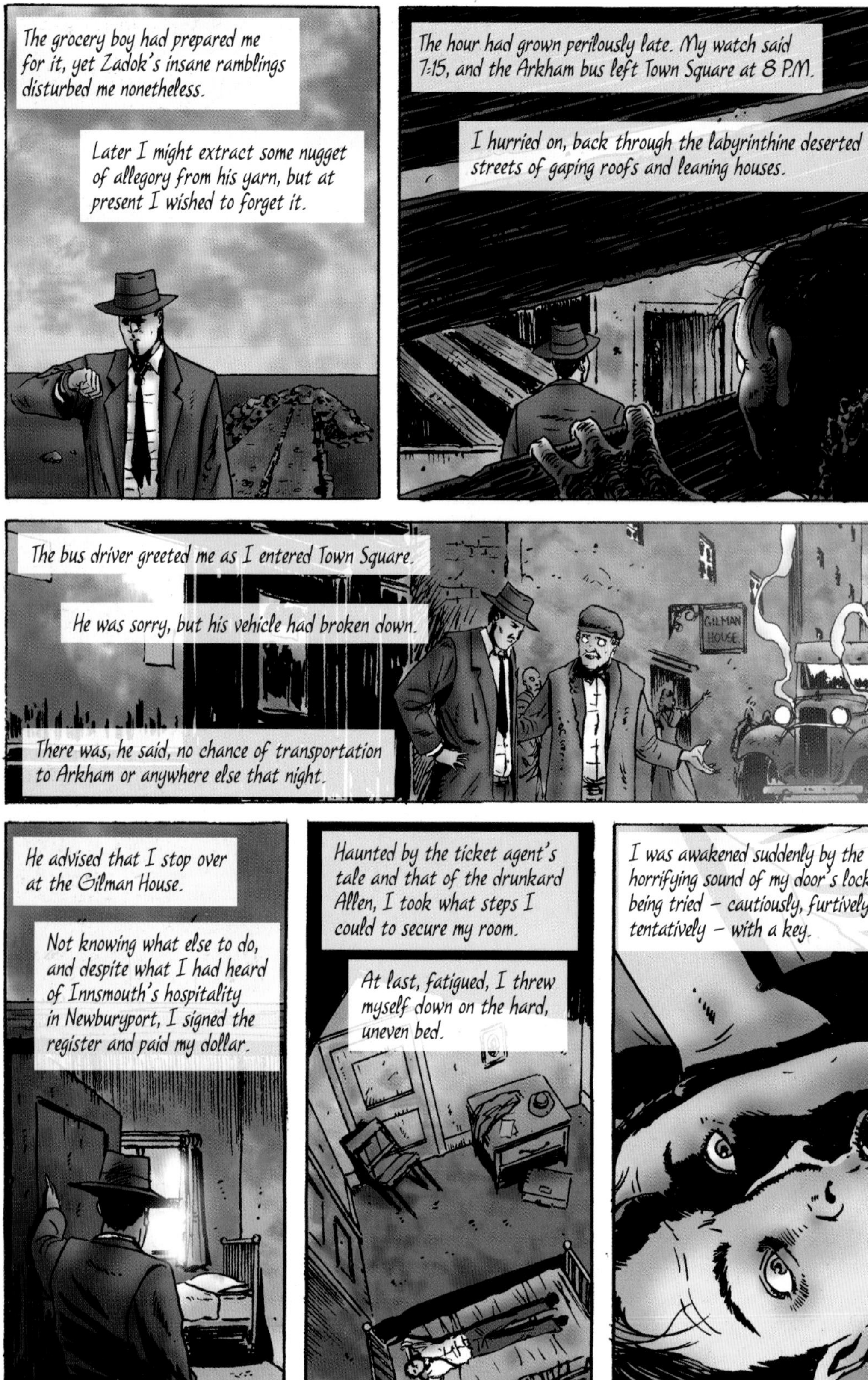
The grocery boy had prepared me for it, yet Zadok's insane ramblings disturbed me nonetheless.
Later I might extract some nugget of allegory from his yarn, but at present I wished to forget it.
The hour had grown perilously late. My watch said 7:15, and the Arkham bus left Town Square at 8 P.M.
I hurried on, back through the labyrinthine deserted streets of gaping roofs and leaning houses.
The bus driver greeted me as I entered Town Square.
He was sorry, but his vehicle had broken down.
GILMAN HOUSE
There was, he said, no chance of transportation to Arkham or anywhere else that night.
He advised that I stop over at the Gilman House.
Not knowing what else to do, and despite what I had heard of Innsmouth's hospitality in Newburyport, I signed the register and paid my dollar.
Haunted by the ticket agent's tale and that of the drunkard Allen, I took what steps I could to secure my room.
At last, fatigued, I threw myself down on the hard, uneven bed.
I was awakened suddenly by the horrifying sound of my door's lock being tried – cautiously, furtively, tentatively – with a key.

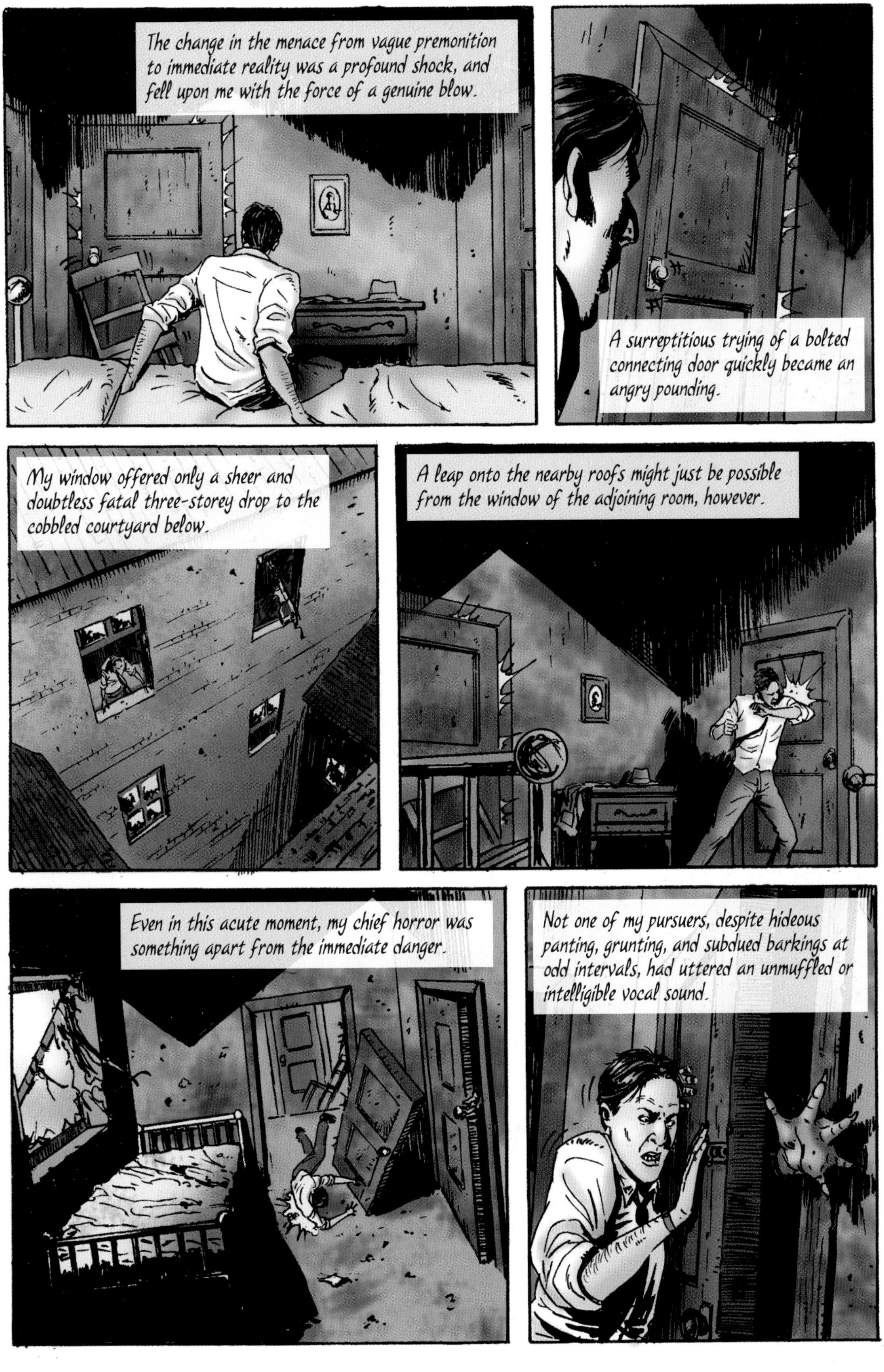
The change in the menace from vague premonition to immediate reality was a profound shock, and fell upon me with the force of a genuine blow.
A surreptitious trying of a bolted connecting door quickly became an angry pounding.
My window offered only a sheer and doubtless fatal three-storey drop to the cobbled courtyard below.
A leap onto the nearby roofs might just be possible from the window of the adjoining room, however.
Even in this acute moment, my chief horror was something apart from the immediate danger.
Not one of my pursuers, despite hideous panting, grunting, and subdued barkings at odd intervals, had uttered an unmuffled or intelligible vocal sound.

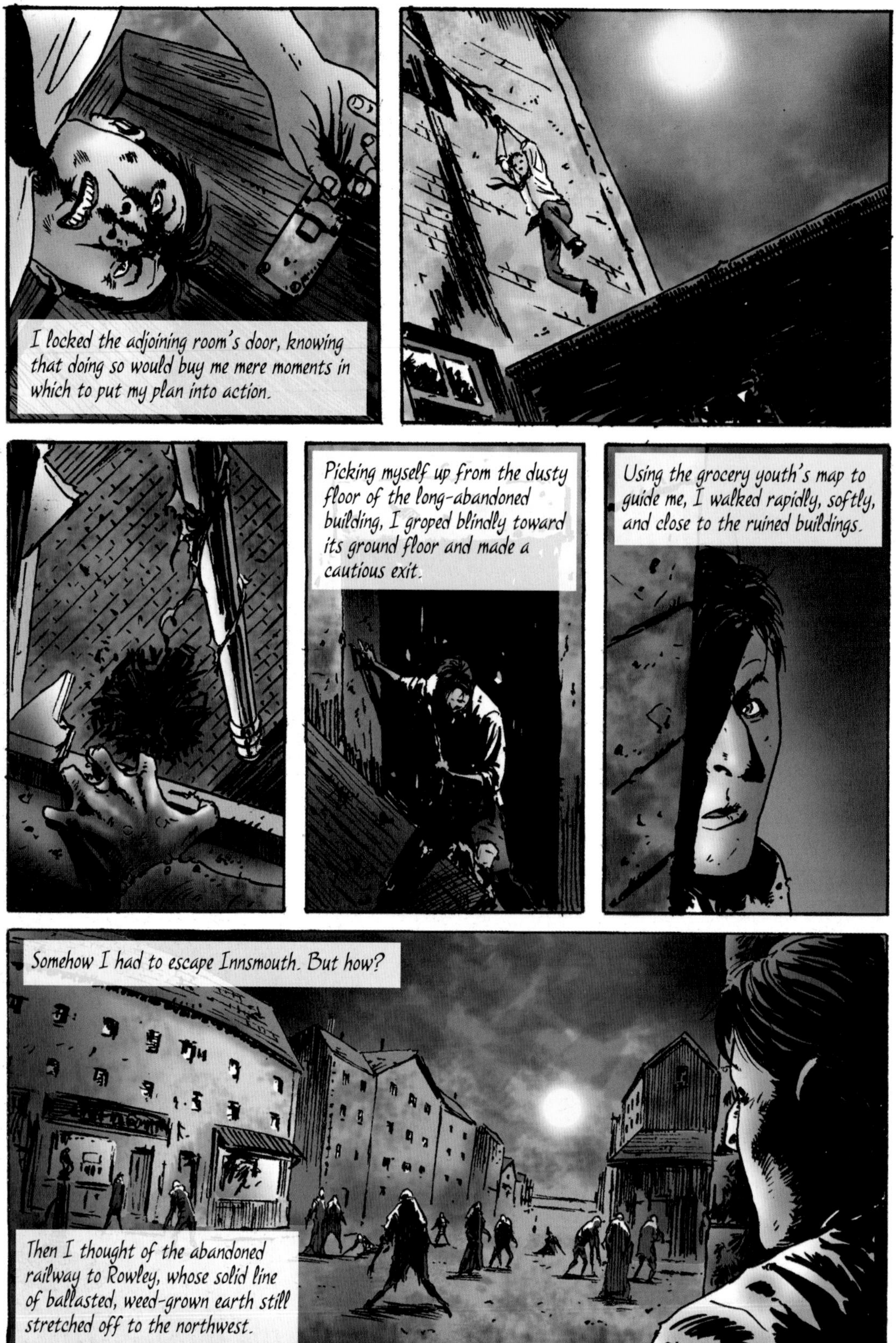
I locked the adjoining room's door, knowing that doing so would buy me mere moments in which to put my plan into action.
Picking myself up from the dusty floor of the long-abandoned building, I groped blindly toward its ground floor and made a cautious exit.
Using the grocery youth's map to guide me, I walked rapidly, softly, and close to the ruined buildings.
Somehow I had to escape Innsmouth. But how?
Then I thought of the abandoned railway to Rowley, whose solid line of ballasted, weed-grown earth still stretched off to the northwest.

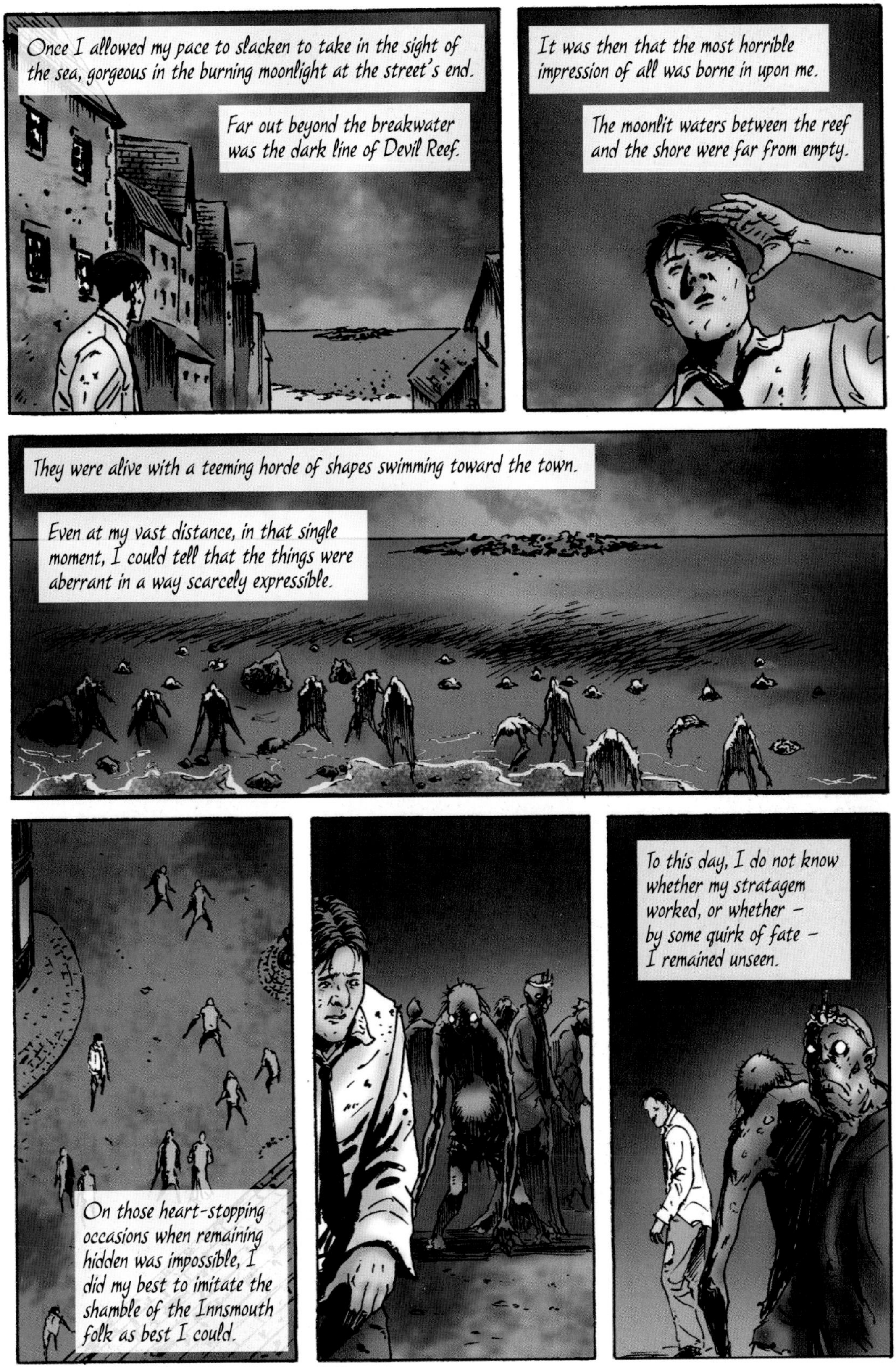
Once I allowed my pace to slacken to take in the sight of the sea, gorgeous in the burning moonlight at the street's end.
Far out beyond the breakwater was the dark line of Devil Reef.
It was then that the most horrible impression of all was borne in upon me.
The moonlit waters between the reef and the shore were far from empty.
They were alive with a teeming horde of shapes swimming toward the town.
Even at my vast distance, in that single moment, I could tell that the things were aberrant in a way scarcely expressible.
On those heart-stopping occasions when remaining hidden was impossible, I did my best to imitate the shamble of the Innsmouth folk as best I could.
To this day, I do not know whether my stratagem worked, or whether – by some quirk of fate – I remained unseen.

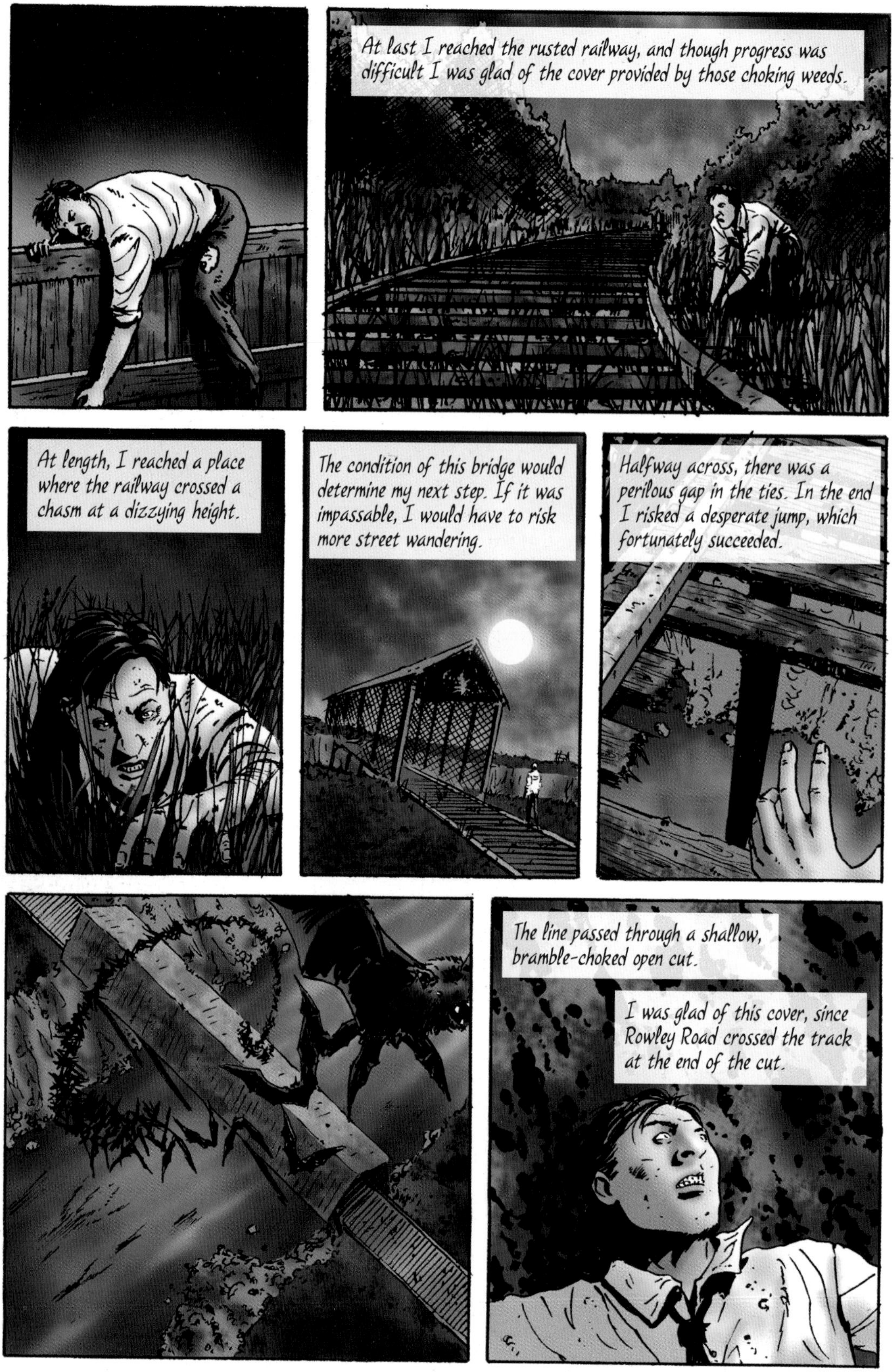
At last I reached the rusted railway, and though progress was difficult I was glad of the cover provided by those choking weeds.
At length, I reached a place where the railway crossed a chasm at a dizzying height.
The condition of this bridge would determine my next step. If it was impassable, I would have to risk more street wandering.
Halfway across, there was a perilous gap in the ties. In the end I risked a desperate jump, which fortunately succeeded.
The line passed through a shallow, bramble-choked open cut.
I was glad of this cover, since Rowley Road crossed the track at the end of the cut.

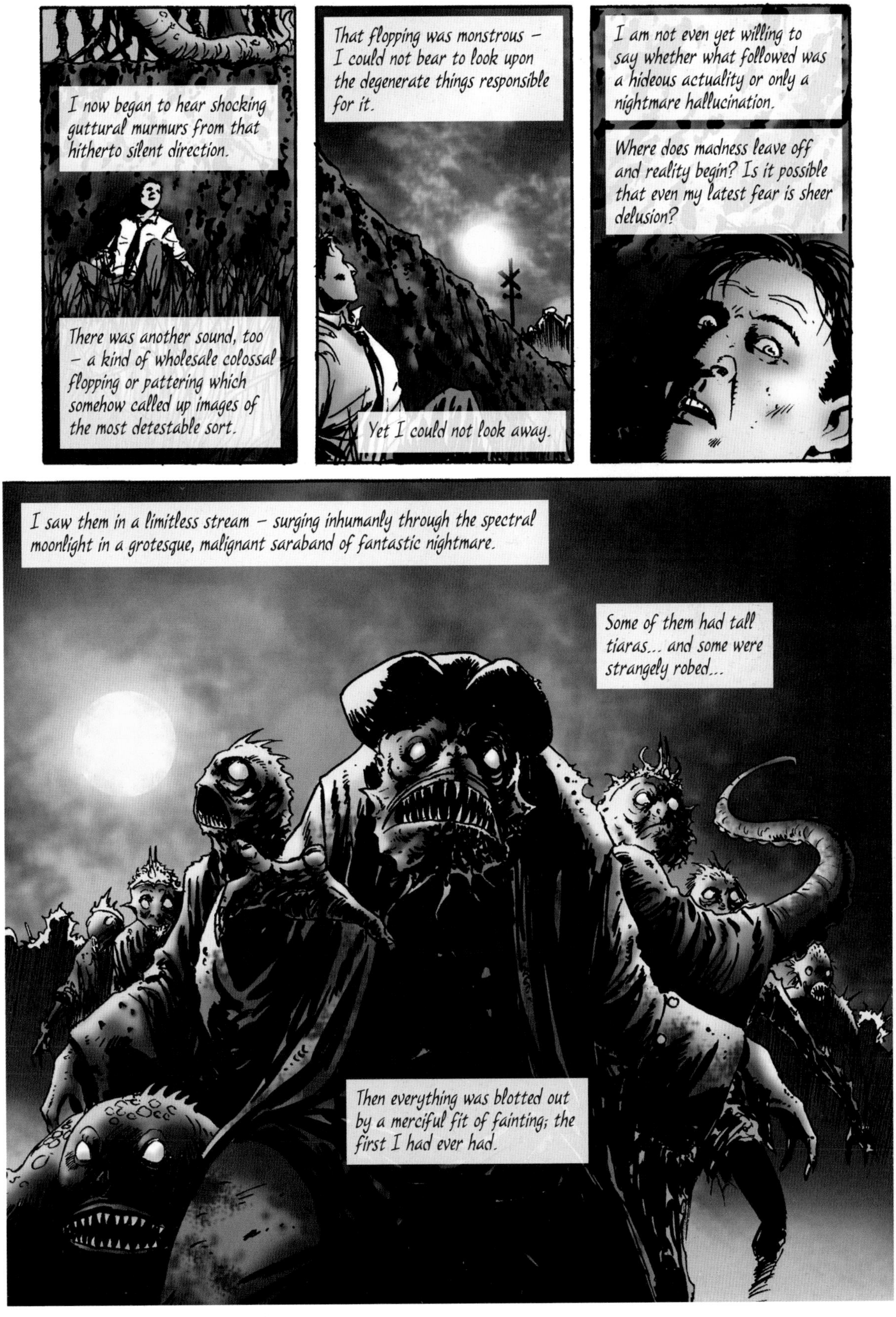
I now began to hear shocking guttural murmurs from that hitherto silent direction.
There was another sound, too – a kind of wholesale colossal flopping or pattering which somehow called up images of the most detestable sort.
That flopping was monstrous – I could not bear to look upon the degenerate things responsible for it.
Yet I could not look away.
I am not even yet willing to say whether what followed was a hideous actuality or only a nightmare hallucination.
Where does madness leave off and reality begin? Is it possible that even my latest fear is sheer delusion?
I saw them in a limitless stream – surging inhumanly through the spectral moonlight in a grotesque, malignant saraband of fantastic nightmare.
Some of them had tall tiaras... and some were strangely robed...
Then everything was blotted out by a merciful fit of fainting; the first I had ever had.

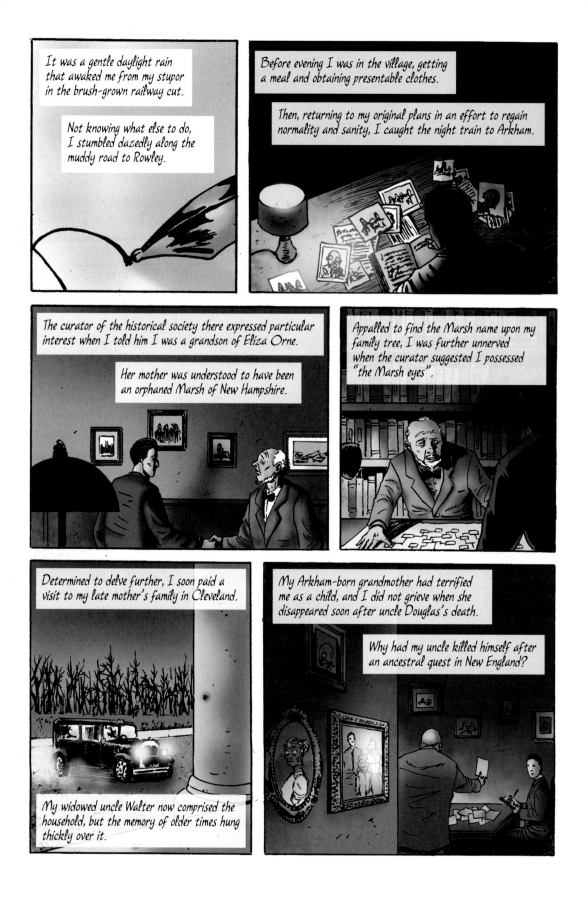

It was a gentle daylight rain that awaked me from my stupor in the brush-grown railway cut.

Not knowing what else to do, I stumbled dazedly along the muddy road to Rowley.

Before evening I was in the village, getting a meal and obtaining presentable clothes.

Then, returning to my original plans in an effort to regain normality and sanity, I caught the night train to Arkham.

The curator of the historical society there expressed particular interest when I told him I was a grandson of Eliza Orne.

Her mother was understood to have been an orphaned Marsh of New Hampshire.

Appalled to find the Marsh name upon my family tree, I was further unnerved when the curator suggested I possessed "the Marsh eyes".

Determined to delve further, I soon paid a visit to my late mother's family in Cleveland.

My widowed uncle Walter now comprised the household, but the memory of older times hung thickly over it.

My Arkham-born grandmother had terrified me as a child, and I did not grieve when she disappeared soon after uncle Douglas's death.

Why had my uncle killed himself after an ancestral quest in New England?

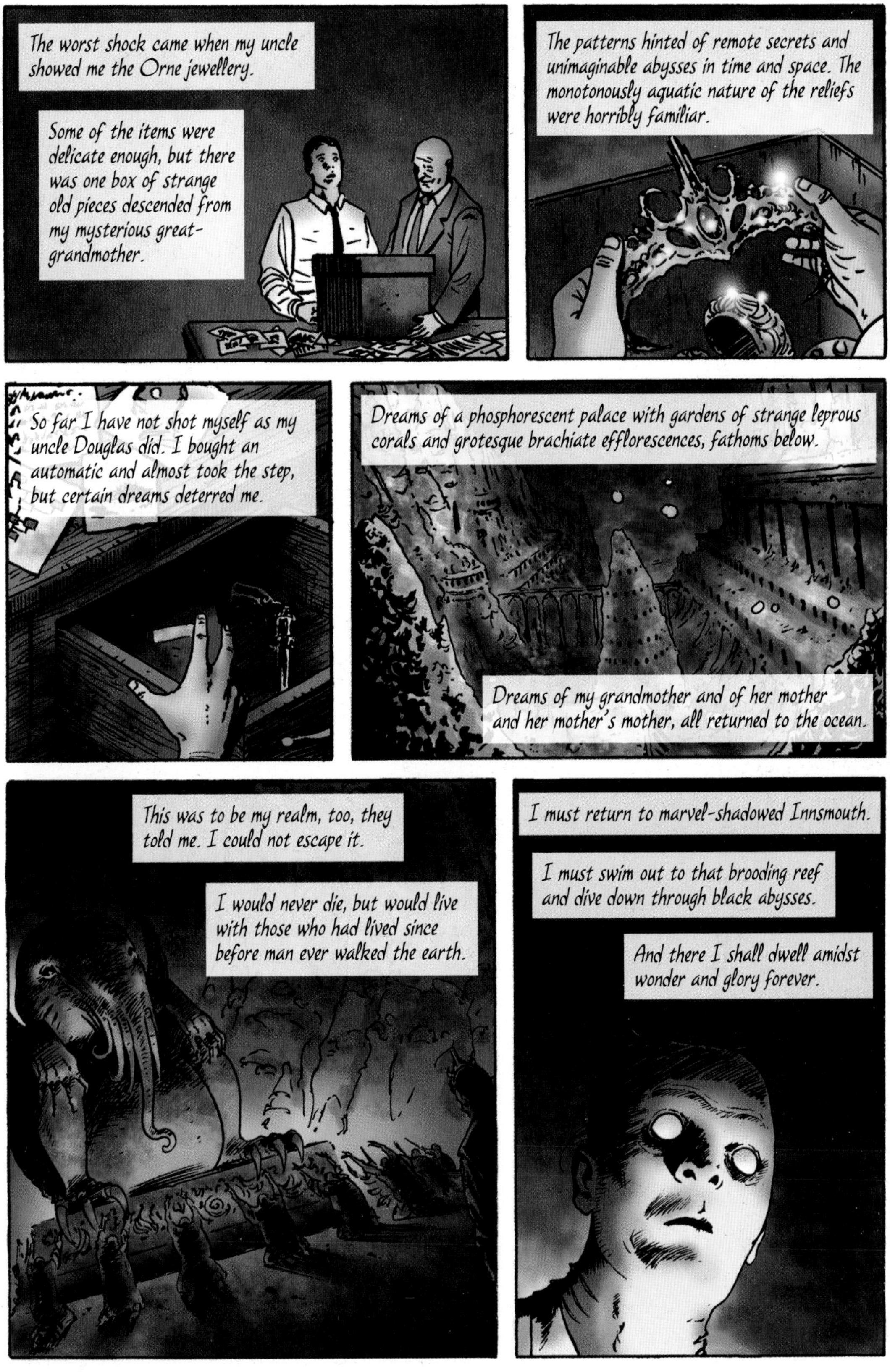
The worst shock came when my uncle showed me the Orne jewellery.
Some of the items were delicate enough, but there was one box of strange old pieces descended from my mysterious great-grandmother.
The patterns hinted of remote secrets and unimaginable abysses in time and space. The monotonously aquatic nature of the reliefs were horribly familiar.
So far I have not shot myself as my uncle Douglas did. I bought an automatic and almost took the step, but certain dreams deterred me.
Dreams of a phosphorescent palace with gardens of strange leprous corals and grotesque brachiate efflorescences, fathoms below.
Dreams of my grandmother and of her mother and her mother's mother, all returned to the ocean.
This was to be my realm, too, they told me. I could not escape it.
I would never die, but would live with those who had lived since before man ever walked the earth.
I must return to marvel-shadowed Innsmouth.
I must swim out to that brooding reef and dive down through black abysses.
And there I shall dwell amidst wonder and glory forever.

The Rats in the Walls

Adapted by
Dan Lockwood

Illustrated by
David Hartman

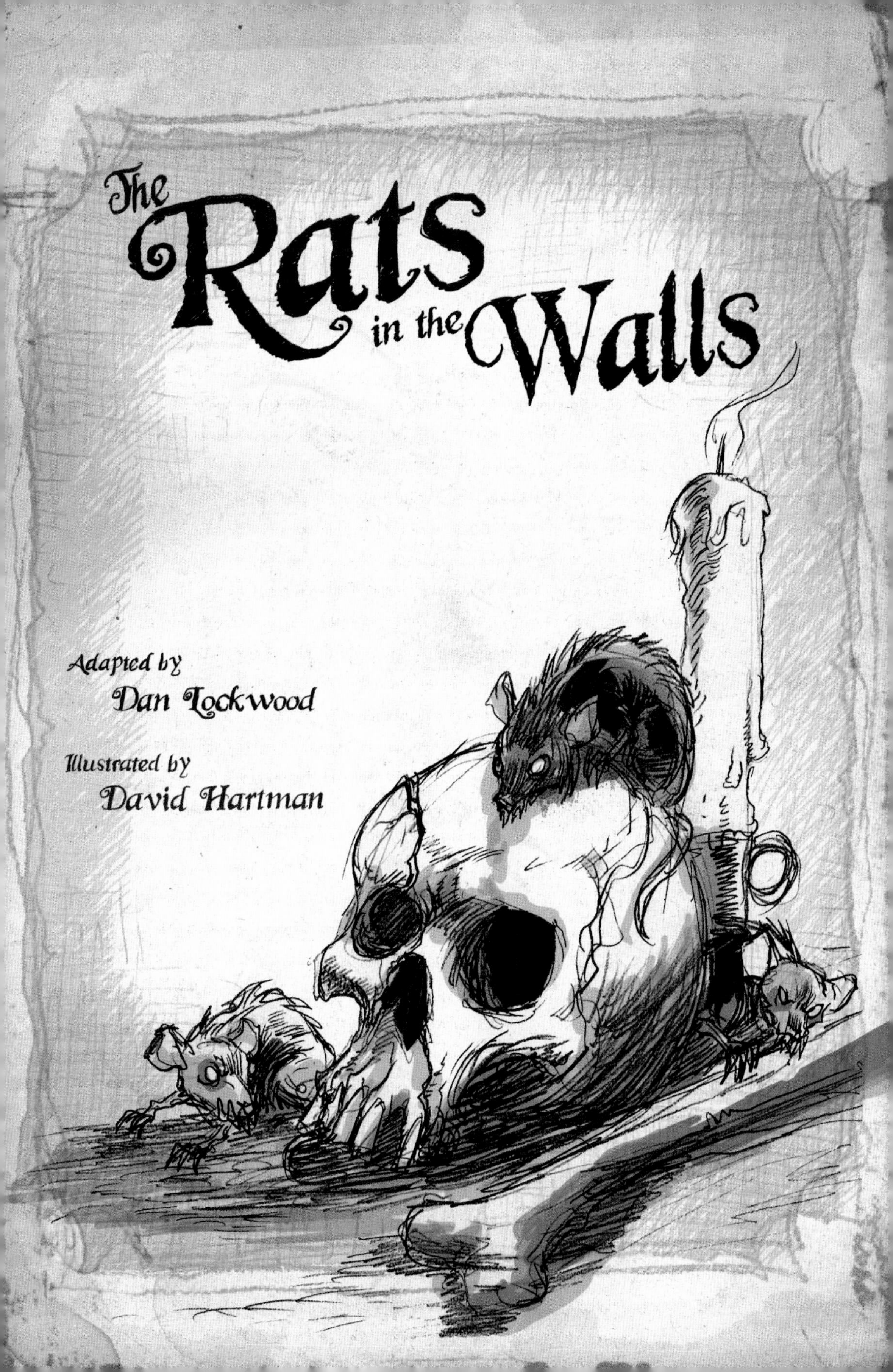

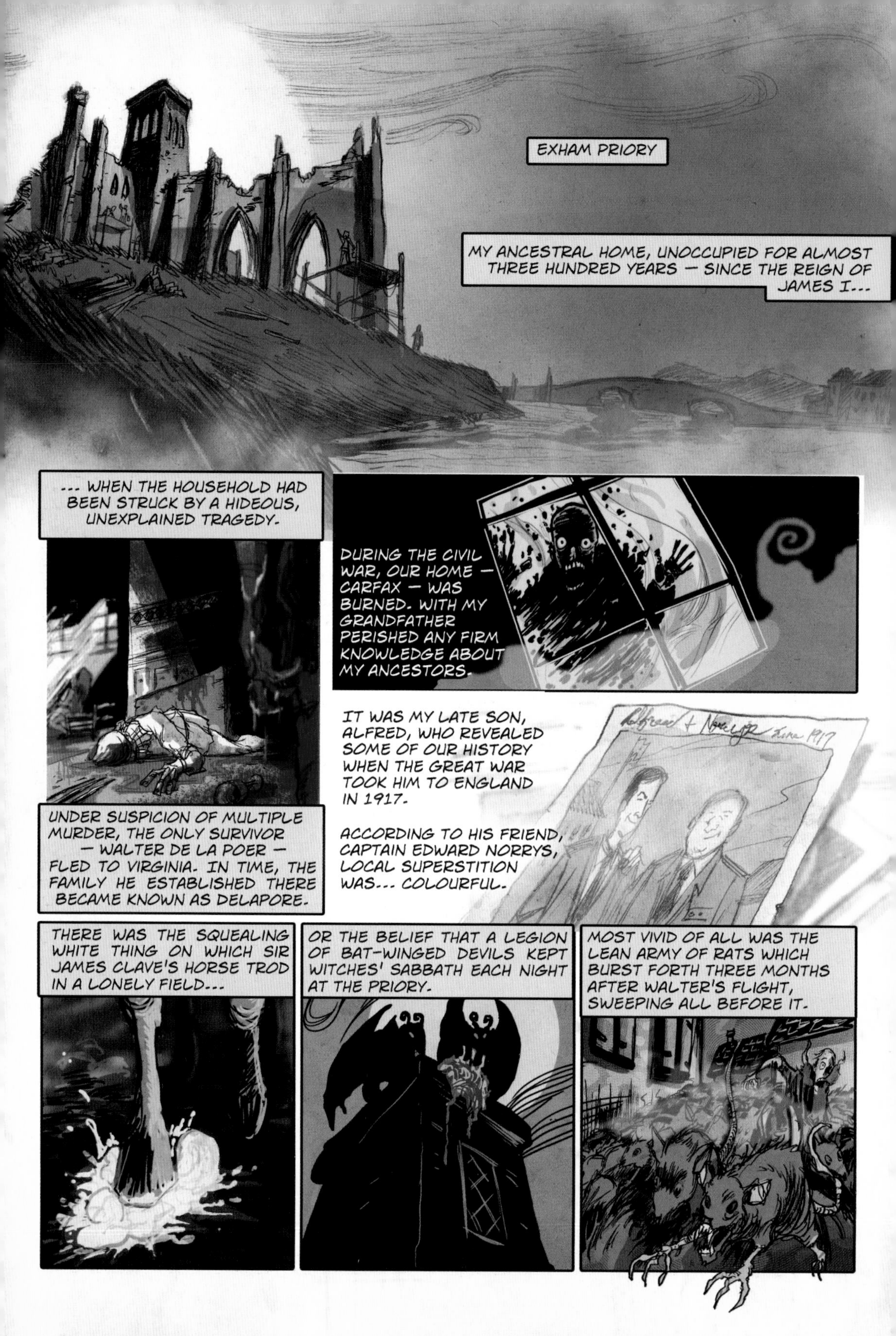
EXHAM PRIORY
MY ANCESTRAL HOME, UNOCCUPIED FOR ALMOST THREE HUNDRED YEARS — SINCE THE REIGN OF JAMES I...
... WHEN THE HOUSEHOLD HAD BEEN STRUCK BY A HIDEOUS, UNEXPLAINED TRAGEDY.
DURING THE CIVIL WAR, OUR HOME — CARFAX — WAS BURNED. WITH MY GRANDFATHER PERISHED ANY FIRM KNOWLEDGE ABOUT MY ANCESTORS.
UNDER SUSPICION OF MULTIPLE MURDER, THE ONLY SURVIVOR — WALTER DE LA POER — FLED TO VIRGINIA. IN TIME, THE FAMILY HE ESTABLISHED THERE BECAME KNOWN AS DELAPORE.
IT WAS MY LATE SON, ALFRED, WHO REVEALED SOME OF OUR HISTORY WHEN THE GREAT WAR TOOK HIM TO ENGLAND IN 1917.
ACCORDING TO HIS FRIEND, CAPTAIN EDWARD NORRYS, LOCAL SUPERSTITION WAS... COLOURFUL.
THERE WAS THE SQUEALING WHITE THING ON WHICH SIR JAMES CLAVE'S HORSE TROD IN A LONELY FIELD...
OR THE BELIEF THAT A LEGION OF BAT-WINGED DEVILS KEPT WITCHES' SABBATH EACH NIGHT AT THE PRIORY.
MOST VIVID OF ALL WAS THE LEAN ARMY OF RATS WHICH BURST FORTH THREE MONTHS AFTER WALTER'S FLIGHT, SWEEPING ALL BEFORE IT.

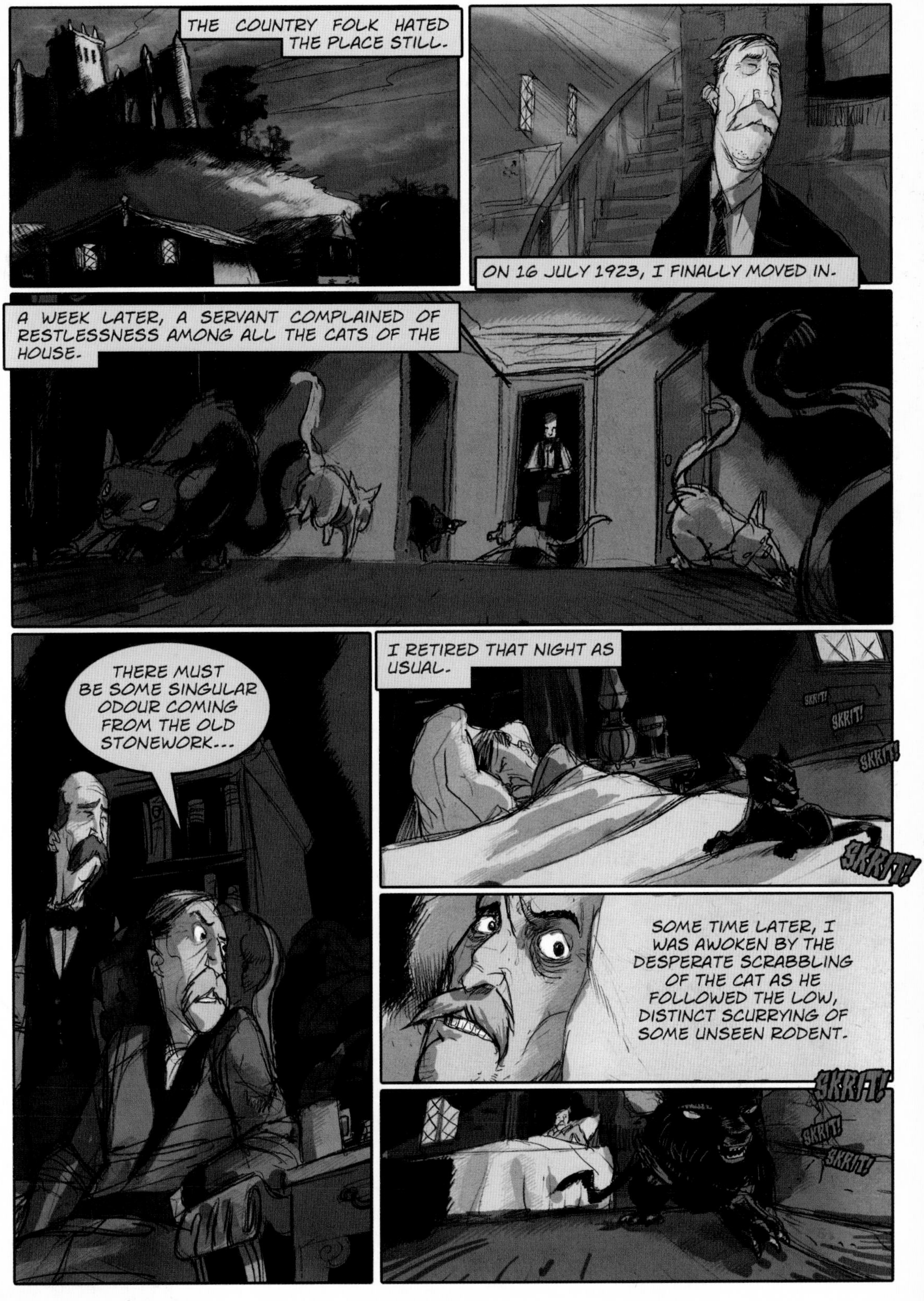
THE COUNTRY FOLK HATED THE PLACE STILL.
ON 16 JULY 1923, I FINALLY MOVED IN.
A WEEK LATER, A SERVANT COMPLAINED OF RESTLESSNESS AMONG ALL THE CATS OF THE HOUSE.
THERE MUST BE SOME SINGULAR ODOUR COMING FROM THE OLD STONEWORK...
I RETIRED THAT NIGHT AS USUAL.
SKRIT!
SKRIT!
SKRIT!
SKRIT!
SOME TIME LATER, I WAS AWOKEN BY THE DESPERATE SCRABBLING OF THE CAT AS HE FOLLOWED THE LOW, DISTINCT SCURRYING OF SOME UNSEEN RODENT.
SKRIT!
SKRIT!
SKRIT!

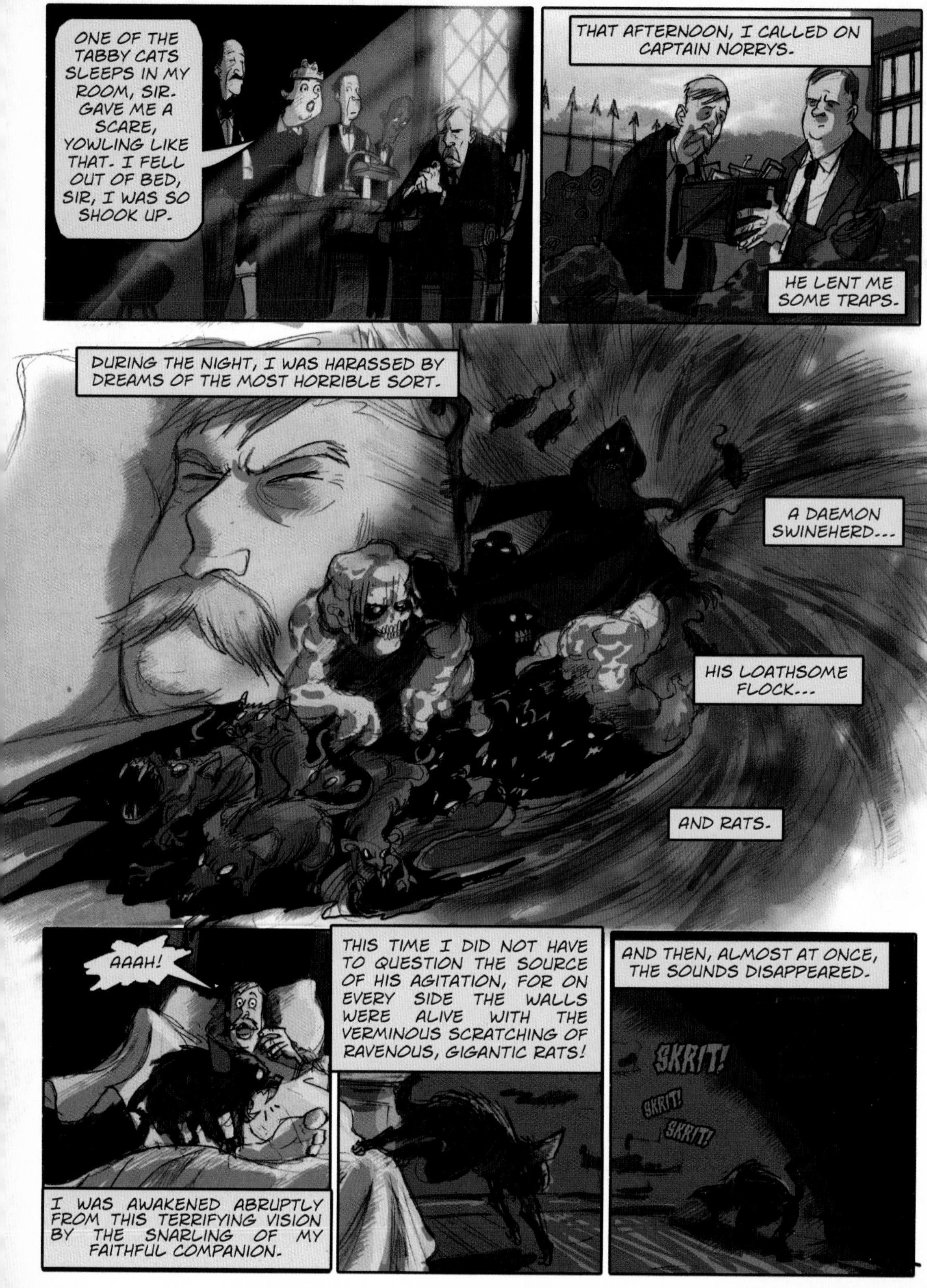
ONE OF THE TABBY CATS SLEEPS IN MY ROOM, SIR. GAVE ME A SCARE, YOWLING LIKE THAT. I FELL OUT OF BED, SIR, I WAS SO SHOOK UP.
THAT AFTERNOON, I CALLED ON CAPTAIN NORRYS.
HE LENT ME SOME TRAPS.
DURING THE NIGHT, I WAS HARASSED BY DREAMS OF THE MOST HORRIBLE SORT.
A DAEMON SWINEHERD...
HIS LOATHSOME FLOCK...
AND RATS.
AAAH!
I WAS AWAKENED ABRUPTLY FROM THIS TERRIFYING VISION BY THE SNARLING OF MY FAITHFUL COMPANION.
THIS TIME I DID NOT HAVE TO QUESTION THE SOURCE OF HIS AGITATION, FOR ON EVERY SIDE THE WALLS WERE ALIVE WITH THE VERMINOUS SCRATCHING OF RAVENOUS, GIGANTIC RATS!
AND THEN, ALMOST AT ONCE, THE SOUNDS DISAPPEARED.
SKRIT!
SKRIT!
SKRIT!

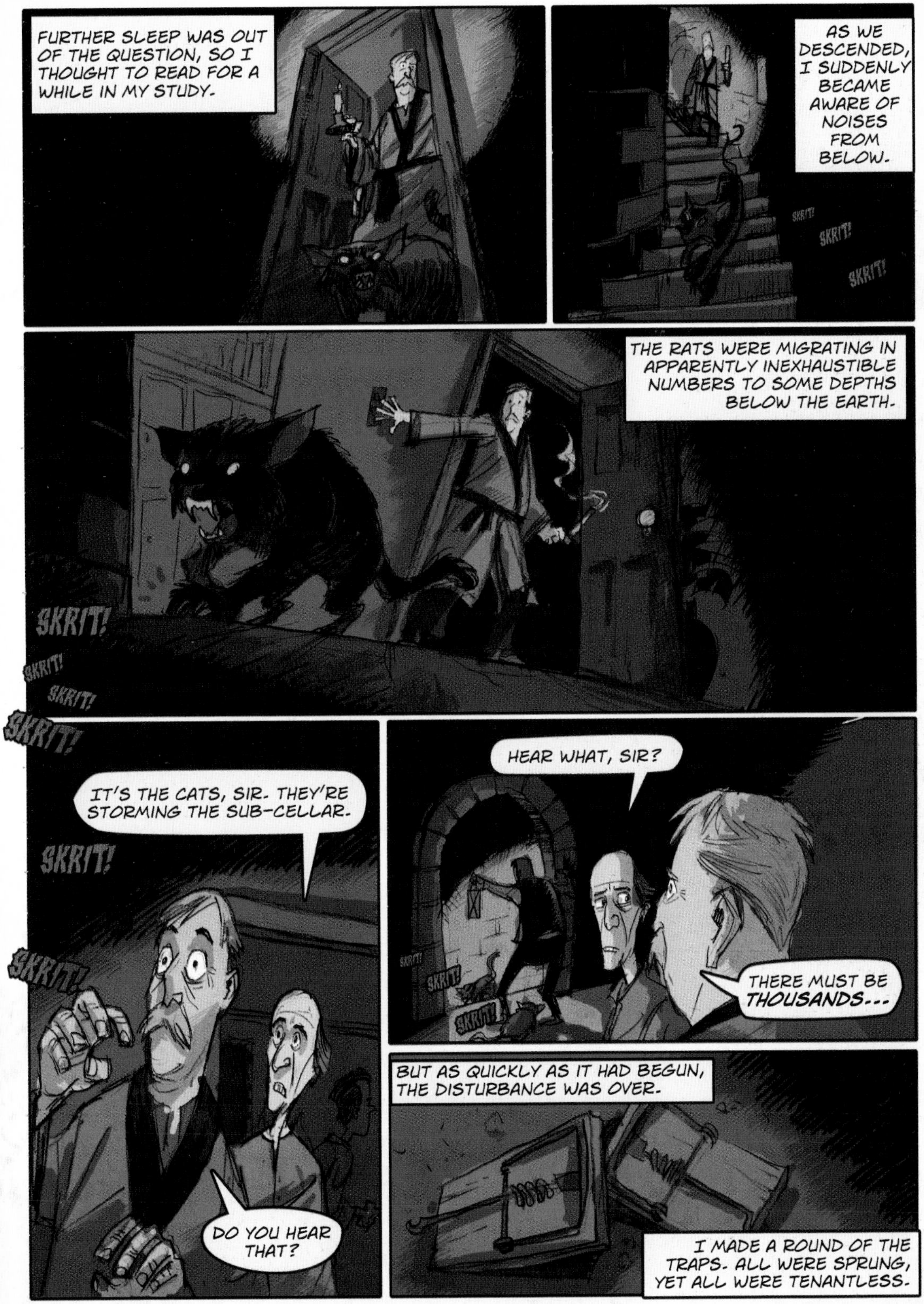
FURTHER SLEEP WAS OUT OF THE QUESTION, SO I THOUGHT TO READ FOR A WHILE IN MY STUDY.
AS WE DESCENDED, I SUDDENLY BECAME AWARE OF NOISES FROM BELOW.
SKRIT!
SKRIT!
SKRIT!
THE RATS WERE MIGRATING IN APPARENTLY INEXHAUSTIBLE NUMBERS TO SOME DEPTHS BELOW THE EARTH.
SKRIT!
SKRIT!
SKRIT!
SKRIT!
IT'S THE CATS, SIR. THEY'RE STORMING THE SUB-CELLAR.
SKRIT!
SKRIT!
DO YOU HEAR THAT?
HEAR WHAT, SIR?
SKRIT!
SKRIT!
SKRIT!
THERE MUST BE *THOUSANDS...*
BUT AS QUICKLY AS IT HAD BEGUN, THE DISTURBANCE WAS OVER.
I MADE A ROUND OF THE TRAPS. ALL WERE SPRUNG, YET ALL WERE TENANTLESS.

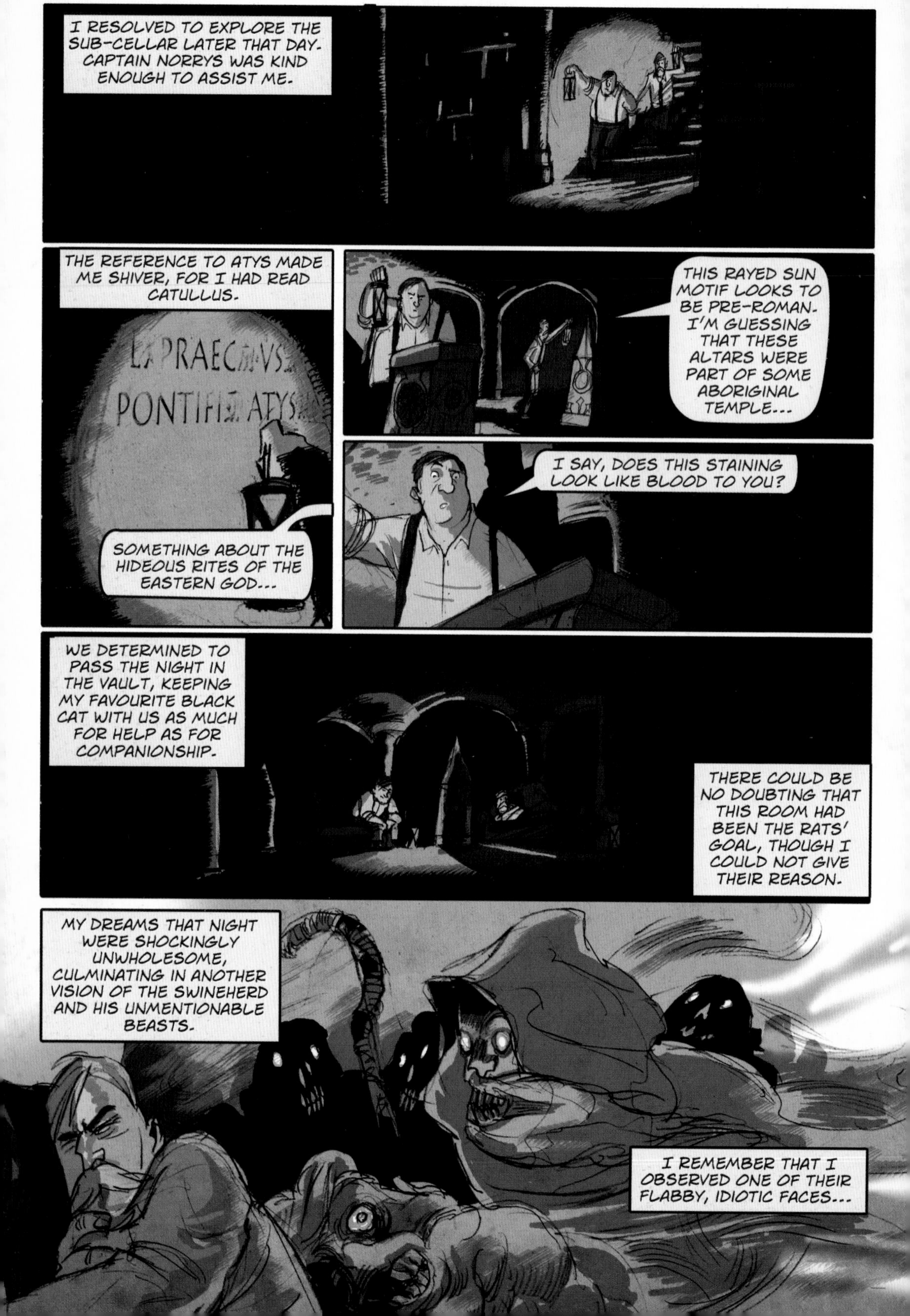
I RESOLVED TO EXPLORE THE SUB-CELLAR LATER THAT DAY. CAPTAIN NORRYS WAS KIND ENOUGH TO ASSIST ME.
THE REFERENCE TO ATYS MADE ME SHIVER, FOR I HAD READ CATULLUS.
THIS RAYED SUN MOTIF LOOKS TO BE PRE-ROMAN. I'M GUESSING THAT THESE ALTARS WERE PART OF SOME ABORIGINAL TEMPLE...
SOMETHING ABOUT THE HIDEOUS RITES OF THE EASTERN GOD...
I SAY, DOES THIS STAINING LOOK LIKE BLOOD TO YOU?
WE DETERMINED TO PASS THE NIGHT IN THE VAULT, KEEPING MY FAVOURITE BLACK CAT WITH US AS MUCH FOR HELP AS FOR COMPANIONSHIP.
THERE COULD BE NO DOUBTING THAT THIS ROOM HAD BEEN THE RATS' GOAL, THOUGH I COULD NOT GIVE THEIR REASON.
MY DREAMS THAT NIGHT WERE SHOCKINGLY UNWHOLESOME, CULMINATING IN ANOTHER VISION OF THE SWINEHERD AND HIS UNMENTIONABLE BEASTS.
I REMEMBER THAT I OBSERVED ONE OF THEIR FLABBY, IDIOTIC FACES...

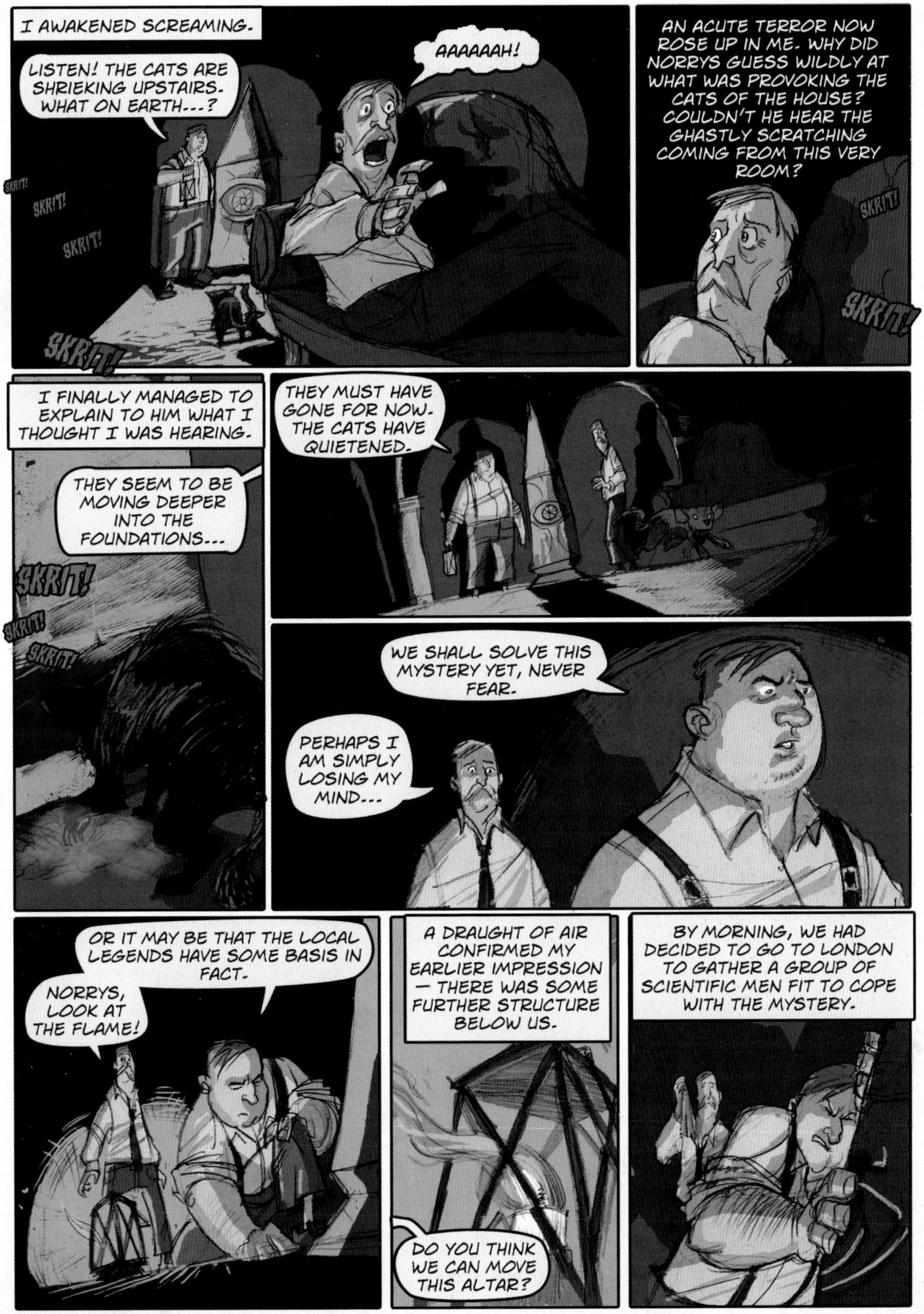
I AWAKENED SCREAMING.
LISTEN! THE CATS ARE SHRIEKING UPSTAIRS. WHAT ON EARTH...?
AAAAAAH!
SKRIT!
SKRIT!
SKRIT!
SKRIT!
AN ACUTE TERROR NOW ROSE UP IN ME. WHY DID NORRYS GUESS WILDLY AT WHAT WAS PROVOKING THE CATS OF THE HOUSE? COULDN'T HE HEAR THE GHASTLY SCRATCHING COMING FROM THIS VERY ROOM?
SKRIT!
SKRIT!
I FINALLY MANAGED TO EXPLAIN TO HIM WHAT I THOUGHT I WAS HEARING.
THEY SEEM TO BE MOVING DEEPER INTO THE FOUNDATIONS...
SKRIT!
SKRIT!
SKRIT!
THEY MUST HAVE GONE FOR NOW. THE CATS HAVE QUIETENED.
WE SHALL SOLVE THIS MYSTERY YET, NEVER FEAR.
PERHAPS I AM SIMPLY LOSING MY MIND...
OR IT MAY BE THAT THE LOCAL LEGENDS HAVE SOME BASIS IN FACT.
NORRYS, LOOK AT THE FLAME!
A DRAUGHT OF AIR CONFIRMED MY EARLIER IMPRESSION — THERE WAS SOME FURTHER STRUCTURE BELOW US.
DO YOU THINK WE CAN MOVE THIS ALTAR?
BY MORNING, WE HAD DECIDED TO GO TO LONDON TO GATHER A GROUP OF SCIENTIFIC MEN FIT TO COPE WITH THE MYSTERY.

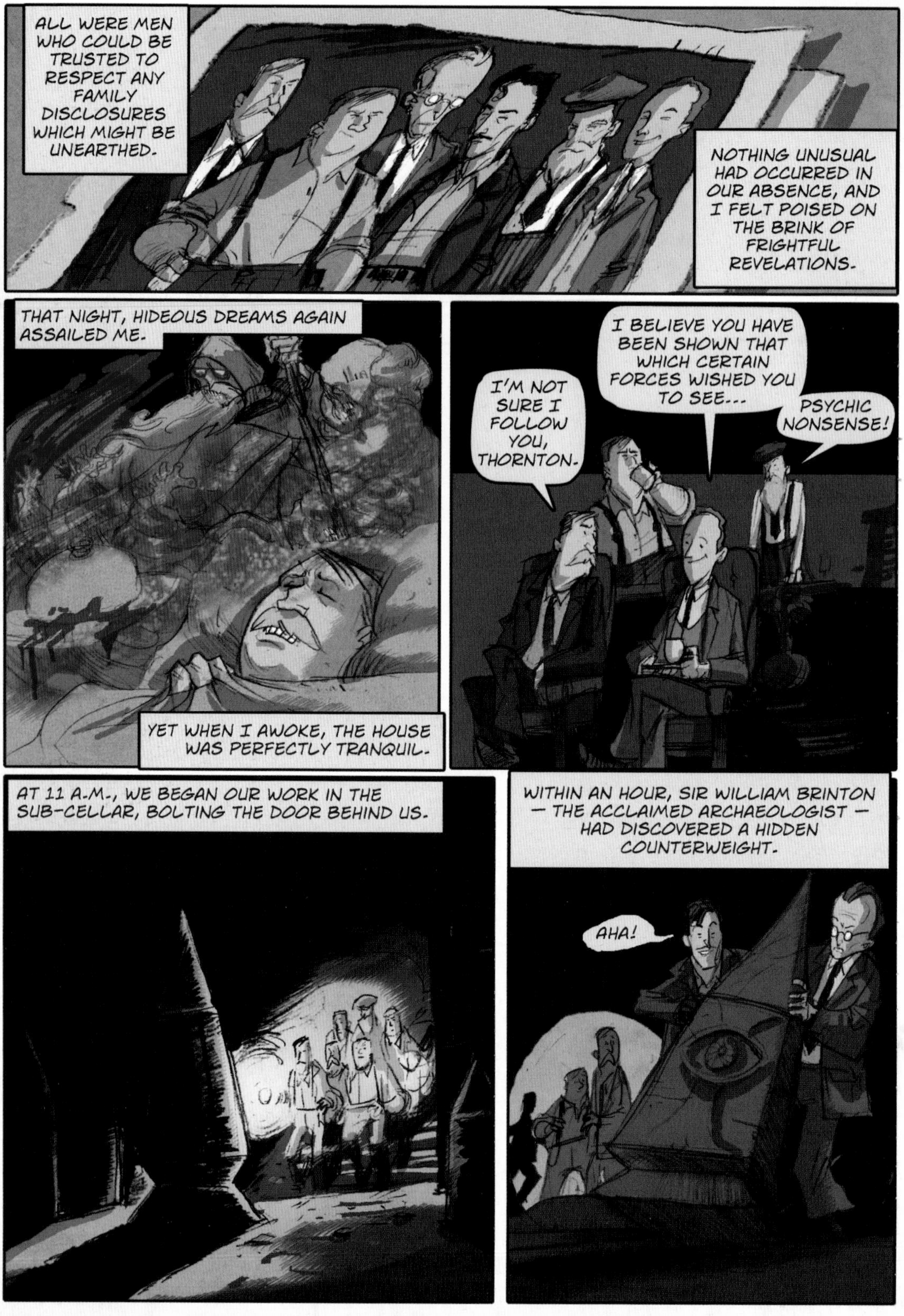
ALL WERE MEN WHO COULD BE TRUSTED TO RESPECT ANY FAMILY DISCLOSURES WHICH MIGHT BE UNEARTHED.
NOTHING UNUSUAL HAD OCCURRED IN OUR ABSENCE, AND I FELT POISED ON THE BRINK OF FRIGHTFUL REVELATIONS.
THAT NIGHT, HIDEOUS DREAMS AGAIN ASSAILED ME.
YET WHEN I AWOKE, THE HOUSE WAS PERFECTLY TRANQUIL.
I'M NOT SURE I FOLLOW YOU, THORNTON.
I BELIEVE YOU HAVE BEEN SHOWN THAT WHICH CERTAIN FORCES WISHED YOU TO SEE...
PSYCHIC NONSENSE!
AT 11 A.M., WE BEGAN OUR WORK IN THE SUB-CELLAR, BOLTING THE DOOR BEHIND US.
WITHIN AN HOUR, SIR WILLIAM BRINTON — THE ACCLAIMED ARCHAEOLOGIST — HAD DISCOVERED A HIDDEN COUNTERWEIGHT.
AHA!

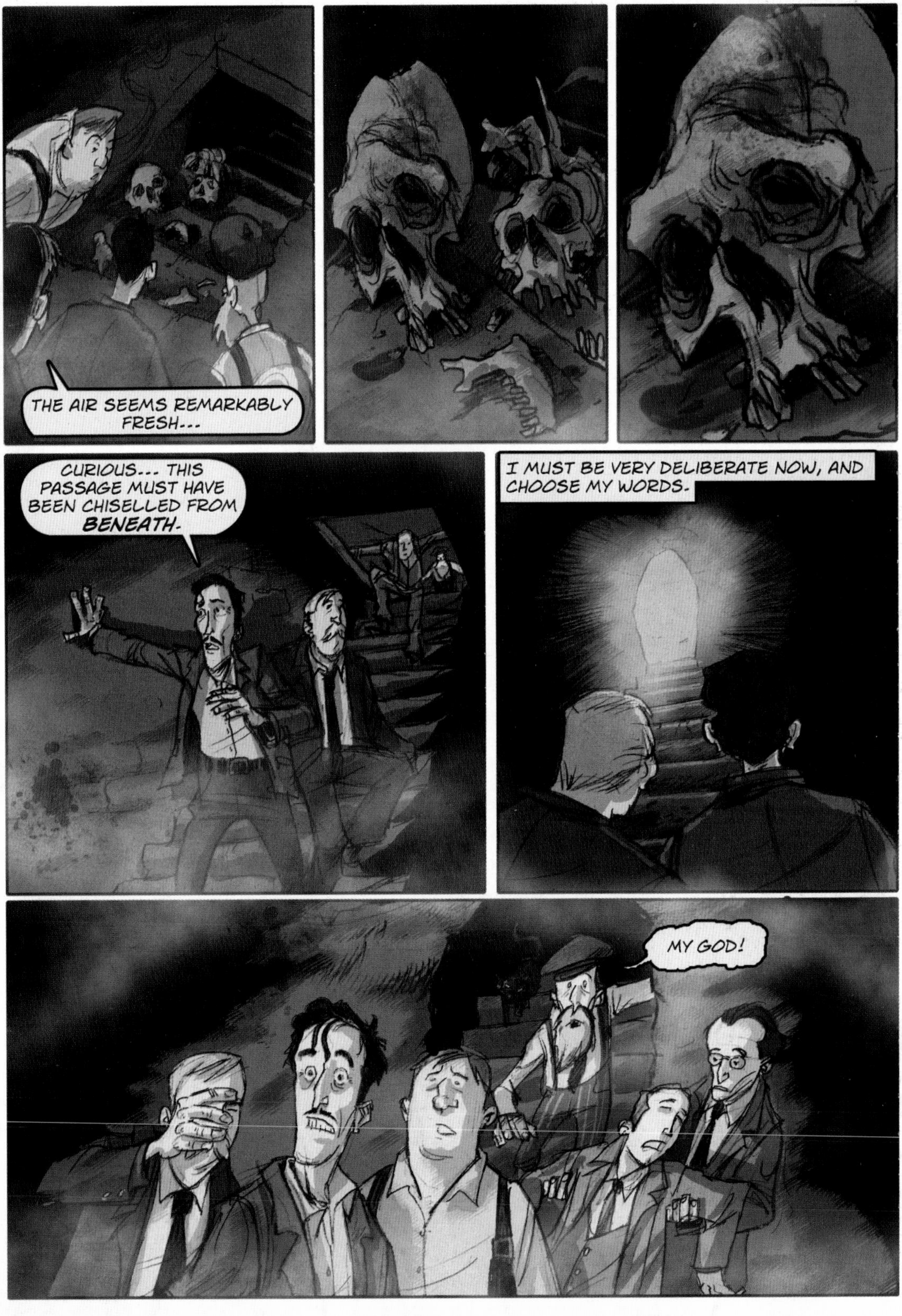
THE AIR SEEMS REMARKABLY FRESH...
CURIOUS... THIS PASSAGE MUST HAVE BEEN CHISELLED FROM **BENEATH**.
I MUST BE VERY DELIBERATE NOW, AND CHOOSE MY WORDS.
MY GOD!

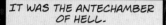

IT WAS THE ANTECHAMBER OF HELL.

I WONDER THAT ANY MAN AMONG US LIVED AND KEPT HIS SANITY THROUGH THAT NIGHTMARISH DAY OF DISCOVERY.

DR TRASK, THE ANTHROPOLOGIST, FOUND A DEGRADED MIXTURE OF SKULLS WHICH UTTERLY BAFFLED HIM.

SOME OF THESE THINGS MUST HAVE DESCENDED AS QUADRUPEDS FOR THE LAST TWENTY OR MORE GENERATIONS.

THORNTON APPEARS TO HAVE FAINTED AGAIN.

HORROR PILED ON HORROR AS WE PROGRESSED. IT SEEMED THAT THE QUADRUPED CREATURES HAD BEEN KEPT IN STONE PENS, OUT OF WHICH THEY HAD BROKEN IN THEIR LAST DELIRIUM OF HUNGER OR RAT-FEAR.

THERE MUST HAVE BEEN GREAT HERDS OF THEM.

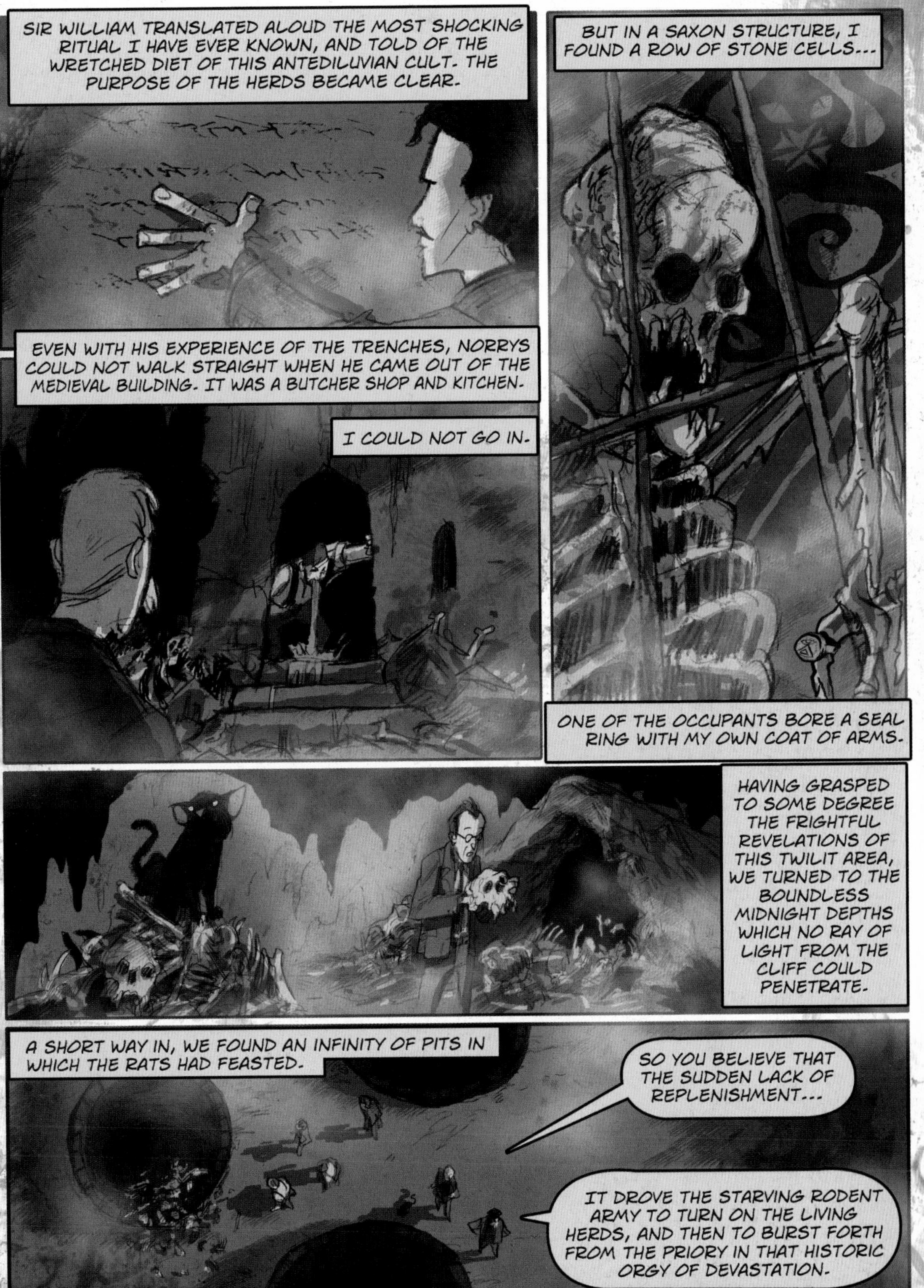
SIR WILLIAM TRANSLATED ALOUD THE MOST SHOCKING RITUAL I HAVE EVER KNOWN, AND TOLD OF THE WRETCHED DIET OF THIS ANTEDILUVIAN CULT. THE PURPOSE OF THE HERDS BECAME CLEAR.
EVEN WITH HIS EXPERIENCE OF THE TRENCHES, NORRYS COULD NOT WALK STRAIGHT WHEN HE CAME OUT OF THE MEDIEVAL BUILDING. IT WAS A BUTCHER SHOP AND KITCHEN.
I COULD NOT GO IN.
BUT IN A SAXON STRUCTURE, I FOUND A ROW OF STONE CELLS...
ONE OF THE OCCUPANTS BORE A SEAL RING WITH MY OWN COAT OF ARMS.
HAVING GRASPED TO SOME DEGREE THE FRIGHTFUL REVELATIONS OF THIS TWILIT AREA, WE TURNED TO THE BOUNDLESS MIDNIGHT DEPTHS WHICH NO RAY OF LIGHT FROM THE CLIFF COULD PENETRATE.
A SHORT WAY IN, WE FOUND AN INFINITY OF PITS IN WHICH THE RATS HAD FEASTED.
SO YOU BELIEVE THAT THE SUDDEN LACK OF REPLENISHMENT...
IT DROVE THE STARVING RODENT ARMY TO TURN ON THE LIVING HERDS, AND THEN TO BURST FORTH FROM THE PRIORY IN THAT HISTORIC ORGY OF DEVASTATION.

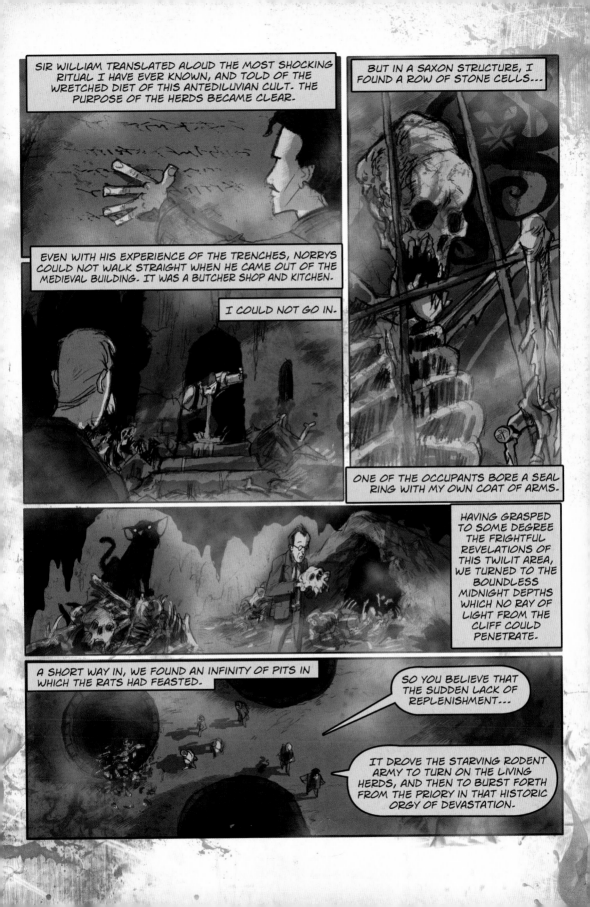

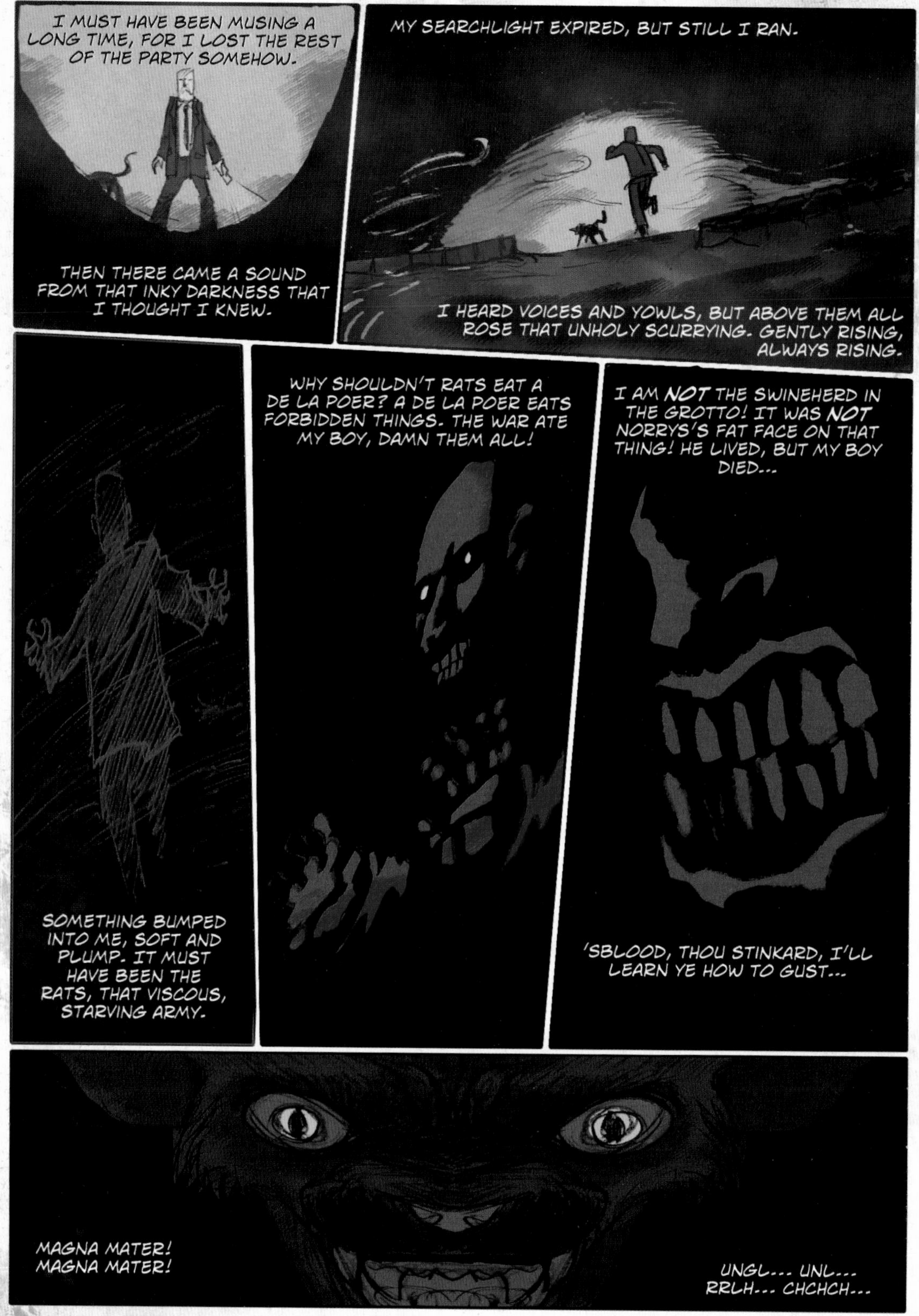
I MUST HAVE BEEN MUSING A LONG TIME, FOR I LOST THE REST OF THE PARTY SOMEHOW.
THEN THERE CAME A SOUND FROM THAT INKY DARKNESS THAT I THOUGHT I KNEW.
MY SEARCHLIGHT EXPIRED, BUT STILL I RAN.
I HEARD VOICES AND YOWLS, BUT ABOVE THEM ALL ROSE THAT UNHOLY SCURRYING. GENTLY RISING, ALWAYS RISING.
SOMETHING BUMPED INTO ME, SOFT AND PLUMP. IT MUST HAVE BEEN THE RATS, THAT VISCOUS, STARVING ARMY.
WHY SHOULDN'T RATS EAT A DE LA POER? A DE LA POER EATS FORBIDDEN THINGS. THE WAR ATE MY BOY, DAMN THEM ALL!
I AM **NOT** THE SWINEHERD IN THE GROTTO! IT WAS **NOT** NORRYS'S FAT FACE ON THAT THING! HE LIVED, BUT MY BOY DIED...
'SBLOOD, THOU STINKARD, I'LL LEARN YE HOW TO GUST...
MAGNA MATER! MAGNA MATER!
UNGL... UNL... RRLH... CHCHCH...

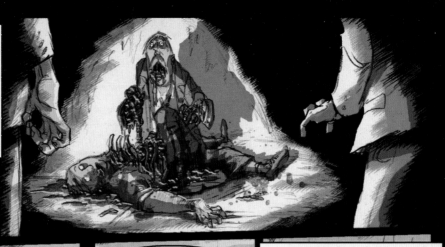

THIS IS WHAT THEY SAY I SAID WHEN THEY FOUND ME THREE HOURS LATER, CROUCHING IN THE BLACKNESS OVER THE PLUMP, HALF-EATEN BODY OF CAPTAIN NORRYS.

SO NOW THE AUTHORITIES HAVE BLOWN UP EXHAM PRIORY AND TAKEN AWAY MY CATS.

BUT THEY MUST KNOW THAT I DID NOT DO IT.

POOR NORRYS...

THEY MUST KNOW IT WAS THE RATS... THE SLITHERING, SCURRYING RATS WHOSE SCAMPERING WILL NEVER LET ME SLEEP.

THE DAEMON RATS THAT RACE BEHIND THESE PADDED WALLS AND BECKON ME DOWN TO GREATER HORRORS THAN I HAVE EVER KNOWN.

THE RATS THEY CAN NEVER HEAR...

THE RATS IN THE WALLS.

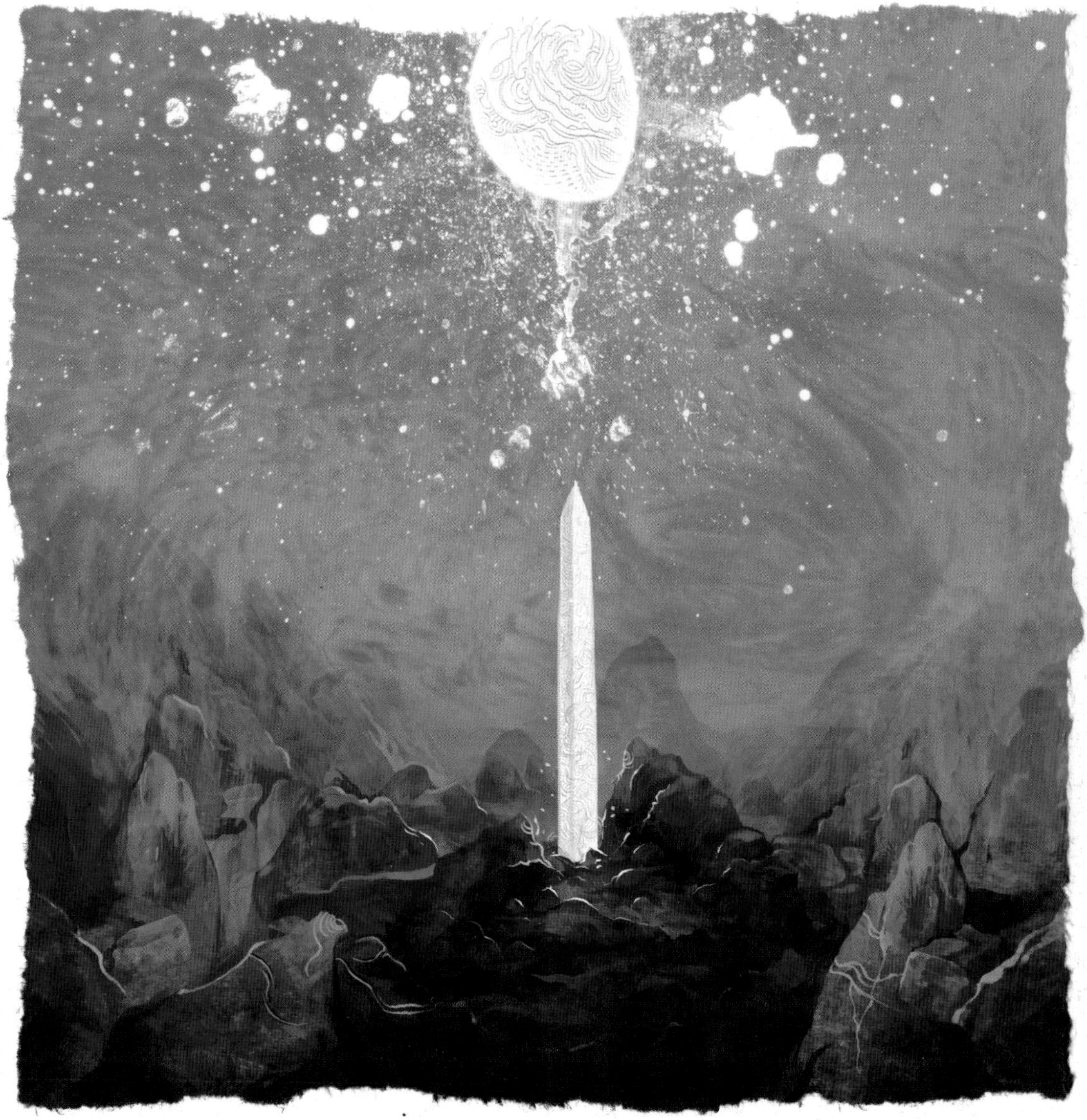

DAGON

Adapted by Dan Lockwood
Illustrated by Alice Duke

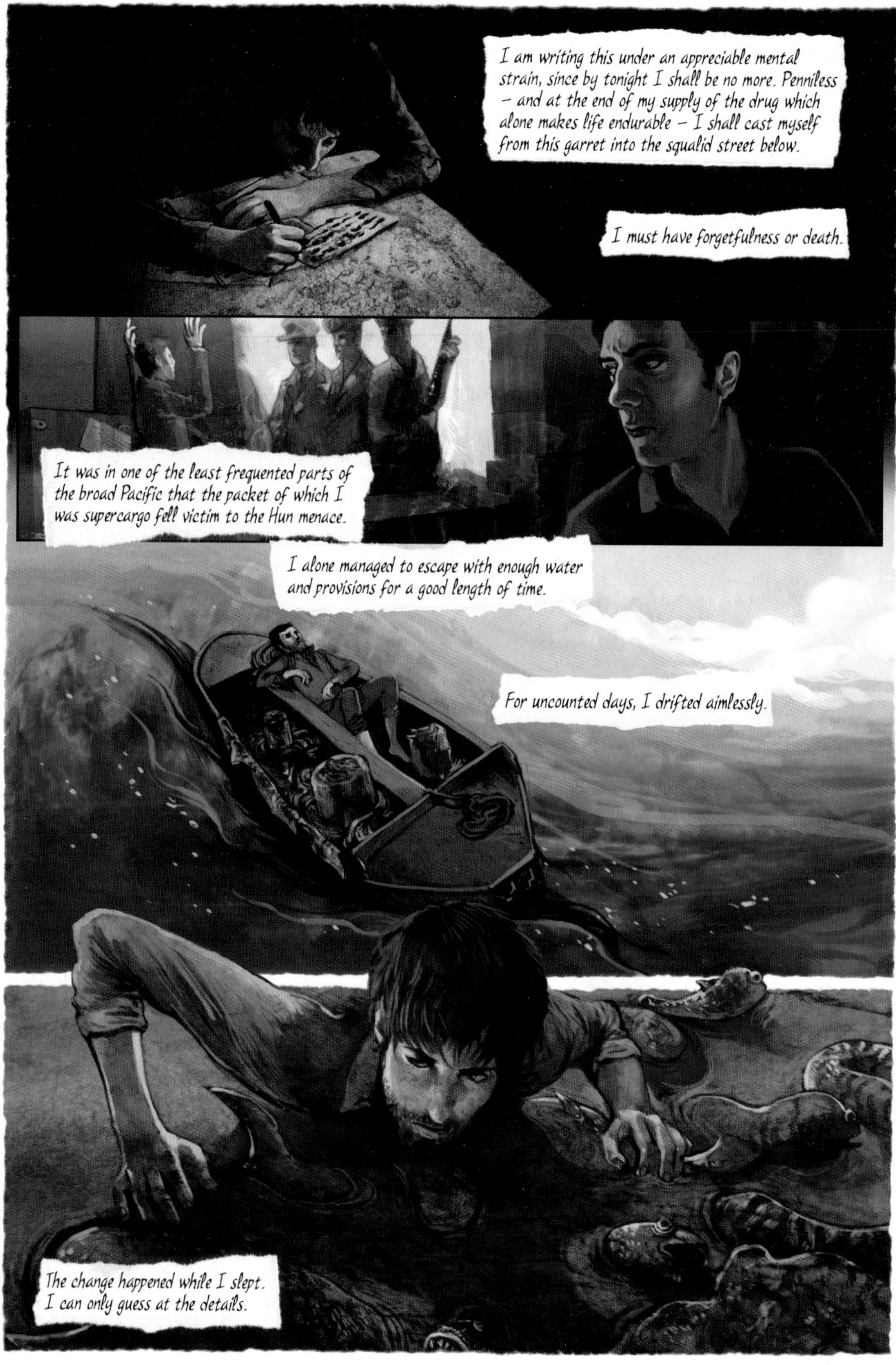
I am writing this under an appreciable mental strain, since by tonight I shall be no more. Penniless – and at the end of my supply of the drug which alone makes life endurable – I shall cast myself from this garret into the squalid street below.
I must have forgetfulness or death.
It was in one of the least frequented parts of the broad Pacific that the packet of which I was supercargo fell victim to the Hun menace.
I alone managed to escape with enough water and provisions for a good length of time.
For uncounted days, I drifted aimlessly.
The change happened while I slept. I can only guess at the details.

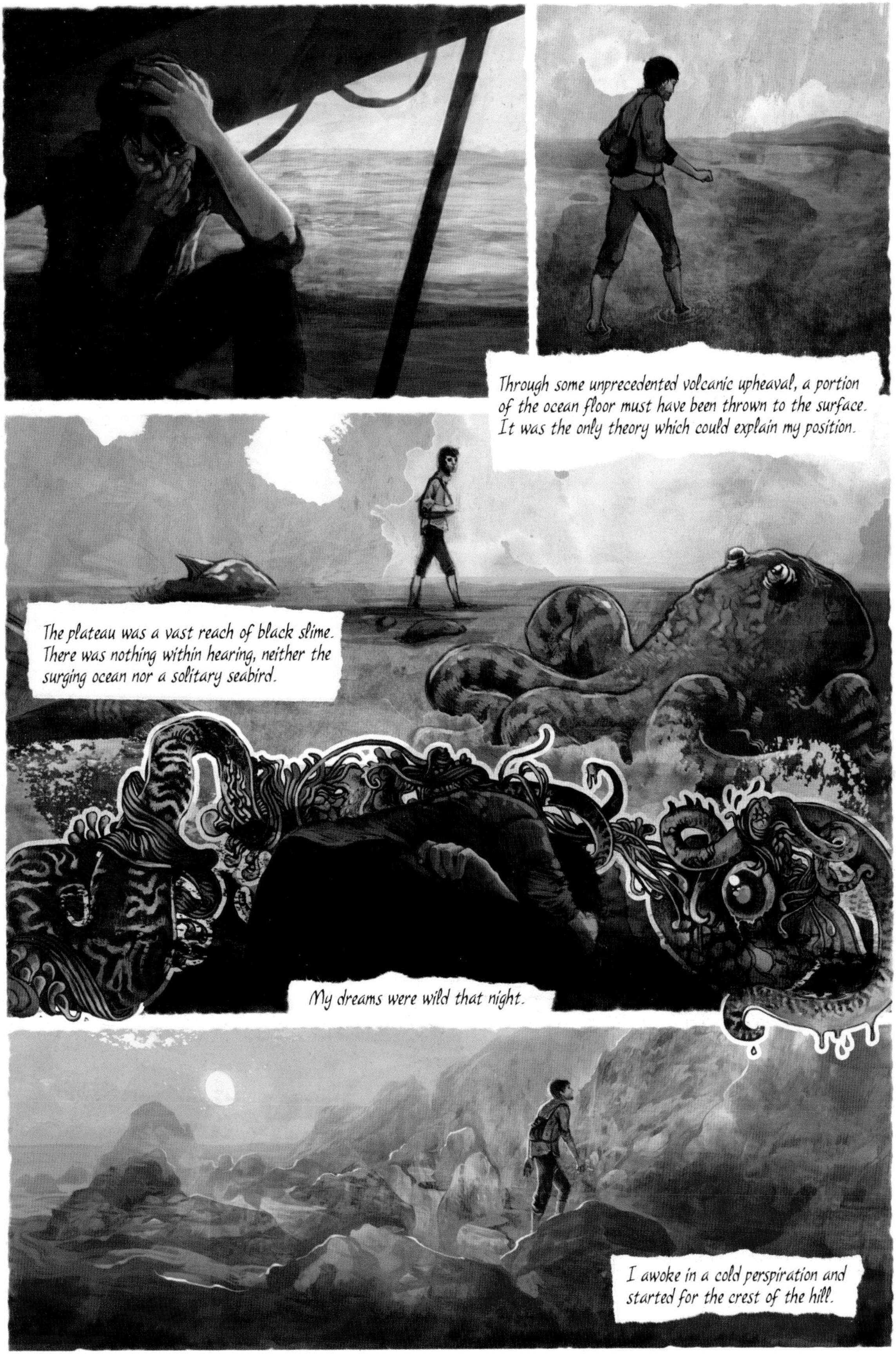
Through some unprecedented volcanic upheaval, a portion of the ocean floor must have been thrown to the surface. It was the only theory which could explain my position.
The plateau was a vast reach of black slime. There was nothing within hearing, neither the surging ocean nor a solitary seabird.
My dreams were wild that night.
I awoke in a cold perspiration and started for the crest of the hill.

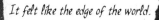

It felt like the edge of the world.

As the moon rose, my attention was captured by a gigantic and singular piece of stone rising from the opposite slope. As I came closer, I realised that its massive bulk had known the workmanship – and perhaps worship – of living, thinking beings.

Grotesque creatures were depicted disporting in the waters of some marine grotto. Some of the carvings were badly out of proportion.

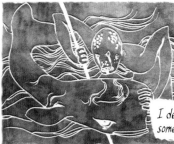

I decided they were merely the imaginary gods of some primitive sea-faring tribe from eras long past.

Then, suddenly, I saw it.

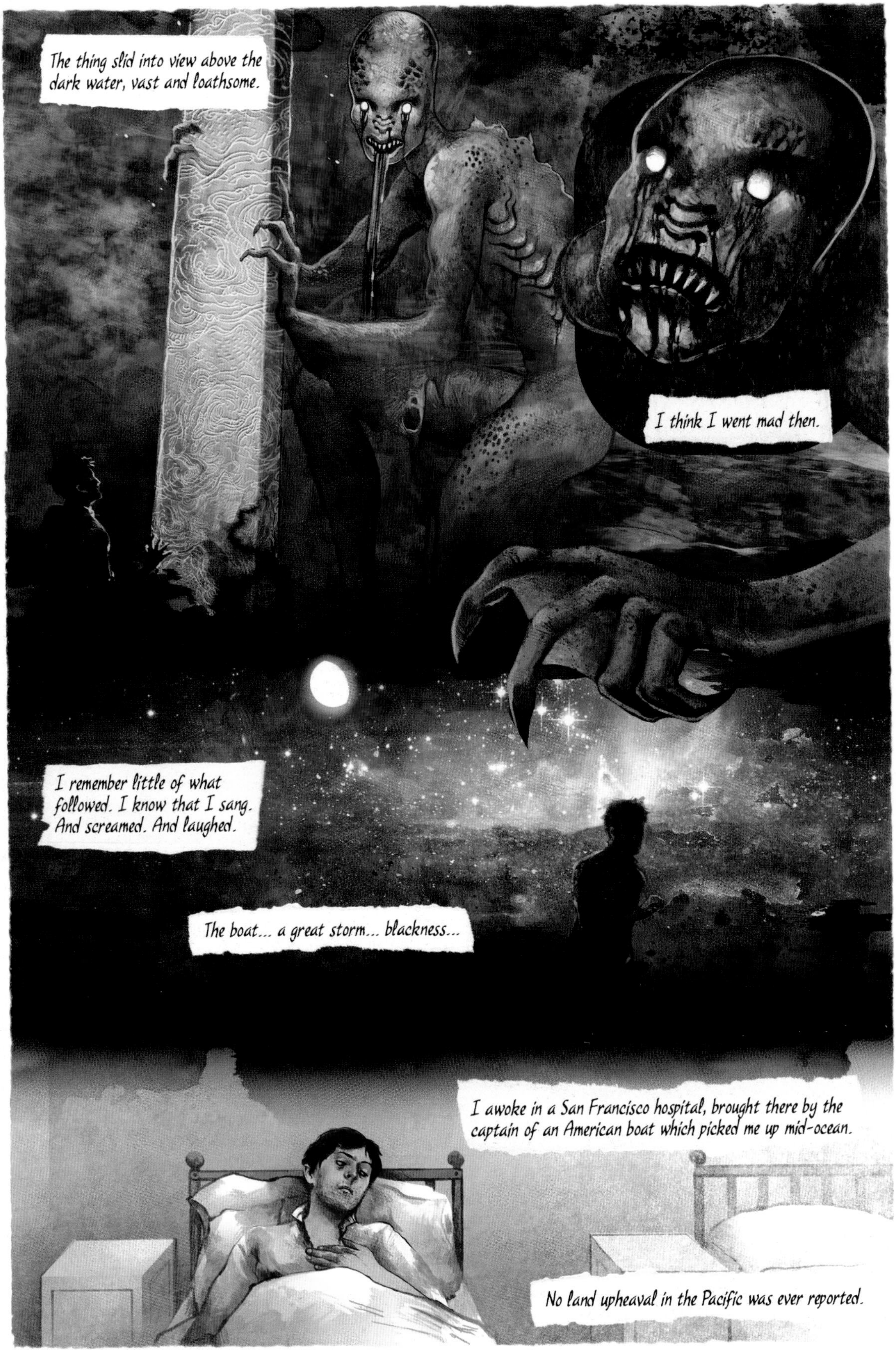
The thing slid into view above the dark water, vast and loathsome.
I think I went mad then.
I remember little of what followed. I know that I sang. And screamed. And laughed.
The boat... a great storm... blackness...
I awoke in a San Francisco hospital, brought there by the captain of an American boat which picked me up mid-ocean.
No land upheaval in the Pacific was ever reported.

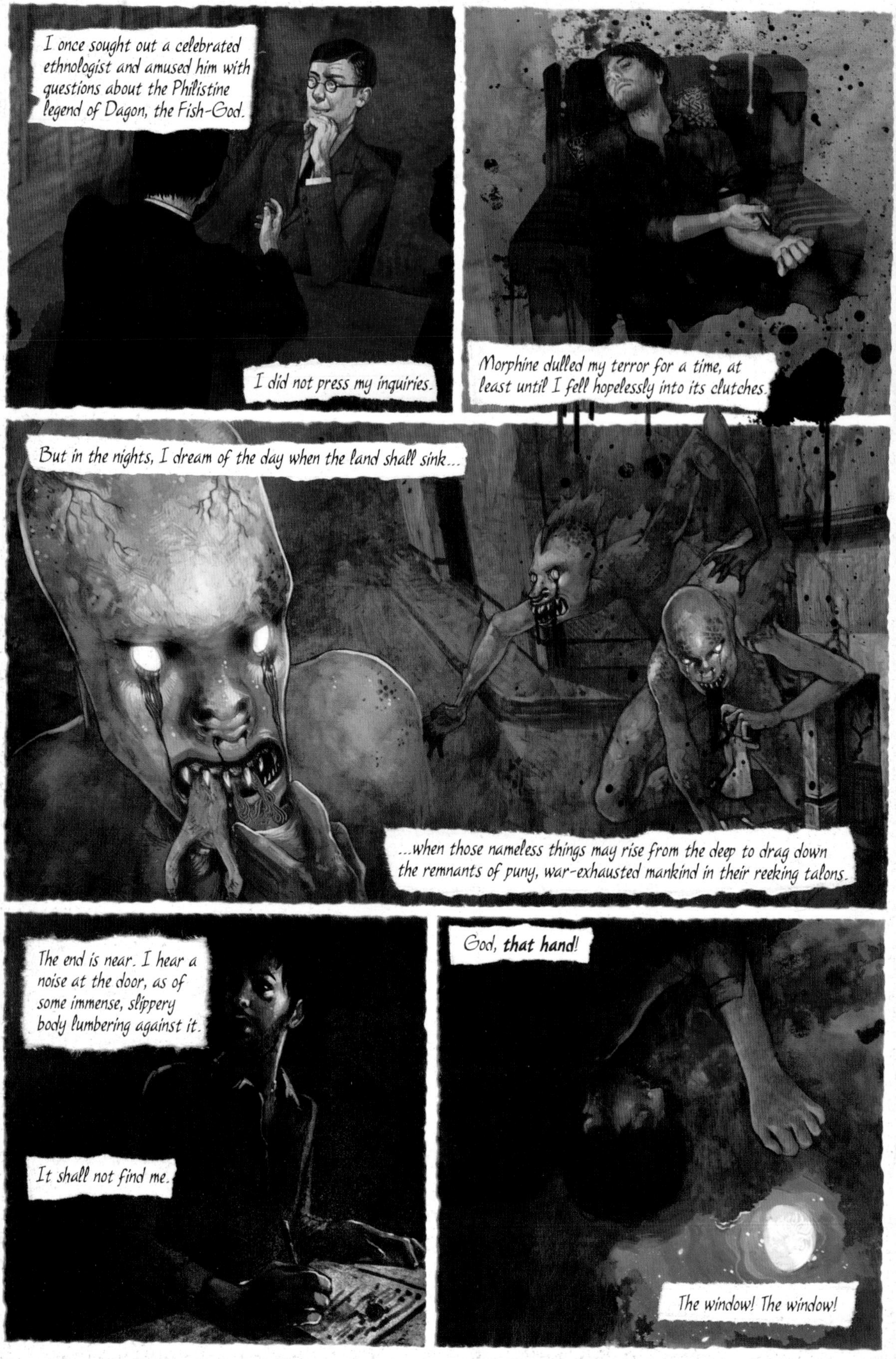
I once sought out a celebrated ethnologist and amused him with questions about the Philistine legend of Dagon, the Fish-God.
I did not press my inquiries.
Morphine dulled my terror for a time, at least until I fell hopelessly into its clutches.
But in the nights, I dream of the day when the land shall sink...
...when those nameless things may rise from the deep to drag down the remnants of puny, war-exhausted mankind in their reeking talons.
The end is near. I hear a noise at the door, as of some immense, slippery body lumbering against it.
It shall not find me.
God, **that hand**!
The window! The window!

ADAPTERS

Ian Edginton, one of Britain's best-known writers, has had a tremendous impact on the world of comics. In his illustrious career he has worked for Lucasfilm, Paramount Pictures and 20th Century Fox to adapt *Star Wars*, *Star Trek*, *Alien*, *Predator* and *Terminator* properties, as well as with the H.G. Wells estate to adapt *War of the Worlds* for Dark Horse. He owes his success to good collaborations with other artists from the industry, most famously D'Israeli (*Scarlet Traces*) and Steve Yeowell (*The Red Seas*). In 2007, his graphic novel *Scarlet Traces: The Great Game* was nominated for Best Limited Series and Best Writer at the prestigious Eisner Awards. He is collaborating with artist I.N.J. Culbard on the Sherlock Holmes series for SelfMadeHero.

Dan Lockwood is a freelance editor and writer, who studied Sanskrit and Greek at the University of Edinburgh before starting work in publishing. He is a huge fan of horror and science-fiction on the page and screen. For SelfMadeHero, Dan has previously edited *The Trial* and *The Master and Margarita*. He lives and works in north London.

Rob Davis began self-publishing his own comic, the highly experimental *SLANG*, in 1989. From there Rob made the leap from experimental into traditional when he was employed by Fleetway to reinvent British comics' icon *Roy of the Rovers*. After a time drawing *Judge Dredd*, he began working as an illustrator and cartoonist for newspapers (including the *Guardian*) and children's book publishers (including Scholastic). In the last few years Rob has returned to comics, writing and drawing *Doctor Who* for Panini. He has recently produced a short story for Solpsistic Pop 3, and is currently adapting and illustrating *Don Quixote* for SelfMadeHero.

David Hine has been working in comics since the early 1980s. After his graphic novel *Strange Embrace* was published in the USA he was hired by Marvel to write several series, including *District X*, *Daredevil: Redemption*, *Silent War* and *Spider-Man Noir*. He also wrote *Spawn* for 3 years, created *Poison Candy* for Tokyopop and *The Bulletproof Coffin* with Shaky Kane for Image. Recent work includes *The FVZA* for Radical and numerous books for DC including *Detective Comics*, *Azrael* and *The Spirit*.

Leah Moore has collaborated with John Reppion on many projects, including *The Trial of Sherlock Holmes*, *The Complete Dracula* (Dynamite Entertainment), *Albion* and *Wild Girl* (Wildstorm). In addition to her writing, Leah enjoys drawing and painting and has provided illustrations for various articles and stories.

John Reppion has collaborated with Leah Moore on many projects, including *The Trial of Sherlock Holmes*, *The Complete Dracula* (Dynamite Entertainment), *Albion* and *Wild Girl* (Wildstorm). John's interests in fortean phenomena, esoterica, folklore, philosophy and weird history have led to his writing articles for magazines and periodicals such as *Fortean Times*, *Paranormal Magazine*, *Darklore*, *The Anomalist* and *Strange Attractor Journal*.

ARTISTS

D'israeli, aka Matt Brooker, has collaborated with many of the best writers and artists, including Shane Oakley (*Fatal Charm*), Warren Ellis (*Lazarus Churchyard*), Ian Edginton (*Kingdom of the Wicked*, *Scarlet Traces*, *Leviathan*) and Paul Cornell (*XTNCT*). These days he mostly works for *2000 AD*, drawing *Lowlife* (written by Rob Williams) and *Stickleback* (written by Ian Edginton). He has also self-published *Timularo,* a collection of his early work for *Deadline*. In between work he paints watercolours, eats too much chocolate and photographs his burgeoning toy Dalek collection.

shane ivan oakley began his career contributing to the alternative comics review *Deadline* in the 1980s (where he created *Fatal Charm* with D'Israeli). Oakley is probably best known for his co-creation of the Wildstorm mini-series *Albion*, with Alan Moore, Leah Moore and John Reppion, which ran from 2005 until 2006. In 2007, he illustrated an adaptation of Edgar Allan Poe's *The Fall of the House of Usher* written by Dan Whitehead and published in SelfMadeHero's *Nevermore* anthology. He recently collaborated with Alan Grant on a four part mini-series called *Channel Evil*.

I.N.J. culbard is an artist and writer. In 2006, he surpassed thousands of other writers and had his work published in Dark Horse Comics' *New Recruits* anthology. He has since appeared in the anthology series *Dark Horse Presents*, the *Judge Dredd Megazine* and *2000 AD*. Culbard is an acclaimed animation director with considerable experience in directing commercials, developing projects for television, and producing and directing short films. He is collaborating with writer Ian Edginton on the Sherlock Holmes series and has adapted and illustrated Lovecraft's *At the Mountains of Madness* for SelfMadeHero.

mark stafford is cartoonist in residence at the Cartoon Museum. He is currently working with Bryan Talbot on the second *Cherubs!* graphic novel, painting dead hillbillies, and writing about cinema for *Electric Sheep* magazine.

Leigh gallagher is a professional comic book artist who has worked on many projects for DC Comics and *2000 AD*, and was also the 2008 artist for the LEGO *BIONICLE* comic. He recently completed illustrating his fourth book of *2000 AD*'s 17th-century zombie hunter *DEFOE*, written by Pat Mills.

David Hartman is an illustrator who has worked in comics and the animation industry for almost a decade, from storyboard artist to Emmy-nominated director and everything in between. His credits include *Transformers Prime*, MTV's *Spiderman*, *Roughnecks: The Starship Troopers Chronicles* and much more. His illustration work for comic books and magazines includes *Steve Niles' Strange Cases*, *The Devil's Rejects*, *The Nocturnals: Midnight Companion* and more. David is currently working on several projects for Rob Zombie.

Alice Duke is an up-and-coming illustrator from Liverpool. Alice illustrated Poe's *Tell-Tale Heart* in SelfMadeHero's graphic anthology *Nevermore* (2007).